The Expert Teacher of Eng

CW00740339

The Expert Teacher of English is for all passionate teachers – both novice and expert – who aspire to become outstanding professionals. It considers what we mean by 'expert' and 'expertise', explores concepts that are vital to understanding what expertise in teaching is 'for', and discusses the characteristics of excellent teaching.

As increasing attention is being paid to the concept of the professional who can model excellent teaching and mentor and develop others, it provides a critical analysis of The Advanced Skills Teacher and the Excellent Teacher, as well as the Chartered Teacher in Scotland and the 'highly accomplished teacher' in the US. Ideas and issues considered include:

- The nature of English as a school subject;
- What it means to be part of a profession;
- Curriculum design, lesson planning and assessment;
- Opportunities for technologies in the English classroom;
- Working collaboratively with colleagues, mentoring and observation;
- Continuing professional development and research.

Drawing on the views, ideas and experiences of a group of skilful teachers, *The Expert Teacher of English* aims to stimulate personal and professional development, help you reflect on the concept of expertise, and support you as you develop as a highly accomplished teacher.

Andrew Goodwyn is Professor of Education and Head of the Institute of Education at the University of Reading, UK.

The Expert Teacher of English

Andrew Goodwyn

Routledge
Taylor & Francis Group

LONDON AND NEW YORK

First edition published 2011
by Routledge
2 Park Square, Milton Park, Abingdon, Oxon OX14 4RN

Simultaneously published in the USA and Canada
by Routledge
270 Madison Avenue, New York, NY 10016

Routledge is an imprint of the Taylor & Francis Group, an informa business

Typeset in Galliard by Exeter Premedia Services
Printed and bound in Great Britain by
TJ International Ltd, Padstow, Cornwall

British Library Cataloguing in Publication Data
A catalogue record for this book is available from the British Library

Library of Congress Cataloging-in-Publication Data
Goodwyn, Andrew, 1954-
The expert teacher of English / Andrew Goodwyn.
   p. cm.
Includes bibliographical references.
1. English language–Study and teaching (Secondary)
2. English teachers–In-service training.   I. Title.
   LB1631.G635 2010
   428.0071'2–dc22
                                    2010008195

ISBN10: 0-415-31695-2 (hbk)
ISBN10: 0-415-31696-0 (pbk)
ISBN10: 0-203-57907-0 (ebk)

ISBN13: 978-0-415-31695-8 (hbk)
ISBN13: 978-0-415-31696-5 (pbk)
ISBN13: 978-0-203-57907-7 (ebk)

In loving memory of my father, Edwin (Ted) Goodwyn, who was not only a lovely man and father, but also, himself, a most dedicated and enthusiastic teacher of English for over thirty years.

Contents

Acknowledgements   viii

Introduction   1

1   The effective, extended professional   9

2   Expertise and models of expert teaching: What do
    you call a 'very good' teacher?   31

3   What is English teaching? Belonging to a subject community   58

4   Teaching English   75

5   Curriculum and assessment   94

6   English teachers and digital technologies   111

7   Working with others   129

8   Continuing to develop   154

Bibliography   179
Index   186

Acknowledgements

I should like to thank all the hundreds of English teachers and student teachers I have had the pleasure of working with over many, many years. I should especially like to thank the six teachers who feature as the case studies in the book.

I should like to acknowledge the importance of NATE (The National Association for the Teaching of English) in my own development and to say 'thanks' to the dedicated members of NATE who I have worked with over three decades. Colleagues from other countries and English organisations have also been a great inspiration, such as Wayne Sawyer, Ken Watson, Cal Durrant, Brenton Doecke, Terry Locke, Dana Fox, Don Zancanella and many others.

I have many colleagues from the University of Reading to thank for their support, and I would pick out, in the English department, Ron Middleton, Judy Baxter, Winston Brookes, Sandy Crocker, Jan Holroyd, Lionel Warner and Sophie Williams; also a special mention for Katrina Harrell, from the University of Christ Church Canterbury.

I say a special thank you for collaborative research over many years with Kate Findlay and, more recently, Carol Fuller.

I offer a personal thank you to Linda Fitzsimons for her patient support throughout the writing of the book.

Introduction

Charlie, Interview 2: *You do need to be an expert really, especially when helping your colleagues, student teachers and so on, but it is not a word anyone actually uses when talking about teaching.*

Teachers tend not to like the word 'expert' when applied to teaching. So why write a book boldly entitled *The Expert Teacher of English*? Partly because, I believe, there are many, many expert teachers, and I wish to challenge what I can see as some professional 'denial'. I profoundly believe teachers need to be more assertive about their expertise and their professional status; of course, there are many other ways to give expert teaching a title, advanced skills teacher? excellent teacher? highly accomplished teacher? chartered teacher?; there will be discussion below of these current terms. Another, essential reason to claim 'expert teacher' now is because of a complex set of factors that combine to give high prominence to the recognition that the teacher is the key variable in improving learning. This may strike readers as something obvious. However, this recognition comes less from teachers themselves and more from the systems within which teachers must operate: educational, professional, social and political. In 1989, Robert Protherough published *The Effective Teaching of English* (Protherough, Atkinson and Fawcett 1989). It was an excellent and intelligent guide to beginning teachers about how to build on their initial training and to develop in their first few years in teaching. Much terminology has changed, but the great majority of its advice remains valuable. An important difference, twenty odd years later, is that we both know more about highly effective (not just effective) teaching and know that we do not yet know enough.

This book is aimed at readers for whom the teaching of English is very important, who may, or may not, be 'expert' or 'novice'; they may simply aspire to become as good a teacher of English as they can. They may now work in 'English' but not as a teacher, perhaps teacher educator, advisor, inspector? Certainly English is a very broad and complex field, problematic in theory and practice. This book is neither a manual nor a handbook; it does not, therefore, claim to *instruct* anyone into how to be 'that expert teacher'. First, it treats its readers as critical and reflective, and invites them to see the text as generative not prescriptive. Second, expertise is susceptible to generalisation and description, but it is experienced and practised individually. Experts are famous for disagreeing with each other, especially in public. There are many explanations for this and certainly ego is one, but more profoundly, having great depth of knowledge leads to questioning that knowledge and how it should be used. Disagreement and challenge are a part of the process of generating new knowledge about a domain. Experts will agree on many, many aspects of their domain; they tend to get excited when discussing finer points and more fundamental points.

One implication of this aspect of expertise is that excellent teachers of English do have many similarities, but they remain individuals with strongly marked individual characteristics. This is a generative, valuable difference not a problem. Our understanding of expertise and specialist forms of expertise is growing rapidly, and much of such new knowledge is contested (see, for example, Selinger and Crease 2006; Collins and Evans 2007). These two texts illustrate that other phenomenon of expertise about experts. There is an interesting debate about how expert one can be without being a practitioner, or more radically, without having ever been a practitioner. In education, an advisory teacher or inspector has always been a teacher initially. On the other hand, principals in the USA have often never taught. They are trained directly to be managers not teachers first, something which is at one level entirely logical; their expertise needs to be in managing schools, but it goes against the grain in the system in England.

In most domains of expertise, the experts have been involved in practice, and this 'practical knowledge' plays a large part in their ability to make decisions and judgements about that field and, very often, to coach and develop everyone from novices to emergent experts. This professional knowledge may not exist in traditional academic forms at all, but it is unquestionably powerful knowledge. It needs to be treated critically at times, and always needs to be separated from mere experience of practice, so that knowledge can exist in each individual and, in that sense, may be deemed *subjective* but, in the community of that practice, there are many ways in which it becomes relatively objectified through observation, dialogue and reflection, all themes to be developed in this book.

Which leads me, appropriately, to summarise my own professional knowledge. I am placing myself in that position of (at least trying) to take an expert stance on something that I no longer practice, but I am confident in saying that I know a very great deal about the school subject called English and how it is taught. This knowledge comes from qualifications in the subject acquired long ago, including a first degree, a subject-related Master's degree, then a postgraduate certificate of education (PGCE), followed by twelve years of teaching (one in the USA), including five years as a head of department. During that time, I put a good deal of energy into creating resources for English teaching from anthologies to text books. Then followed a period of about twenty years that has involved eighteen as a PGCE English course leader, seventeen as a course leader of an MA in English in Education and increasing levels of managerial and leadership responsibilities in a teacher education/university environment. One development has been an increasing attention to teaching about expertise both generically and specifically in relation to English. During all that latter period, I have made hundreds of school visits to observe student teachers, practising teachers and to evaluate departments, and held countless meetings of English teachers about a whole range of topics and issues. I have conducted many research projects about English and English teaching, all of which I will draw on, in one way or another, in this book. This research has found its way into the community of practice through workshops, conferences, articles, chapters, books, etc. The very great majority of the research has been focused on English, but some has been more generic, including investigations into Advanced Skills Teachers and, most recently, how very good teachers adapt technology into their teaching.

One study is at the heart of the book and was undertaken between 1999 and 2001; it was a set of six case studies of very good English teachers (the details are given in the opening to Chapter 4). These teachers generously gave of their time so that I might observe them, record very in-depth interviews and enjoy vigorous discussion of the nature of English teaching and its context. Comments from these teachers head each chapter, but their voices are strongly present in two central chapters (Chapters 4 and 5). They do not dominate the book, and they would not wish to, but their professional dedication, their personal modesty, but real creativity, pervade it; it was a privilege to work with them. Pam, interview 2: *Well, no, I do not feel 'ordinary', I really have learnt so much, I hope what you are learning might be of use to other English teachers perhaps?* Whenever I quote from one of these teachers, it will be italicised to distinguish a voice from a more conventional quotation.

Returning to my own development, one consistent thread has been membership, since the age of twenty-two, of the National Association for the Teaching of English and an active role, throughout most of my career, within it locally and nationally. This membership has been a source of tremendous professional development and also great enjoyment with all the ups and downs of belonging to a kind of extended family; it has been a very emotional place as much as professional. In this book, this is the 'I' that is trying to contribute to our knowledge of how to teach English to young people as best we can. I accept my subjectivity and, at times, I am going to say things that may be construed as opinionated and without firm evidence. When I can, I will appeal to the more objectified forms of knowledge that come from sources such as research and evidence. And in that combined way, I will aim to 'speak' very directly to teachers whose highly pressured lives I know a good deal about. I will aim throughout the book to try and connect with that busy world and write in a way that is trying to interest and to inform and also, especially at some points, to challenge. Handbooks and manuals should not be challenging, they should be designed to be simple and clear. But being emphatic about *not* writing a manual is no excuse for not being clear and accessible, least of all when you expect your reader to have been given little time for their own professional development during a busy working life. Some of the challenge of the text will come not from its style or language, but from concepts it explores and from topics it covers. At times, the topics might seem lacking in immediacy for teachers faced by the urgency of the class-room. But this is the point: professional understanding reduces that urgency by putting matters into a comprehensible perspective; this might be theoreti-cal or historical or, very often, both. This book then is essentially an attempt to help teachers of English generate a deeper professional understanding of their profession. English teaching and its history is too expansive a topic for a book on expertise, but it will make its presence felt throughout and will be used as a reference point or to provide examples whenever possible. Some of the more extended examples feature particular phases or initiatives, some over twenty years old, because part of professional expertise is a deep understanding of the context of the expertise; many 'reforms' in education, especially in relation to English, are politically short sighted, and it is vital to develop a true perspective allowing for much more reasoned understanding and the potential to resist such impositions when necessary.

The end of the first decade of the twenty-first century is an excellent time to review expertise, not least because, in England, the term 'excellent teacher' has been added (2006) to the official categorisation of teachers, joining 'advanced skills teacher' (AST), first formulated in England in 1997, but as a term, originally from Australia. The book will discuss these terms and their histories in detail; here, it is sufficient to point out that expert teaching does have an official title and role in the English system, principally through the key recognition that it was not in the best interests of the education system for its best teachers to become managers in order to progress in their careers, achieve status and a decent salary. It has been recognised globally that retain-ing the best teachers in the classroom and rewarding them with status and pay is crucial to improving learning. Therefore, several models of the 'expert teacher' have evolved around the world, and this international dimension will pervade the book. The English 'advanced skills teacher' was a term imported from Australia, but is the term the best one? And is the role as defined making the best use of very good teachers? The introduction of 'excellent' teacher as distinguished from AST seems at first nonsensical; its origins (see Chapter 2) are more pragmatic.

These official roles are currently occupied by a mere 1 per cent of the teaching force; surely the system wants all teachers to be excellent; surely all teachers want to be excellent? It is neither as simple as that in terms of expertise nor as straightforward in terms of the teaching profession. Good teachers can become demotivated and deskilled; expert teaching is quite 'situated' in both context and chronology; teachers have lives and they change as their lives change. Any systemic attempt to make all teachers 'better' is much more realistic than expecting 100 per cent experts. However, any intelligent system will want to identify its best teachers and give them roles that have maximum benefit for students, colleagues and the system as a whole. This book then does not predicate itself on the AST model or the 'excellent' model; it critiques both for their undeniable benefits and their disadvantages and problems. This book is for anyone, title regardless, who wants to be a better English teacher or to influence English teaching for the better.

These terms 'advanced skills teacher' and 'excellent teacher' and their associated standards and role definitions are important elements within this book, and they do signal the key recognition mentioned above. This recognition also has other courses and facets. The global move is well represented through the 2007 McKinsey report (Barber et al. 2007), which examined 'high performing education systems' to determine what might explain their success. Ultimately, they conclude that, fundamentally, an education system is only as good as its teachers, and that student achievement has an absolutely direct link to the individual teacher. This rather obvious point actually is a landmark recognition.

Its importance is easily illustrated by taking the simple example from England of 'The Strategies', the 'National Literacy Strategy' and the 'Framework for English', these being the most spectacular examples. These were vast government-backed policies attempting to enforce a change in practice from the top down. They were vastly expensive and characterised by prescriptive models of pedagogy, nationally produced teaching materials, narrowly focused 'one size fits all training' backed up by 'manuals' and policed by a potentially punitive combination of 'advisers' and also inspectors. To those who might see this description as a travesty of a well-intentioned investment in teachers and schools, the research evidence incontrovertibly demonstrates that this is how they were both perceived and experienced by teachers (Goodwyn 2004a, 2004b). These schemes treated the teacher as a kind of unit of production needing retooling to do a better job. This whole book will demonstrate just how important individual expertise, given an appropriate balance of autonomy and intelligent accountability, is to successful student achievement. I write of these initiatives as if in the past tense when technically they are not. However, their time has now passed and, inevitably, the reason is not really educational. Politically, they did not 'deliver' the raising of standards, and it is now officially recognised, by Ofsted for example, that the obsessive testing regime distorts teaching and leads to lower student achievement. This extraordinary process of what was laughingly called 'school improvement', in a sense, tried to bypass teachers' expertise rather than maximise it. The whole high stakes edifice is falling under its own enormous weight.

It is no paradox to say that this was also the period of closer attention to teacher 'performance'. In England, the Hay McBer Report (2000) outlined a system for performance management. The report itself has some interesting points to make about teacher expertise and puts outstanding teachers as a concept at the heart of the report. The impact of the report was actually very different (as it was designed to be), because it required schools to monitor and assess teacher performance; this will be further discussed later in the book. Although it describes very good teaching in an intelligent way, it was intended to provide a framework for the management of teacher performance. As the system became operational during the era of prescription and high stakes testing, so the context was simply 'all wrong' for performance management to become a valuable tool for teacher development; however, this might well be what happens longer term.

Ultimately, this book comes at a time when an era of what can realistically be called 'teacher oppression' is ending; this is not to say that teacher liberation automatically follows. What it does mean is that teacher expertise, not mere 'performance', is entering the spotlight and for positive reasons. The consistent success of systems such as Finland's in the Programme for International Student Assessment (PISA) tests is convincing politicians that the Finnish model of teacher autonomy is the most productive. In Finland, teachers are highly respected, relatively well paid, highly autonomous and have almost no external tests to contend with; no wonder that, in Finland, top graduates choose teaching and that parents do not worry which school their children attend; the schools are all considered equally good, because their teachers are also equally good. Finland also conceptualises teaching as a Master's level profession, one factor that has influenced government to introduce a Master's degree in teaching and learning (see discussions below).

So, these are exciting times for very good teachers whose effectiveness should be given far more respect and whose influence will be much greater. Among those teachers will be many English teachers. English as a subject continues to be conceptualised as the most important of all subjects, and English departments are always one of the larger teams in any school.

The structure of the book

As a book about the expert teaching of English, much of the text concerns the nature of the subject itself. However, it begins by contextualising English teaching within the larger world of teaching. Secondary teachers have very powerful subject identities and loyalties, but they always remain part of the larger enterprise of their collective profession. Becoming a highly effective practitioner may involve deep and specific knowledge, but it also involves a broad awareness of the profession and its issues. Chapter 1, therefore, explores some key concepts that are vital to understanding what expertise in teaching is 'for', that is what are its purposes. Such concepts include being part of a profession, evaluating the status and meaning of teaching as one profession within a number of professions in a complex social order. Professions have rules and regulations, and so the place of the unions, professional associations and the General Teaching Council for England (GTCE) are all reviewed. The GTCE exemplifies the productive tension between teacher autonomy and forms of accountability, of which the GTCE, as regulatory body, is one. The term teaching and its history are considered especially in relation to judgements of whether it is 'effective' or not. Teaching is analysed in relation to other influential paradigms such as the reflective practitioner, the notion of competence and models of development. Notions of competence lead on to a discussion of the proliferation of standards produced to describe teaching as a series of levels of achievement. The chapter concludes with a discussion of Hattie's characteristics of expert teaching (Hattie 2003); these descriptors are then used as a framework throughout the text.

Chapter 2 focuses more specifically on what we mean by 'expert' and 'expertise'. It is important to review these terms as contested and evolving, not blandly consensual and fixed. The study of expertise is examined and especially in relation to development, for example many English teachers are teachers for of all their professional lives, others take career breaks, some adopt different but influential roles; they may, or may not, continue to develop as teachers of English or as commentators upon it. The current standards for teaching are analysed and reviewed as to what extent they do, and do not, provide a developmental model, leading to a discussion of what to call an expert teacher and a critical analysis of the advanced skills teacher and the excellent teacher. These are discussed in the much wider context of an international perspective and what other systems have determined, for example the 'highly accomplished teacher' in the US and the 'chartered teacher' in Scotland. Finally, there is a review of two models that are specifically 'English'; the 'highly accomplished teacher of language arts' in the US and the 'Standards for Teachers of English Language and Literacy in Australia' (the STELLA project). Both models provide very rich and appropriately complex descriptions of English teaching.

This concluding focus on English teaching itself provides the link into Chapter 3, which explores the nature of the subject as a school subject. Chapters 4 and 5 draw extensively on the research study mentioned above and on the views and ideas of one group of very good English teachers. Chapter 4 focuses on the teaching of the subject and Chapter 5 on curriculum design and assessment. Even since that study was undertaken (1999–2001), technology has moved on remarkably. Chapter 6 explores some of the issues around technology for teachers and students and draws on another research study (Goodwyn et al. 2009; Goodwyn 2009) considering whether teaching with technology requires an extended form of expertise. Chapter 7 focuses on working with others. Whereas almost all the research on expert teachers focuses on the individual teacher, there is no doubt that the extended professional has a very significant impact on colleagues. The AST and excellent teacher in England and the chartered teacher in Scotland place huge emphasis on the best teachers as models of best practice who support others. Indeed, the conceptualisation of the AST in England is almost unique in its emphasis on outreach, although the specific impact of this role has little systematic evidence to support it. The idea of the influence of expertise remains a fascinatingly complex one. The chapter explores the very valuable role that an expert teacher can play in collaborating with other professionals. The final chapter addresses the need for and reality of continuing to develop. One of the characteristics of the best teachers is a self-awareness and a criticality; this is not mere perfectionism, it is a deep desire to stay committed to learning, that is the learning of students but also of the teacher constantly learning. It is hoped that this book might make a contribution to that desire to learn and constantly improve that is a marked characteristic of the best teachers.

Chapter 1

The effective, extended professional

Polly, Interview 3: You know locally, as it were, your kids, the parents you talk to, they really do respect teachers and they surprise you with how much they appreciate you, but the media, politicians and so on, seem always to be trying to blame all kinds of things on school and teachers – it is a wonder we keep doing it!

The challenge of 'status' as a profession

Expertise does not exist in a vacuum. Although it may be argued that one might be expert at almost anything, cleaning your own teeth for example, being expert at any old thing is not the point. Expertise is associated with knowledge and skill, but also with value. Some expertise is highly valued and highly rewarded, other forms much less so, and those two elements, value and reward, exist in a creative tension. Before examining expertise per se, it is important to establish some fundamentals about effective teaching and teaching as a profession and about professions more generally. A concept such as expert teaching cannot be understood in a vacuum, and this book is addressed to readers who want to understand such expertise in its context. Comparisons with other forms of professional expertise are highly illuminating, and the term 'professional' is essential in defining the context in which teaching takes place. All kinds of teaching take place in many 'amateur' settings, and these are of interest; for example, in the performing arts, the concept of the master class will be discussed below. However, the kind of teaching we are focused upon has developed within a professionalised environment. The term *teaching* also needs some scrutiny, partly because it does not begin to capture the multiplicity of roles and functions that a teacher makes use of to create students' actual learning. It also needs examination in relation to what is considered to be *effective teaching* before it is reasonable to examine what may be called *expert teaching*.

Being a 'professional'

The teaching profession has had a long struggle with defining itself, especially in relation to other professions (Eraut 1994). Although it has always wished to be taken very seriously, especially by the public, it has often rather undermined its own status. 'Everyone knows about teaching' is an obvious point but all the more important to state, because of that loose generalisation. As every parent, politician and media commentator has experienced school, so they do have a genuine, if completely partial, knowledge base from which to pass opinions on teachers and teaching. This knowledge is chiefly of the 'passenger in the car' kind, that is passengers have been present while a great deal of driving has taken place, but have neither experienced the challenge of driving nor really observed it closely. It is also reasonable to say that everyone does some 'teaching', that is if you define teaching as helping someone else learn how to do something, either something new (learning to ride a bike) or improving (learning how to avoid falling off a bike).

Another highly defining element is that teachers themselves are also chiefly driven by intrinsic concerns for their students, rather than for themselves. They therefore share, with other 'caring professions', nursing, counselling, social work, etc., a tendency to describe what they do in terms of the benefits to students rather than the extraordinary difficulty of what they do in their daily work.

These factors combine at times to produce a curious but powerful paradox. There is a consensus, even among politicians, that teaching is really very important; at the same time, it is absolutely taken for granted and, especially given the passenger perspective, seen as really rather an easy job; the old cliché 'think of the holidays' is never far away. There is evidence (Goodwyn 2004a) that the last twenty years have seen some shift in this perspective, but it is not yet a fundamental one. The phrases 'a top lawyer' or 'an expert financial adviser' are commonplace and have an immediate credibility that 'top teacher' simply does not. What we actually call a 'top teacher' will be much discussed in this book. However, here we are initially concerned with the status of teaching and how that may, or may not, add kudos to expert teaching.

When teaching is compared with other well-established professions, it shares only some of their characteristics (Eraut 1994). Any term as general as 'profession' is bound to have many and often competing definitions and, given rapid change in the workplace, a necessarily evolving definition. For example, is a teaching assistant (TA) a straightforwardly professional role, or is it, as seems more currently accurate, a 'paraprofessional role' like a 'paramedic'? Is a 'higher level teaching assistant' a more professional role than just a 'TA'; the answer seems, almost certainly, 'yes'. Finally, on this point, it may well be that the establishment of a well-defined paraprofessional role such as teaching assistant raises the status of teaching per se by implication. How do expert teachers, for example, work productively with another trained adult in the classroom, or might there be an implication that such teachers do not need assistance?

Given this book is aimed at teachers of English, then a short section devoted to the linguistic and semantic origin of the term professional is appropriate.

There are many sources to draw on but any hefty dictionary will do (for example *The Shorter Oxford English Dictionary*), and this analysis draws on a summary of some key points, not least because a key, sociological study of English teachers by Margaret Mathieson called English teachers back in the 1970s, *The Preachers of Culture*. This has a fundamental relevance because the origins of professional come from the medieval religious notion of 'professing', that is to profess the vows of religion, to 'declare them' (1510). The act of professing was crucial to being accepted into the community of the preferred religion and, by implication, a particular 'order'. By the late 1500s, the term had already extended to mean both laying claim to some particular knowledge and expertise in a form of art or science and *to teach some subject as a 'professor'*. Simultaneously, the idea of a profession as a vocation, a chosen calling, develops, tending still to be associated with religion but also including medicine, the law and the military.

In the late 1700s, the term 'professional' appears as pertaining to or being proper behaviour in relation to a chosen occupation, taking on the sense of having values and a moral code, not just about having knowledge but being concerned with how that knowledge is used. In the mid-nineteenth century, 'professionalism' had come to mean having a professional quality, the stamp of a profession and, by the 1880s, the distinction in sport emerges between amateur and professional, bringing in the inevitable question of financial reward. Therefore, what can be considered to be the ideological underpinnings of the concept of a professional were established by the end of the nineteenth century. For example, the first use of the term 'unprofessional' meaning contravening what is expected of a professional is in 1899.

In the twentieth century, the notion of the professional has become absolutely established as a normative role within a highly structured economy and within defined characteristics. However, these defining features (see below) must be seen as contested and contestable. For example, with the idea of professional status may come accountability, but how much is a true professional autonomous, and how much accountable, and if so, to whom? This latter point has been a particular issue for teachers, especially highly effective ones, in the late twentieth and early twenty-first century.

Therefore, although particular professions will set out lists of skills, as does teaching, these can fragment into microscopic items that become almost pedantry. All professions then are skilled, and they debate, principally internally, exactly what the 'skill set' is at any one time. The professions are best understood, as Michael Eraut sums it up, 'as an occupational ideology' (Eraut 1994: 227). In his excellent discussion of *Developing a Knowledge Base within a Client-centred Orientation*, he argues that the debate about professional characteristics has become sterile and that 'professionalization can then be viewed as a strategy for gaining status and privileges in accordance with that ideology – the three central features of the ideology of professionalism are a specialist knowledge base, autonomy and service' (ibid.: 227). But, Eraut points out, teaching struggles to be a full profession, especially as politics exerts increasing influence down to classroom level and because of the ever increasing numbers of stakeholders who demand influence. Teachers are perhaps confused because, as Eraut puts it, 'Are they meant to be serving the pupils, the parents, the local community, the school district, or the whole nation?' (ibid.: 228).

In a 'top tier' profession such as medicine or law, there is clearly a very strong element of client service and a very distinctive knowledge base, so distinctive in fact that most 'lay people' define themselves as completely lacking that knowledge. As discussed above, that is not quite the case with teaching (Goodwyn 2004b); lay people definitely believe they can express a view and should be entitled to do so. On these grounds, 'old' professions such as medicine (still doctors rather than nurses although that status is changing in an interesting way), law, architecture, etc., are 'top'. Teaching has enough of these characteristics to be almost a top tier profession.

Although Eraut defines the professions as principally having in common an ideological stance, it is reasonable just to note what are relatively common features associated with professional status. For example, the knowledge base usually comes from an initial period of graduate-level study in the key subject or a related one. In top professions, there is then a period of further study, possibly vocational, very often postgraduate. At some point, the novice actually enters the profession, is, as it were, *through the gate*. As the individual professional becomes established, this tends to be through developing a specialism, which demands further study and ongoing upskilling (continuing professional development or CPD). Such specialists then have students and novices of their own who they induct into the profession. Most such professions also have a strong, sometimes direct relationship with a discipline studied in higher education; this academic subject (say mathematics) may have a very long history. Education as a discipline still struggles to hold its own in the academy, not least because populist views cluster around it, but also because teachers themselves frequently undermine it as a subject and its 'theories'. Much of this view comes from the experience of the academic study of education during initial teacher training (ITT); other professions insist on much more post-initial training studies.

Professions are also marked by their very particular language and technical vocabulary. They have a regulatory body of some kind and the capacity to 'practise' is dependent on belonging to that body. As well as having codes of practice set down in great detail, they tend to have ways of behaving that are much less defined but are the 'culture' of that group. 'Never smile until Christmas' is not a technical term, it is more of a folklore phrase, but it carries meaning within the professional group that are teachers. Teachers do not wear uniforms (compare nurses) or particular gowns (compare barristers), but each setting tends to have a strong dress code, although it may not be written down.

Teaching has most of the markers of a top profession; it has, for example, the appropriate level of esteemed qualification (it is almost entirely a graduate-level group), an appropriate initial training period with a strong gatekeeping function and certification of practice that can be revoked. It does now require teachers to maintain their own professional development (see the Standards section of the Department for Children, Families and Schools website), although the lack of any real system persists; teacher in-service development is haphazard at best. There is a well-defined, although constantly changing, career structure. Perceptions of teaching as a career change over time and international comparisons are very interesting. The McKinsey Report (Barber et al. 2007) discusses how vital the status of the teaching profession has become to attracting the best graduates; this is linked to history and culture; but they stress how influential teachers themselves can be and how, in synergy with positive government policy, status can quickly (over five years) be raised.

The importance of a regulatory body? The role of a 'General Teaching Council'

So expert teachers work in a profession that is clearly service oriented and is respected for that dimension, but also has some ongoing issues about its status and its knowledge base. On the point about status, the emergence of the General Teaching Council for England (GTCE) relates to the initial discussion above, i.e. does the GTCE add to or diminish teachers' status? There is little hard evidence to review here.

The establishment of a regulatory body for the profession generally, and potentially to its expert practitioners, should have been a very significant 'step up', given the eminence of a body such as the General Medical Council. The 1998 Act that set up the Council gave it two aims: 'to contribute to improving standards of teaching and the quality of learning, and to maintain and improve standards of professional conduct among teachers, in the interests of the public'.

Therefore, 'The General Teaching Council exists to support teachers' professional efforts to offer children and young people high quality teaching that meets their needs and enables them to learn and thrive' (GTCE website 2009).

The GTCE has the power to 'strike off' a teacher from the official list of practitioners and, very occasionally, does exercise this power. The perception among teachers is that this particular function is certainly necessary and to be recognised as such, but that, as the body that fulfils this function, the GTCE is without much significance or influence. It is also not seen as a threat to the autonomy of teachers; this comes from other sources. Put simplistically, the GTCE does not 'feel' like a recognition of self-regulation, a mark of a top profession; instead, it is perceived as a bureaucratic and remote entity. It is never seen as the authoritative 'voice of the profession', a function more associated with the teaching unions. This can be contrasted with the equivalent body in Scotland, which has much recognition and influence among teachers and carries out some of the functions of government agencies such as the Training and Development Agency (TDA) (see below).

It might be argued that it is a relatively young body in comparison with other professions; this is a reasonable point. However, there is little evidence that it is maturing or gaining authority; it seems more to be tolerated than respected. Certainly one very important reason is that the powerful bodies in relation to teaching in England are the TDA for Schools and the Office for Standards in Education. The GTCE essentially has no visible power in relation to these hugely important agencies (more discussion of them will follow).

The role of the unions

Returning to teaching and its status, the role of the teaching unions is also significant. Internationally, it varies considerably as to whether the teaching unions are significant players or not; Canada's unions are, for example, both powerful and assertive about the status of teaching. In the UK generally, they have focused on pay first, and conditions second. How well teachers are paid is always contentious, especially in relation to *what it is that they are being paid for* (remember 'the holidays'). The unions have been very influential in bargaining and, at some points, in uniting the profession to take industrial action. They have had considerable influence, especially in more recent years, in defining the actual conditions of teaching. The National Union of Teachers (NUT) was formed in 1870 and remains a powerful influence on policy and teachers' career possibilities. For example, in the last decade, the NUT (and other unions) have certainly helped to challenge the testing regime set up in the 1990s, leading to the abolition of the Key Stage 3 test.

However, the unions are not perceived as raising the status of teaching. One simple reason is that there are several, and they publically squabble with each other. Another is that collective bargaining is often seen as a sign of the weakness of the individual practitioner's position, hence the need to be collective. Architects and lawyers do not engage in such public displays of desperate demands to their employers. Equally, teachers do not have to belong to a union, even though the advantages are very obvious, especially in terms of professional indemnity. A teacher is much better protected in a union than by being in the GTCE. Despite some specific historical episodes, teachers in the UK are not generally militant.

It is worth noting that the GTCE appears to have no opinion on the concept or status of expert teaching. The unions, especially the NUT, have generally been negative about the establishment of any kind of formal recognition. The advent of the advanced skills teachers (ASTs) was not supported by the unions, and their prevailing view still seems to be that such a role is more divisive than positive. There will be further discussion of ASTs below.

To sum up, the unions are powerful and important, but do not add status to the profession. The GTCE is tolerated but is seen as insignificant. It might well be argued that it is the culture of teaching itself that undermines the GTCE. If teachers were more concerned about their public status, it seems probable that they would demand to have a more assertive regulatory body. So, teachers do have a degree of self-regulation, and continue to have a modest level of autonomy, but they work within a very dominant accountability regime that, it can be argued, does not encourage innovation or genuine expertise.

The tensions between autonomy and accountability and the use of 'standards'

A genuine professional must be reasonably accountable, but must also retain a significant degree of autonomy and be able to exercise reasoned professional judgement. What degree of accountability is reasonable for teaching as a profession? Do differing degrees of accountability act as a developmental pressure on improving teaching or can they produce a compliance culture which restricts innovation and nullifies expertise? This is an especially challenging question in relation to expert teaching; should not such teachers, if they are agreed to be expert, have a great deal of autonomy as leaders within the profession?

This book is not a history of the teaching profession but, on occasion, the longer perspective is valuable. Teaching in England, in the 1990s, became a highly accountable, punitively observed activity. That is to say that, in England specifically, the regime of Ofsted has been perceived by teachers as essentially negative and obsessively judgemental. It is ironic that, in a period in which teaching has been subject to more professional observation than ever before, teachers themselves feel that they have learned very little from this at least potentially rich database of observation. Ofsted were given the enormous power to rate all teaching on a scale that includes the terms 'good' and 'outstanding'. This recognition of the quality of teaching per se might have been a powerful stimulus to the profession, especially as the observers were recording their observations in a systematic way. However, Ofsted adopted a secretive model in the literal sense that only reports and summaries were ever made available to the public domain. Equally, Ofsted were, themselves, made unaccountable to the profession; therefore no dialogue about the accumulated evidence of good teaching could be discussed or debated.

It might be argued that teaching had been too unaccountable pre-Ofsted, and that teachers could get away with poor teaching very easily. However, there is no evidence to support this view and no evidence, apart from Ofsted's own claims, that teaching itself has improved as a direct consequence of inspection. An extraordinary opportunity was missed. The essential conceptualisation of Ofsted as a body charged with hunting down bad practice and failing schools meant that the gaining of a positive report was seen as a pleasant escape. It also engendered a culture of compliance towards Ofsted descriptors. Research (Cullingford 1999) has shown that schools, and individual teachers, learned how to 'play the game', although they found the effects of an inspection highly unproductive. The three-step formulation of building up to the inspection, coping with the inspection period and recovering from the inspection led to huge amounts of time and effort being diverted from teaching and from students' learning.

Had Ofsted been conceptualised as employing a sampling, best practice model, then teachers might have been able to welcome every inspection as a chance to demonstrate what they were genuinely doing and to receive professional feedback from highly qualified and broadly experienced colleagues. The benefits for expert teaching could have been substantial. Not only might there have been a publically accessible database of descriptions of expert teaching, but this might have been refined and developed over time and fed back into the profession.

The emergent, self-evaluative model may well be a step forward on a number of dimensions, and the reduction in direct observations of teaching is not a loss on the basis of the old, negative model. However, it means that there will be no independent observations of teaching except from minor players such, perhaps, as ASTs as part of their outreach role. The one very positive development, certainly in relation to developing expertise in teaching, has been the acceptance throughout teaching that observation per se is an essential part of teacher development. In simple terms, teachers' doors are generally 'open' rather than 'closed', and both teachers and students are entirely used to observers in classrooms; this will be further discussed below, especially in Chapters 7 and 8.

This cultural change towards an open door can be understood as stemming from several complementary sources, all contributing to a better developed knowledge base in schools in relation to teacher expertise. One key but contentious and problematic development has been performance management for teachers. The introduction of performance management in 1997 required head teachers to justify their recommendations for teacher reward. Whatever the complications of such a system, it meant that teachers had to be observed, and the basis on which they were being observed had to be explicitly stated. This is equally the case for the initial assessment of advanced skills teachers (see below). From the perspective of developing a knowledge base for increasingly expert teaching, the performance management initiative offers great potential. Although it is designed to attribute relatively simplistic quality indicators to an individual teacher's performance, it is an annual entitlement and is linked to other factors, such as a portfolio of evidence including professional development work undertaken since the last assessment.

It does, therefore, offer a developmental perspective. The 'setting of targets', if used imaginatively, also provides a focus on, and evidence of, a teacher's developing expertise.

The relatively recent introduction of standards for all teachers is another two-edged sword (Slee and Weiner 1998) with real potential for teacher development, not least because of the category of 'excellent teacher', discussed below. Standards for initial teacher training (ITT) have been in place for over ten years (1998), and those for newly qualified teachers since 1999; the importance of standards will be discussed later in relation to the competency paradigm. One potent effect of the standards for ITT, predicated as they are on a partnership model, has been to make far more teachers directly involved in both teacher training and its gatekeeping function. Teachers' much greater involvement in ITT has undoubtedly led to far more teacher knowledge about 'learning how to teach'. A great deal of this knowledge has been generated through teachers making regular observations of ITT trainees and through having to articulate, against explicit standards, how the trainees are accumulating evidence of their teaching expertise and of specific advice on how they need to improve.

The role of the ITT mentor has risen significantly in status and responsibility since the move to more school-based training. Such mentors are usually well trained, typically by a higher education institution (HEI), and generally are given a certificate to acknowledge their skills. In many such schemes, there are opportunities to undertake more demanding levels of training and then to take on a more senior role such as lead mentor. There are often opportunities to undertake MA-level work related to mentoring and teacher development, typically through critically informed investigations of practice. All these developments in school-based ITT have built capacity, and many more teachers have become skilled in observation, feedback and the interpretation of standards-based evidence gathering. What is most important, in this incremental change, has been the crucial positioning of serving teachers as the gatekeepers for the profession. This has strengthened one of the key elements in marking teaching as a potentially top tier profession. In relation to this change, the introduction of the graduate teacher route, often perceived as damaging to the status of teaching (Brookes 2005), has placed more emphases on schools as training environments. Although a minor route into teaching and still questioned by many in the profession, the graduate teacher programme (GTP) has stabilised into a route of particular suitability for career changers and for teaching assistants upgrading to qualified teacher status (QTS).

Training schools are another equivocal development. Their establishment would appear to add credibility to the idea that schools can be powerful agents in professional development and in initial training, especially recognition of the GTP route. However, their distribution across England is extremely uneven and their own status seems unclear and without a certain future.

Effective teaching

The apparently consensual term 'teacher' does not come close to capturing what a teacher actually does, *teaching* being only one element within a teacher's actual role. Given that this issue is a global one and could fill a book in itself, the discussion below will limit itself to some relevant initiatives in the English-speaking world.

It is worth reflecting, very briefly, on the evolution of the concept of 'teacher' as a term (for more detail, see Ericsson et al. 2007). This evolution also prefigures some of the conceptualisations of contemporary teaching that will be discussed below. The first accounts of teaching in Western history are associated with Socrates and his 'student' Plato. What is significant about this early conceptualisation is that teaching was largely individual and therefore personal, and that it was characterised by an open, dialogic approach; it was not didactic. The term 'Socratic dialogue' remains in common use. That model of the wise teacher enabling the student has a long influential history. In the Middle Ages, when universities became established and when texts (although hand written) became available, the additional dimension developed with the individual student devoting great periods of time to literal 'study' of the authoritative texts. Alongside this development, which was principally associated, as with the term 'professor' above, with religion, was the emergence of the craft guilds. In the latter model, the craftsman was the expert maker, and his apprentice or apprentices learned 'on the job' and through observation and imitation. This model has an immediate resonance with much contemporary vocational training, including teaching.

The huge change came with industrialisation and the fundamental change to factory models of production and to the development of schools with very large number of pupils needing a basic level of competence in order to function in an industrial society. This is when the teacher emerges as the professional, at the same time as teaching becomes a very commonplace activity. The important point to reflect on here is that schools are still dominated by a factory concept and that highly skilled teaching is mostly associated with large groups of students; this kind of performative teaching is the dominant paradigm and clearly strongly influences ITT. Concepts of personalised learning currently exist in tension with the performative model, but a distinguishing feature of expert teachers (see below) is their capacity to address individual needs. It seems probable that one role for expert teachers in the longer term is to enable other teachers to develop this facet of personalised attention. One of the rationales for developing the advanced skills teachers in England was just that notion, that ASTs could directly influence the quality of teaching of their colleagues.

Conceptualising teaching: what is the point of teaching?

As we noted above, the concept of teaching has been through a massive paradigm shift as a result of industrialisation, so it must be examined for ways of thinking about it. Squire's 1999 analysis is a very helpful starting point. He describes teaching as an activity as typically conceptualised in one of six dominant ways: as 'a common sense activity', 'an art', 'a craft', 'an applied science', 'a system', 'a reflective practice' and 'a competence' (Squires 1999). All of these conceptualisations have a very definite real world presence and influence and are useful not only for helping us think critically about teaching, but also for understanding how others view it. For example, the 'common sense' view may well be that of many parents, whereas the 'system' view may be much favoured by politicians and is evidenced in the McKinsey Report's preference for high- and low-performing descriptions of teaching. Turner-Bissett offers a clear analysis and application of Squires to effective teaching (Turner-Bissett 2001: ch. 1).

For our purposes, it is worth recognising that these paradigms are present in most discussions about teaching quality and may well influence judgements about what is expert teaching. Considering the paradigms from that perspective, then, the common sense view is a pragmatically grounded approach to doing 'what works' and to 'getting on with things' without too much reflection. It is antipathetical to any recognition of real expertise. Whereas the teaching as art model immediately offers a rich perspective as it treats teaching as not only complex and highly skilled but also as an aesthetic and emotional activity. For example, Eisner in 1985 characterised good teaching as 'some times performed with such skill and grace that it can be described as an aesthetic experience; it involves qualitative judgements based on an unfolding course of action; it is contingent and unpredictable rather than routine; and that its outcomes are often created in the process' (Eisner 1985: 175–76). One interesting dimension to this paradigm is that it positions the performance of good teachers in a comparative relationship to musicians and other 'performers'. This is valuable because it suggests that such performances can be truly outstanding, not least because they are affective as well as effective. Perhaps most importantly, this paradigm suggests that, as with music, the individual artist is the interpreter and so in a very creative relationship with the notes/script, etc. Undoubtedly a weakness in this paradigm is that it implies that, as with great performers, there will only be a very few such individuals. Teaching may well be an art form, but it will always need to position the audience very differently from the passive listeners at a concert.

In opposition to the artistic mode, much work has been done to establish teaching as based more on scientific principles, the 'applied science' model. This would imply that the 'rules' of teaching can be discovered and then applied rationalistically. There is plenty of evidence that teaching requires rationalist and systematic approaches, especially at the planning level; however, psychology has demonstrated that professions such as teaching are very concrete and situational – strict adherence to rules is a problem and not a solution.

The craft model continues to feature strongly in many education systems as it does in many vocational training models. The essential notion that teaching is learnt partly by 'doing it' and partly by copying others who can already 'do it' is very close to the common sense approach. However, it is fundamentally faulted by the fact that merely reproducing practice is not the way forward and by an absolute reliance on whoever the 'demonstrator' may be.

The 'system' model has had an influence on teaching, sufficient to be credited with a strong influence because it focuses on processes and how they might be improved. This rightly treats teaching as a complex activity that cannot be simplistically understood. However, it does tend to simplify teaching overall as part of the 'school' and 'education' systems. In this respect, it is possible to see why a government would create a top-down reform such as the National Literacy Strategy, believing that 'informed prescription' would actually force all teachers to teach in a certain way that was considered to be best practice; this led to huge training manuals and highly scripted lessons. The research evidence about teachers' views demonstrated how absurd they found these prescriptions and how it both undermined their performance and eroded their self-esteem (see Beverton 2000, 2003; English 2003; Goodwyn 2004a).

The most influential paradigm among many educators has been that of the reflective practitioner; the most powerful among government agencies and politicians has been that of competence. These two models, therefore, have sections of their own.

Reflective practice

The notion of 'reflective practice', it can be argued, has been one of the most powerful influences on thinking about teacher development and especially the idea that teachers (and other professionals) can continuously develop. The great exponent of this notion is Donald Schon, and his book *The Reflective Practitioner: How Professionals Think in Action*, published in 1983, is still the bible of this whole idea. His thinking has been widely influential in many professions, but it has dominated teaching at all levels, especially teacher education where, for example, the practice of insisting that student teachers keep reflective diaries or journals is widespread on a global scale. There is little solid empirical evidence of a direct link between individual reflection and improved practice. The process of both self-evaluation and evaluation from others, e.g. through observation and feedback, has plenty of evidence of direct impact on practice.

It is important to examine Schon's original ideas and then to consider their relationship to current concepts of expertise. Schon drew heavily on the traditions of John Dewey. This summary will not do justice to the complexity of his thinking; this would involve looking at his major books in detail. However, it is clear that his original formulation has remained the most significant influence. To Schon, reflective practice (RP) was necessary to counteract simplistic and reductive notions of teaching; it both helped teachers get beyond such approaches but also revealed how remarkable is the thinking of such professionals. He critiques the simplistic approach, 'If the model of Technical rationality is incomplete, in that it fails to account for practical competence in divergent situations, so much the worse for the model. Let us search instead for an epistemology of practice implicit in the artistic, intuitive processes which some practitioner do bring to situations of uncertainty, instability, uniqueness and value conflict' (Schon 1983: 49). He then outlines some key components of RP. Reflection is both continuous (reflection in action) and retrospective (reflection on action). At all times, it is defined by the professional's 'dialogue with the situation', that is generating questions related to the situation that need an answer and a solution. It is important to state that Schon was very interested in a range of professions and can often generalise very broadly across several; this can be very stimulating and generative of ideas, but it certainly elides some obvious differences between being an architect and a teacher.

The attraction for teachers is that this model puts them very much in control of their development. The key issues are how to consciously engage in reflection, i.e. 'reflection on the action' and also, most crucially, how to do this in ways that are time efficient. The relentless business of teaching in the classroom and the typically frenetic atmosphere of school life would appear to militate very strongly against opportunities for reflection, even to be by their nature 'anti-reflective'. Other professions do have, both formally and informally, what might be described as a more reflective professional paradigm (Schon 1987). However, Schon's formulation of a 'dialogue with the situation' means that much reflective thinking is done 'in action'.

There are some simple points to add that may take us beyond Schon's model without diminishing its value per se. One is that his fascination with highly effective practitioners led him often to focus on the individual to the exclusion of the group and the wider community. It seems likely, if hard to prove, that we can 'do reflection' socially as well as privately. In Chapter 8, we will consider the role of professional development in supporting the ongoing improvement of expertise, usually something experienced by teachers in groups. It might be argued that Schon's individualistic model has done teaching something of a disservice as a profession by suggesting that it is simply all about reflection, something that individuals do, as it were, in their own time. It might be one reason why ITT has been so overloaded because its formulation may imply that, as long as student teachers can learn how to reflect, then they can carry on developing regardless of the 'situation' they find themselves in. This may be a somewhat parodic version of ITT, but teaching as a profession is woefully short of formally provided development time, a part of which should surely be reflective.

Here, it may be useful to consider the rather broader notions of reflectiveness and their relationship to expertise which can be formulated reductively as merely 'skill'. Underlying all these models is the importance of working memory and cognitive capacity. Teaching, in the best sense, has much that is routine and regular about it; equally, it is full of variety and surprise. Effective teachers develop many strategies for becoming able to distinguish between what does and does not need attention in a classroom. As this capacity increases, it releases mental space for focusing on what is significant in the moment of interaction with students.

Competence and standards

It is worth framing this discussion first through the following conceptualisation of conscious competence. It is argued that, in acquiring a skill, there are, typically, four broad stages:

1   unconscious incompetence;
2   conscious incompetence;
3   conscious competence;
4   unconscious competence.

It is especially interesting to consider (1), because it relates to the earlier discussion of the perception by so many adults that teaching is 'easy'. This was characterised as the 'passenger model', i.e. teaching looks easy when just observing or receiving it but, if you really try to do it, then immediately (2) comes into play. After some time, perhaps two or three years, then teaching begins to feel like (3). Very experienced and competent teachers reach (4).

Two points emerge here. Very effective teachers may well lack some self-awareness of 'how they do it', especially as the difficulties of learning how to do it recede with time, making them, potentially, very unsympathetic to both the novice and the incompetent. This, for example, is why mentorship training is so important for experienced teachers who need to re-examine how teaching is learnt so that they can help novices move on from stage (1). The second point is that, as well as a desirable and necessary stage, 'unconscious competence' may also be a plateau; competent is not expert. Semantically competent can mean merely 'adequate' and may even be somewhat negative; 'that was just a competent performance' can suggest that much was missing.

One outcome of the effort to treat teaching as a set of competences has been the rapid rise of standards, that is descriptive statements of what effective teaching should be like. In this section, the focus will be on the pros and cons of this approach, not the detail. Much reference will necessarily be made to standards throughout the book, especially where they try to capture expert/excellent levels. The strength of the competence approach is that it offers definitions of aspects of teaching that can be used by a range of professionals to discuss actual teaching. So a novice teacher can be helped to understand what an experienced teacher is achieving by a joint discussion of a particular 'standard'. Such descriptions allow reasonable judgements to be made against evidence accumulated by a teacher. However, the objectivity of standards is fundamentally an illusion. They are very 'of their time', and they are always open to interpretation; indeed, the best teachers use them as a starting point not a finishing point. At worst, competence descriptors produce long checklists that are administered mechanistically and without reasonable judgement. Inevitably, they may become especially limited when applied to expert and innovative performance.

Overall, they have brought more benefits than disadvantages to teachers and researchers because they have helped articulate our knowledge base about teaching and have begun to open up dialogues about how best to capture and describe 'good practice'. The creation in several systems of either a continuum of standards, e.g. England (DCSF website), or standards aimed at the *more than competent* teacher, e.g. the National Board for Professional Teaching Standards (NBPTS) in the US (NBPTS website), chartered teacher in Scotland (GTCS website), mark a decidedly new departure and offer a very new set of opportunities for the highly effective teacher. They are not, in themselves, necessarily any more reliable than other such standards; however, they potentially bring into the dialogue the very best teachers, and they have certainly begun to establish the concept that such teachers not only exist, but can be both helpful to all other teachers and can themselves continue to improve.

Effective teaching?

There are some valuable sources for considering the nature of effective teaching; this section is a selective summary. An important starting point is a relatively recent research study, the Hay McBer report (Hay McBer 2000), which divides teachers into competent, effective and outstanding. This report was especially important for a number of reasons, the most striking of which is that it formed the basis for the introduction of performance management into English schools ('performance' will be considered below). A second important factor was that the research was conducted by a management consultancy, not educational researchers. This was an interesting tactic as it meant that the authors could ignore all the existing research evidence and 'start afresh'. Such an approach is not entirely without merit, and the report itself does have some valuable ideas (these are considered below). The report revealed some of its political inflections by using the term outstanding as a given term; 'outstanding' is the term adopted by Ofsted throughout the 1990s. Overall, however, in simply ignoring previous work, the report has a superficiality that undermines its very conclusive rhetoric (it will be discussed further below).

A number of substantial studies have tried to define what is good about teaching, for example 'good teaching' (Brown and McIntyre 1993), effective teaching (Perrot 1982; Cullingford 1995; Cooper and McIntyre 1996; Kyriacou 1997), 'creative teaching' (Woods and Jeffrey 1996), 'veteran teachers' (Shulman 1987) and 'quality teaching' (Stones 1992). A very substantial, recent examination of teacher effectiveness, the VITAE project (Variations in

Teachers' Work, Lives and their Effects on Pupils), published in book form as *Teachers Matter: Connecting Lives, Work and Effectiveness* (Day et al. 2007), also uses the term 'teachers who break the mould' and places a high emphasis on 'resilience'. The 2007 McKinsey Report, which boldly states 'the quality of an education system is only as good as the quality of its teachers', adopts the terms 'low performing' and 'high performing' (performance will be considered below).

Over this period, the term effective has been used consistently and is most helpful to us because of its general applicability. There are a number of texts that cover 'effective teaching' in some detail, Kyriacou's *Effective Teaching* (1997) being a good example. He points out that research began quite early in the twentieth century, mainly focusing on teacher attributes. For example, a 1930s study gathered the views of a number of what might now be termed 'stakeholders' (including teachers and pupils), and they considered the most important qualities to be 'personality and will', 'intelligence', 'sympathy and tact', 'open-mindedness' and 'a sense of humour'. It seems unlikely that this list has changed much, indicating, as it actually does, what makes teachers likeable as much as effective. Much early research tended to be of the 'black box' variety (Kyriacou 1997: 5), that is trying somehow to measure the existing attributes of teachers and pupils and then the examination results produced by a particular combination. This was a 'black box' approach because it entirely ignored what actually happened in classrooms. Since the 1960s, a much more valid model has emerged, generating much more robust and realistic evidence. Indeed, it laid some foundation for the more recent recognition, as in the McKinsey Report, that the absolutely key variable is teacher quality.

The evidence produced has suggested that the key focus is always the learning task and activities undertaken by students as generated by the actual teacher. The most productive way to investigate this focal point is through examining the variables associated with context, process and product. The *context* is everything that characterises the situation such as the teacher's knowledge and training, experience, age, gender, social class and personality, the nature of the class being taught and the occasion (end or beginning of the day, early or late in the school year), the subject or subject matter, the school as an environment and culture, the immediate community and so on. Even this list is clearly a simplification especially in a period of government policy prescription that has had a very marked effect on the subject of English. This key subject, which is, like teaching itself, always given very high status, is also the most 'interfered with' of all secondary subjects. The teaching of the subject English really is remarkably different to teaching, say, mathematics. Expert teachers have a very great deal in common, but secondary teachers also have strong subject identities. The concept of both subject knowledge and subject pedagogical knowledge will be discussed in Chapters 3 and 4.

Process refers to such elements as the teacher's enthusiasm, organisation, clarity of explanations, questioning technique, use of praise and comment, management strategies, approach to discipline, classroom climate, design of learning tasks and use of resources. Equally, students contribute to process because of the level of their engagement with the lesson, their own interaction with the teacher and each other and their own strategies for learning. Much emphasis is now being placed on the capacity of students to reflect and to 'learn how to learn'.

Product, put simply, is the result of all this interaction between context and process and, in the early twenty-first century, the preferred term is 'outcomes'. Examples of 'product' would be increases in student skill and knowledge, interest in the subject or topic, better intellectual motivation, improved confidence and self-esteem, greater autonomy and independence, and increased social development. A collective term for all this might be 'self-efficacy', i.e. that all these products are increasing together in a positive way. However, there can obviously be marked increases in one area and even decreases in another simultaneously. For example, an increase in academic knowledge may be combined with a loss of confidence.

A final point is that product suggests something measurable and objectively verifiable. If we were to use the 'common sense' paradigm here, then clearly payment by results would make sense, i.e. test them before the teacher starts whatever episode is determined significant (one lesson? one year?) and then repeat the test; if the students do better, then effective teaching must have occurred. In an era of 'high stakes testing', this will lead to incessant testing, a great deal of 'teaching to the test', huge emphasis on highly visible results per teacher, per school, per school district and per system. This might produce what could be called efficient teaching, i.e. a very narrow focus producing some very particular outcomes, but the evidence is clear that this is not effective education and it is also highly damaging to teaching quality (see Day et al. 2007). Certainly one of the underpinning principles in this book is that such a regime is counterproductive to the development of really expert teachers in any phase or subject. Ultimately, the measurement of educational outcomes clearly has its place, and the continued application of research and experiment may lead to genuine increases in the accuracy and validity of such measurement.

However, the obsession with measurement and with what might be termed the medical model of research is unquestionably highly problematic. The 'medical model' adopts a random trial of a large population to see what works, i.e. does drug x work with all ages and types of people? If not, which ones does it work with and who should therefore avoid it? Over time, these findings can be progressively refined. It is also important to consider that this model is usually predicated on trials on animals first. It is not surprising that governments find this notion appealing, as in, does intervention x produce good outcomes for all students; hence, in England, the design of the National Literacy Strategy and the obsessive attempts to measure its 'benefits'. However, teachers and students are not rats, not that rats should be treated inhumanly either.

The key point in considering both effective teaching and expert teaching is that the inter-relationship of context, process and product variables is highly complex and difficult to measure in a simple and reliable way. This does not lessen its importance or the value of constantly seeking to find better ways to achieve it. The point is that teachers themselves are a part of this development, not merely subjects in a highly controlled experiment. Indeed, something that should be treated as experimental and not permanent is the introduction of standards to teaching, the ultimate use of the competence paradigm.

Standards and accountability

The introduction of standards into teaching is a global phenomenon. In one respect, it can be welcomed as further evidence of an ongoing trend to define what good teaching looks like in practice. At the same time, it is hugely problematic if it merely prescribes practice and is really driven by managerialist attempts to both measure (in a simplistic way) and control effective teaching. As with many points in this book, very good teachers have very specific issues with a standards model, not least because their special qualities may lie beyond or above what such a model can capture. However, it seems inevitable that standards are likely to be used, for the foreseeable future, in the service of both developing teachers and controlling them; this will be a real tension and expert teachers have a key role to play in exerting influence towards development.

The very term 'standards' is applied to so many things for so many reasons that it is in danger of becoming a linguistic morass. In an effort for some clarity, it is worth stating that the next section will endeavour to avoid any debate about the 'standards in schools are rising/no they are falling' agenda. Later in the book, there will be some discussion of the impact of the standards agenda on experienced and successful teachers, but in relation to their resilience and their determination to develop. The focus here is on the competence paradigm as it is enacted through the development and use of standards to describe teaching, especially very good teaching.

It is worth noting that the development of national style standards stems initially from the emergence of the teacher appraisal model in the 1980s at a time when schools and teachers were the subject of particularly fierce criticism. A recommendation in *Better Schools* (DES 1985) became a scheme in 1991 (DES), and this was mirrored in many countries (Millman and Darling-Hammond 1990; Hickcox and Musella 1992). The teaching unions were extremely suspicious of these schemes and tend still to be so, being concerned that such schemes are not only principally managerialist, but also driven by a desire to prove incompetence rather than to celebrate expertise.

The three main purposes for appraisal can be summed up quite simply (see Kyriacou 2001: ch. 9). There is a managerial function which should essentially be about understanding teacher quality in a school so that the management (head teacher, head of department, etc.) can understand a teacher's performance and make the best use of it by also diagnosing any school issues. Equally, it is a tool for professional development (this will be discussed in more depth in Chapter 8). As in professional development, there are two key aspects: one is feedback on actual performance, especially the observed teaching episode; and second, there is feedback on longer term and career development. When appraisal is undertaken successfully, these two major purposes can be very complementary, especially for increasingly effective teachers who may be able to undertake much wider roles in the school if their quality is understood, for example, becoming an advanced skills teacher or an excellent teacher. Such teachers may themselves become very valuable as appraisers, especially as they may be perceived as not managerial and solely developmental.

It is the third purpose, that of public accountability, that connects most directly with this particular standards agenda. In other words, by assessing the quality of teaching in a school, some kind of measure can be awarded to the school and therefore cumulatively to the school area and then the whole system. If such evidence were reliable and robust, it would be possible to state year on year whether standards of teaching were improving. The entire model of inspection in England was based on such an assumption for a considerable period, leading to massive statements in the Chief Inspector's report about the quality of teaching across the whole of the system. This whole approach also led to the draconian 'failing school' concept and the notion of 'special measures'. This entire conceptualisation of schools and teaching is deeply flawed and highly controversial. It also makes accountability seem principally predicated on the need to fail teachers and schools. There is abundant evidence (for example, see Day et al. 2007) that the effect of this model of inspection was corrosive and destructive. Very good teachers who received an Ofsted 1 as confirmation of their quality were typically pleased, but mostly relieved, a rather paradoxical outcome. The self-evaluative model of inspection that is under development in England may shift paradigms and become a much more reflective model.

One simple initiative to emerge from this complex period of high prescription of both the curriculum (National Curriculum introduced in 1988) and of teachers (appraisal introduced in 1991) was the introduction of standards for ITT in 1999. It is worth reflecting on the fact that standards were first introduced for student teachers (novices), then later for ASTs ('experts'), and that the middle part of the continuum (competent) came last! It is also of note that the creation of standards for ITT was bound up with the reformulation from initial teacher *education* to initial teacher *training* and the significant shift from *student* teacher to *trainee* teacher. Much of this stemmed from another government accountability agency, the Teacher Training Agency (TTA). It emerged in 1993 and was conceptualised as very much part of the competence/incompetence paradigm. It can certainly be argued that this was all part of a profoundly negative shift towards downgrading teaching as a profession and imposing massive negative control on it at classroom level. Part of this was symbolised by the destruction of the previous Her Majesty's Inspection of Schools model of inspection and the creation of the Office for Standards in Education in 1992 (Ofsted). It is notable that the TTA changed its name in 2005 to the Training and Development Agency for Schools, clearly signalling a shift in role towards support for teachers.

From effective to expert

Chapter 2 explores the idea of expertise in a broad sense and then focuses on some current 'models' of expert teaching in England and beyond. This chapter concludes by bringing together the idea of the professional with a meta-analysis of expert teaching. Hattie's seminal review of the existing research evidence, based on half a million studies from around the world (Hattie 2003), provides a framework for considering expert teachers throughout the rest of the book. He synthesises the findings first into five dimensions.
  Expert teachers:

- A: can identify essential representations of their subject;
- B: can guide learning through classroom interactions;
- C: can monitor learning and provide feedback;
- D: can attend to affective attributes; and
- E: can influence student outcomes.

He then outlines the specific characteristics:

A1. Expert teachers have deeper representations about teaching and learning.
A2. Expert teachers adopt a problem-solving stance to their work.
A3. Expert teachers can anticipate, plan and improvise as required by the situation.
A4. Expert teachers are better decision-makers and can identify what decisions are important and which are less important decisions.
B5. Expert teachers are proficient at creating an optimal classroom climate for learning.
B6. Expert teachers have a multidimensionally complex perception of classroom situations.
B7. Expert teachers are more context dependent and have high situation cognition.
C8. Expert teachers are more adept at monitoring student problems and assessing their level of understanding and progress, and they provide much more relevant, useful feedback.

C9. Expert teachers are more adept at developing and testing hypotheses about learning difficulties or instructional strategies.

C10. Expert teachers are more automatic.

D11. Expert teachers have high respect for students.

D12. Expert teachers are passionate about teaching and learning.

E13. Expert teachers engage students in learning and develop in their students self-regulation, involvement in mastery learning, enhanced self-efficacy and self-esteem as learners.

E14. Expert teachers provide appropriate challenging tasks and goals for students.

E15. Expert teachers have positive influences on students' achievement.

E16. Expert teachers enhance surface and deep learning (Hattie 2003: 6–10).

Hattie explains that these are not prescriptive or uniform, but facets:

> Our claim, from a review of literature and a synthesis of over 500,000 studies, is that expert teachers can be distinguished by these five dimensions, or 16 attributes. This is not aimed to be a checklist, but a profile. We see these attributes as 16 facets of the gem-stone, we see there is no one necessary facet, nor the equal presence of all, but the overlapping of many facets into the whole.
>
> Hattie (2003: 10)

He also points out that there is nothing here about 'content knowledge' but explains:

> Our argument is that content knowledge is necessary for both experienced and expert teachers, and is thus not a key distinguishing feature. We are not underestimating the importance of content knowledge – it must be present – but it is more pedagogical content knowledge that is important: that is, the way knowledge is used in teaching situations.
>
> Hattie (2003: 10)

This is an important distinction for this book, which does focus on a key content area called English, difficult to define but 'real' nevertheless; it is the subject of Chapter 3. Hattie is also very deliberately focusing on the teacher as the individual variable inside the classroom; this book treats the expert teacher also as an expert professional and as a major potential influence on other teachers (see Chapter 8). For the purposes of the book, I offer a slightly simplified version of Hattie's characteristics:

• Deep understanding of teaching and learning;
• Problem-solving approach;

- Anticipate, plan and improvise;
- Excellent decision-makers – prioritise decisions;
- Optimal classroom climate for learning;
- Recognise the multidimensional nature of the classroom;
- They recognise that teaching is context dependent and highly situated;
- Constantly monitoring student progress and providing valuable feedback;
- Testing 'hypotheses', i.e. is this working?;
- More automatic, i.e. they keep plenty of 'mental space' available;
- High respect for all students;
- Passionate about teaching and learning;
- Highly motivating – building students self-regulation, self-efficacy, self-esteem;
- Set appropriate but challenging goals and tasks;
- Positively impact on achievement;
- Enhance surface and deep learning.

Hattie's characteristics therefore offer a very useful framework for considering the expert teaching of English, but they will not capture the full picture of the extended professional who is an expert teacher of English.

Chapter 2

Expertise and models of expert teaching

What do you call a 'very good' teacher?

Sally, Interview 3: *I think it does and doesn't matter what we call very good teachers. I don't like Advanced Skills much, sounds like train driver or something, and expert is a bit clinical, but just 'very good' carries no weight I know, it is a tricky one...*

Defining expertise

The creation in England of the 'excellent teacher' grade in September 2006 looks like an important moment in the increasing recognition of the importance of expert teaching, and it may well be. However, the previous establishment of the advanced skills teacher role in 1998, some ten years before, partly suggests an uncertainty in deciding what to call 'expert teachers' and also equally complex issues around role definition; what do you do with expert teachers once you are sure you have correctly identified them? The establishment of these two named categories also demonstrates how reluctant teachers and policy-makers are to use the term 'expert'.

However, from expert comes expertise, a much less divisive notion. What all the cited professions above (Chapter 1) have strongly in common is a powerful focus on identifying what characterises expertise in their particular field and ensuring that they 'control' and develop that expertise.

The term 'expert' has enjoyed a much simpler history than 'profession'. Deriving originally from the Latin meaning 'experienced' and 'practised in', the term has had a simple acceptance as a consistent definition. There is the occasional mention in literature, for example, in Chaucer's *General Prologue to The Canterbury Tales*, in introducing the Mancible and his learned advisers, there occurs the line 'That were of lawe expert and curious', and in Shakespeare's *Othello*, Cassio remarks about Othello's ship 'his Pylot Of verie expert, and approu'd Allowance'. In the nineteenth century, expert becomes more about having both specialised knowledge and being a specialist, but this was already implied in both Chaucer's and Shakespeare's usage. Late in the nineteenth century, the definition includes having an expert opinion, implying that others would want to access such an opinion and also pointing to the later development of the 'expert witness'.

Expertise is variously defined, but these points are fundamentally agreed (see Ericsson et al. 2006: 1–17):

First, it is the characteristics, skills and knowledge that distinguish the experts from novices and less experienced people. For example, it is very easy to hear differences in musical performance, even without having musical expertise.

Second, experts are able consistently (although not perfectly) to reproduce high levels of performance. For example, experienced and expert doctors typically make correct diagnoses. This aspect of expertise is often called 'superior reproducible performance of representative tasks'; this is a very clear distinguisher in teaching between the novice and the expert teacher.

Third, although the notion of the 'precocious' is powerful and especially impresses the general public in certain domains, particularly in musical performance, chess-playing, various sporting domains, etc., experts are highly experienced in their domain. This can be simplistically quantified, i.e. 'she has been teaching for forty years'.

Fourth, being experienced does not guarantee expertise. Experts have mental organisations of their experience that make them vastly superior to equally experienced peers. However, although there is increasingly a body of evidence to support this point, it is, by its mental nature, not easily susceptible to 'proof'. At a pragmatic level, most teachers do develop a sense of who, among their colleagues, is open to maintaining a developmental perspective on their teaching, however experienced they are. There is a danger here of mere 'folk lore' conceptualisations, one argument, therefore, in favour of more professional attention to identifying and studying true teacher expertise.

Fifth, and less certainly, expertise is acquired through deliberate training and practice, rather than through merely repetitive practice. This point seems very obvious, but it is more complex than it seems at first. It might imply that, if one practised a skill in isolation for long enough, one would become expert, for example in playing the violin. And expert violinists spend huge amounts of time doing just that. However, they also learn from watching others, from direct instruction and from indirect means such as reading about the lives of musicians.

This last point is especially important in teaching. One reason is because there is a strong folk lore in teaching that 'you can only learn by doing it'; this extends to the idea that one is only credible if you have taught for many years and if you still regularly do teach. This affects perceptions of head teachers and other senior staff who no longer teach; similarly, teacher educators who are now 'removed' from the classroom can be perceived as too 'theoretical'.

I would argue strongly that this is one of the myths that keeps teaching in a second tier mode as a profession and tends to make competence, i.e. a reasonable level of practice, a dominating paradigm. The second reason for this point's importance to teaching is the notion of deliberate practice, and this will be elaborated in Chapter 7. At this stage, it is important to summarise this complex issue with an example. Teacher questioning is increasingly identified as one of the key skills in any subject domain or age phase. If that is the case, what might be the best way to move, as rapidly as possible, from novice to expert application of this skill? We do not have a definitive answer, partly because it is very difficult to create a domain in which to study teacher questioning; the 'real' classroom is such a complex arena. Equally, how might we create a 'practice environment' for teachers that bears any approximation to a classroom? These difficulties tend to mean that the individual teacher can be left to 'reflect' on their own practice in isolation.

Models of expertise

A useful starting point for identifying an operationally useful definition of expertise for teachers is the Dreyfus Brothers model. This is a model that fits well with the research evidence about the stages of teachers' long-term development and also because of its genesis. The Dreyfus brothers worked in the emerging field of artificial intelligence (AI) in the 1970s. Their hypothesis was not that robots and AI would come to be more significant than human beings, but quite the reverse. They considered that human beings' capacity to learn, especially from experience, made them infinitely adaptable and capable of improvement (Dreyfus and Dreyfus 1986).

Essentially, they first put forward a five-stage model and then revised it to become: novice, advanced beginner, competent, proficient and expert. Interestingly, in their very first outline, they did not include advanced beginner but had 'master' above expert. This is a very challenging element and will be discussed below when referring to what to call 'expert teachers', for example the term 'master teacher' has had some currency in the US (e.g. the University of Georgia, Master Teacher program).

The five-stage model, including advanced beginner, fits well in broad terms with our understanding of teacher development, and is helpful in that it identifies the necessity of going through stages to become an expert teacher. It helps to conceptualise the possibility of both being able to characterise such stages with evidence from teaching, making observers and assessors more able to plan development and training opportunities, and also teachers' being self-aware of these stages and so having relevant and intelligent expectations. Practically, for example, novice might be equated with trainee seeking qualified teacher status (QTS) and advanced beginner with newly qualified teacher (NQT). However, individual professional development should never be overly tied to real time, i.e. simplistic notions of a 'training year'.

In terms of real impact on the professions, Benner's seminal 1984 work, *From Novice to Expert: Excellence and Power in Clinical Nursing Practice*, applied the Dreyfus model to nursing, and developed the model into a much more grounded and usefully detailed modus operandi:

> The Dreyfus model posits that, in the acquisition and development of a skill, a student passes through five levels of proficiency: novice, advanced beginner, competent, proficient and expert. These different levels reflect changes in three general aspects of skilled performance:
>
> 1. One is a movement from reliance on abstract principles to the use of past concrete experience as paradigms.
> 2. The second is a change in the learner's perception of the demand situation, in which the situation is seen less and less as a compilation of equally relevant bits, and more and more as a complete whole in which only certain parts are relevant.
> 3. The third is a passage from detached observation to involved performer. The performer no longer stands outside the situation but is now engaged in the situation.

Benner's interpretation closely aligns with Schon, especially over point 3, and highlights how experts retain, as Hattie notes, that passion and enthusiasm for their teaching. Benner elaborates on each stage:

> • Stage 1: Novice
>
> Beginners have had no experience of the situations in which they are expected to perform. Novices are taught rules to help them perform. The rules are context free and independent of specific cases; hence, the rules tend to be applied universally. The rule-governed behavior typical of the novice is extremely limited and inflexible. As such, novices have no "life experience" in the application of rules. "Just tell me what I need to do and I'll do it."

These are certainly the characteristics of the beginning teacher and usefully highlight that experience of life, i.e. being a mature student, is not the same as the life experience of the role of a teacher.

> • Stage 2: Advanced beginner
>
> Advanced beginners are those who can demonstrate marginally acceptable performance, those who have coped with enough real situations to note, or to have pointed out to them by a mentor, the recurring meaningful situational components. These components require prior experience in actual situations for recognition. Principles to guide actions begin to be formulated. The principles are based on experience.

Certainly in teaching, this would be a minimum to pass training. It also emphasises that training must offer many real life situations and that a mentor is vital. The increased emphasis on the role of mentoring for trainees, NQTs and all colleagues is a huge step forward in developing teacher expertise (see Chapters 7 and 8).

- Stage 3: Competent
Competence, typified by the nurse who has been on the job in the same or similar situations for two or three years, develops when the nurse begins to see his or her actions in terms of long-range goals or plans of which he or she is consciously aware. For the competent nurse, a plan establishes a perspective, and the plan is based on considerable conscious, abstract, analytic contemplation of the problem. The conscious, deliberate planning that is characteristic of this skill level helps achieve efficiency and organization. The competent nurse lacks the speed and flexibility of the proficient nurse but does have a feeling of mastery and the ability to cope with and manage the many contingencies of clinical nursing. The competent person does not yet have enough experience to recognize a situation in terms of an overall picture or in terms of which aspects are most salient, most important.

Again, this is very recognisable in teaching, especially the general sense of 'having arrived' and having developed confidence and self-efficacy. Teaching is peculiarly orchestrated by the school year and its rhythm of terms, half-terms and key assessment points. After experiencing three years, a teacher is likely to have become accustomed to the rhythm and will usually have taught the same year group twice, perhaps seen a two-year course completely through (e.g. GCSE, 'A' level). Such a teacher will also have seen students mature over time and begun to appreciate what 'long-term goals' can be for a teacher and a school.

- Stage 4: Proficient
The proficient performer perceives situations as wholes rather than in terms of chopped up parts or aspects, and performance is guided by maxims. Proficient nurses understand a situation as a whole because they perceive its meaning in terms of long-term goals. The proficient nurse learns from experience what typical events to expect in a given situation and how plans need to be modified in response to these events. The proficient nurse can now recognize when the expected normal picture does not materialize. This holistic understanding improves the proficient nurse's decision making; it becomes less labored because the nurse now has a perspective on which of the many existing attributes and aspects in the present situation are the important ones. The proficient nurse uses maxims as guides which reflect what would appear to the competent

or novice performer as unintelligible nuances of the situation; they can mean one thing at one time and quite another thing later. Once one has a deep understanding of the situation overall, however, the maxim provides direction as to what must be taken into account. Maxims reflect nuances of the situation.

It is interesting that this stage can clearly be linked to the 'threshold' notion in England when the teacher finally becomes the full professional. It is also clear how important that 'deep understanding' is; this comes out very strongly in the case study teachers featured in Chapters 4 and 5. One of their strongest characteristics is their ability to make confident generalisations about teaching and learning, i.e. what is 'typical', but always to recognise and respect individual differences, i.e. what is 'special'. Each situation and each student is a potential nuance within their expert field.

- Stage 5: The expert
The expert performer no longer relies on an analytic principle (rule, guideline, maxim) to connect her or his understanding of the situation to an appropriate action. The expert nurse, with an enormous background of experience, now has an intuitive grasp of each situation and zeroes in on the accurate region of the problem without wasteful consideration of a large range of unfruitful alternative diagnoses and solutions. The expert operates from a deep understanding of the total situation. The chess master, for instance, when asked why he or she made a particularly masterful move, will just say: "Because it felt right; it looked good." The performer is no longer aware of features and rules; his/her performance becomes fluid and flexible and highly proficient. This is not to say that the expert never uses analytic tools. Highly skilled analytic ability is necessary for those situations with which the nurse has had no previous experience. Analytic tools are also necessary for those times when the expert gets a wrong grasp of the situation and then finds that events and behaviors are not occurring as expected. When alternative perspectives are not available to the clinician, the only way out of a wrong grasp of the problem is by using analytic problem solving.

There are very powerful echoes here of both Schon and Hattie and of the paradox of unconscious competence; the expert is very automatic and goes with intuition at such a speed that even recalling decisions may be very difficult, hence making the explanation of expertise and expert performance very difficult to explain. This description of stage 5 also highlights the point that deliberated thought will slow down any process of decision making and therefore hamper the quality of the problem solving. This is explored thoughtfully in *The Intuitive Practitioner* (Atkinson and Claxton 2000); the subtitle sums this up neatly: *on the value of not always knowing what one is doing.*

I would argue that, if the word 'teacher' is substituted for 'nurse', most highly effective teachers recognise themselves immediately. However, the fact that Benner's detailed account of the model is, in fact, about a very different domain from teaching is both interesting in itself and striking because nursing is also perceived as a 'second tier profession', yet clearly Benner is positing a very high level of expertise that would normally be associated with a top profession. I would add that teaching, like nursing, is a too modest profession very often, and that is part of its problem. I would suggest that status is not arrogance, that confidence is not complacency.

The Dreyfus model has been influential in the caring professions, but there are others. For example, Hoffman (1998) conceptualises a 'proficiency scale'. He begins with 'naive', 'one who is totally ignorant of a domain', and then calibrates novice, initiate, apprentice, journeyman, expert and, finally, master (the experts preferred expert); this model could be used to analyse expertise in teaching. A much more fine-grained model of 'perceptual learning' (Goldstone, Schyns and Medin 1997) can offer some insights into teaching as it 'happens' in the classroom situation. Their model suggests that these five 'mechanisms' operate together to produce an expert reading of a situation: attention weighting (knowing what to pay attention to), detector creation (working out what the various components are in a situation), dimensionalisation (knowing what matters most within a situation), unitisation (by knowing individual components in a situation, developing control over the whole situation), contingency detection (realising that the situation is changing). One fundamental teaching skill is summed up as 'reading the classroom', i.e. a very complex, multivariant situation happening in real time; perceptual understanding of its dynamics is vital to effective teaching and learning. Models of expertise and/or skill acquisition are numerous and can help analyse and understand teaching expertise both holistically (like Dreyfus) and in aspects (like Goldstone et al.).

Is there a 'model' in England?

Strictly speaking, the current model in England is not defined as a model of expertise at all, but if examined then its stages are:

* Achieving qualified teacher status, i.e. initial training;
* Passing 'induction' and achieving the core standards, i.e. 'probation';
* Post-threshold;
* Excellent;
* Advanced skills.

The 2009 version of the standards for teachers is set out to suggest that they are a continuum, with the advanced skills teacher (AST) positioned as the ultimate 'level'. However, they are described in the guidance as essentially career and reward stages:

> The framework of professional standards for teachers set out below defines the characteristics of teachers at each career stage. Specifically it provides professional standards for:
>
> - the award of qualified teacher status (QTS) (Q);
> - teachers on the main scale (core) (C);
> - teachers on the upper pay scale (post threshold teachers) (P);
> - excellent teachers (E);
> - advanced skills teachers (ASTs) (A).
>
> DCSF website

This mode of description immediately highlights the underlying ideology of the use of the standards, as opposed to the nature of the standards themselves; their use is both 'performance related' in a managerial sense and hierarchical rather than developmental. The Guidance (DCSF 2009) makes this even more explicit:

> The standards provide the framework for a teacher's career and clarify what progression looks like. As now, to access each career stage a teacher will need to demonstrate that he/she has met the relevant standards. The process for this varies depending on the standards concerned. Teachers seeking Excellent Teacher or AST status need to apply and be assessed through an external assessment process. Teachers seeking to cross the threshold are assessed by their head teacher. The standards for Post Threshold Teachers, Excellent Teachers and ASTs are pay standards and teachers who are assessed as meeting them also access the relevant pay scale.

For the aspiring or existing expert teachers, this is a clear reminder that 'standards' are always of their time and are very likely to be ideologically inflected. They have their uses, as discussed above, but they should be treated critically and as subject to constant revision and even improvement. Indeed, a characteristic of an expert teacher would be to adopt this stance towards standards and to treat them as generative not prescriptive. Before considering the more apposite excellent teacher and the AST standards in more detail, it is worth noting again that this is a global movement and that most developed systems are trying out this mode of teacher characterisation, producing a variety of 'titles' (see below) as a result.

One development worthy of mention, partly as a contrast, is the initiative in Scotland to introduce the 'chartered teacher' (GTCS 2009). This is underpinned by a similar wish to retain the best teachers in the classroom and, at first glance, looks very comparable to England, for example the Scottish scheme identifies these components:

- professional values and personal commitments;
- professional knowledge and understanding;
- professional and personal attributes;
- professional action.

In England, the components are (DCSF 2009):

- professional attributes;
- professional knowledge and understanding;
- professional skills.

However, the chartered model is intended for all experienced teachers who wish to achieve 'the standard'; this can be done either through a Master's-style programme or through 'stating a claim' to the GTCS, which then has to be validated. The chartered model was developed consensually in Scotland and has given the Scottish GTC a really important role in improving the status of the profession, something completely missing in England. The use of the term also implies a strong equivalence with other professions that identify and celebrate their own chartered professionals. This model has also been adopted for teachers in Wales, and some subject associations in England are developing their own chartered teacher model, notably science and geography. The Geography Association's description (see GA website) is interesting for a number of reasons, first:

- Honours degree in geography or related subject (60% geography content) or BEd with geography (or fifteen years' teaching experience if no relevant degree is held);
- at least six years' teaching experience;
- commitment to continuing professional development (CPD), embedding it in your own practice and supporting others.

This is straightforward and it naturally stresses subject knowledge, but it also emphasises demonstrating working with others (see Chapter 7). It then stresses the status that is on offer:

If you are successful in your application for Chartered status you will also become a Fellow of the Royal Geographical Society (with IBG) if you are not so already.

You can use existing documentation to support your application, such as:

- your Professional Development Record, which can be used as evidence for the CPD portfolio required for award of CGeog (Teacher);
- evidence you have collected for performance management.

Where did these criteria originate? The criteria for Chartered Geographer (Teacher) were set by the Privy Council.

This is a much more ideological inflection and reminds us of Eraut's point (see Chapter 1) that professions are essentially ideologies; what could be more distinguished than recognition by the Privy Council?

The Association of Science Education combines an emphasis on the skilled nature of teaching:

> Science teaching is a demanding and complex process. Skilled science teachers, knowledgeable in pedagogy, science education and science deserve professional recognition. The ASE has worked in collaboration with the Science Council to create a mechanism which recognises and celebrates high quality science teachers and science education profession-als through the award of Chartered Science Teacher (CSciTeach) status.
>
> The introduction of the CSciTeach designation provides for the first time an opportunity for individuals to gain an award which accredits and val-ues their all round expertise in science education and their commitment to updating the knowledge, skills and understanding they require. CSciTeach, as our current President, Professor Sir Gareth Roberts, noted:
>
> "... *will provide science teachers, working in a wide range of settings, with a professional status recognising and rewarding their high quality expertise which is in turn underpinned by a commitment to CPD. Ultimately the main beneficiaries, however, will be our pupils and students.*"
>
> *Education in Science* Feb 2005 (ASE website)

What is CSciTeach?

CSciTeach, or Chartered Science Teacher, is a chartered designation in line with other awards, such as Chartered Scientist, Chartered Engi-neer, Chartered Accountant or Chartered Surveyor, that recognises the professional standing of an individual working in that field. The awards are made under powers granted by the Privy Council to par-ticular organisations and incorporated in their Royal Charters. As a chartered designation CSciTeach recognises the unique and demand-ing combination of skills, knowledge, understanding and expertise that are required by individuals involved in practising and advancing science teaching and learning.

Chartered Science Teachers, therefore, are professionals, teachers and educators, who are practising and/or advancing science teaching and learning and for whom knowledge and skills in pedagogy, science edu-cation and science are essential elements in their role. They will have a critical awareness of current issues which is informed by developments in educational practice, pedagogy and scientific endeavour.

The ASE rightly stresses that this kind of teacher recognition is not susceptible to government policies and has an equivalence that might make it globally recognisable:

Who awards CSciTeach?

ASE awards CSciTeach. Under the terms of its Royal Charter, ASE, as a licensed body of the Science Council, is empowered to award CSciTeach to individuals who meet the requirements and to maintain a register of holders of the designation. This register in turn is a special section of the register of Chartered Scientists (CSci) which underpins the quality and equivalence of the awards. In other words it means that CSciTeach will be widely accepted alongside other chartered qualifications.

Finally, it relates the intrinsic rewards and the extrinsic and returns to the key concept of expertise:

What are the benefits of CSciTeach?

As CSciTeach is in its infancy the benefits relate mainly to raising the overall profile of science teaching and learning and, for individuals, to providing recognition of their expertise and commitment. In time, as with other chartered designations, it is hoped that CSciTeach will provide access to more tangible benefits and rewards. Currently CSciTeach aims to:

- promote high quality science teaching and learning;
- recognise high and improving professional expertise;
- reflect best effective practice in science education;
- provide evidence of a commitment to continuing professional development.

This use of 'chartered' as a term is clearly a thoughtful attempt to give teaching a comparable status to, say, chartered engineers, accountants, librarians and so on. It also places the award outside the vagaries of political policy changes; the AST and excellent teacher are not a 'status' and, as pay levels, could be abolished or diminished overnight. Equally, the AST role, after ten years, has not evolved into a realistic expectation for the majority of experienced teachers; figures in 2009 suggest about 4,500 ASTs out of about 500,000 teachers.

Scotland is aiming for 5,000 chartered teachers within five years, and this will be a very significant proportion of the teacher population. This model is worth considering in some detail as it is arguably the most developed of its kind in Europe (Connelly and McMahon 2007).

The GTCS makes clear that the focus is on staying in the classroom and achieving more recognition at the same time:

What are the benefits of Chartered Teacher status?

Experienced teachers have faced a difficult choice: to gain further rewards and respect for their professionalism, they have to move away from the classroom into a management post. However, by gaining Chartered Teacher status, with CPD advantage, you will:

- increase your earning power;
- enhance your professional recognition and career progression;
- gain membership of the City and Guilds of London Institute (MCGI): a qualification comparable to a Master's degree;
- remain a classroom based professional.

By obtaining Chartered Teacher status, you can gain the respect and financial rewards appropriate for an experienced professional and you will gain additional knowledge, skills and abilities that will enable you to enhance the quality of learning experiences and achievements of the students you teach.

GTCS website

However, the standards for chartered status clearly articulate an extended professional model, including the idea of professional *action*:

The Standard

The Standard consists of four key components:

- Professional values and personal commitments;
- Professional knowledge and understanding;
- Professional and personal attributes; and
- Professional action.

Scottish Government website

The stress is very much on the teacher as a caring, imaginative human being; this contrasts quite sharply with the AST:

Professional values and personal commitments

The Chartered Teacher, having developed beyond the basic requirements of the Standard for Full Registration, *should demonstrate four central professional values and personal commitments:*

- Effectiveness in promoting learning in the classroom

Since teaching is about promoting learning, the Chartered Teacher must be strongly motivated to be effective in securing the well-being and educational progress of learners.

- Critical self-evaluation and development

No matter how effective the Chartered Teacher may be, there is a commitment to enhanced performance. Practice is subject to regular review and there is a continuing search for new and improved ways of supporting pupils' learning through discussion with others and by reading and research.

- Collaboration and influence

The Chartered Teacher will be committed to influencing and having a leading impact in team and school development, and to contributing to the professional development of colleagues and new entrants to the profession. As a member of a wider professional community, he or she will be committed to influencing the development of teaching and learning, and to strengthening partnerships with other professional groups, parents and other agencies.

- Educational and social values

The Chartered Teacher is committed to core educational and social values, such as concern for truth, personal responsibility, equality, social justice and inclusion, and to pupils' personal, social, moral and cultural development.

The characteristics that teachers must demonstrate map very closely to Hattie, but also emphasise the teacher as not just a reflective practitioner but also a deeply informed professional with a real awareness of research and publications:

Professional knowledge and understanding

The Chartered Teacher *should demonstrate through his or her work a critical understanding of:*

- current approaches to teaching and learning;
- current research on teaching and learning;
- changing social and cultural contexts of education;
- the school curriculum, its knowledge base, and how the curriculum relates to life in the community, including citizenship and the world of work;
- educational assessment and its interpretation;

- responses to pupil differences and to pupils experiencing barriers to learning;
- principles and practices of social justice, inclusion, equality and democracy, and strategies to counter discrimination;
- education and the promotion of personal well-being, and community and environmental development;
- teachers as co-educators with parents and other professionals;
- the nature of professionalism;
- current policy debates;
- ICT and its importance in teaching and learning.

This standard even mentions information and communications technology (ICT), something also missing from ASTs but discussed in depth in Chapter 6. Both the professional and the personal are articulated:

Professional and personal attributes

The Chartered Teacher *should be able to demonstrate a range of skills and attributes that are characteristics of all forms of professional work*:

- having enthusiasm and the capacity to motivate;
- communicating effectively;
- being resourceful and positive, and adopting a problem-solving approach;
- being creative and imaginative, and having an open attitude to change;
- being systematic and well organised, focused, determined and hard-working;
- demonstrating empathy and fairness, being caring and approachable;
- showing consistent performance across all professional areas.

Finally, the emphasis is not on just gaining the status but using it in the real world of school:

Professional action

As noted earlier, these professional values and personal commitments, knowledge and understanding, and professional and personal attributes must interact and result in professional action of various kinds.

The consultation process confirms support for identifying *nine forms of professional action*. These can be categorised to correspond to the four professional values and personal commitments, namely, *Effectiveness in promoting learning in the classroom; Critical reflection, self-evaluation and development; Collaboration and influence; and Educational and social values.*

One example of such action is:

articulating a personal, independent and critical stance in relation to contrasting perspectives on educational issues, policies and developments.

And the instances given are:

- undertaking critical evaluations of official educational documents, research reports, articles or books in relation to the current debates in the educational and wider community;
- engaging with others in the critical discussion of educational policy and practice.

Whereas the AST tends to be characterised as carrying out policy (see below), the chartered teacher is far more critical and independent. However, the excellent teacher does at least have some requirement of this kind (see below). Overall, for the aspiring expert teacher, the chartered model is one to watch; it may prove to be the best of its kind in Europe, possibly the world. Some might argue that being within the reach of all experienced teachers may devalue that status. In the end, it will come down to professional credibility and to the development of a robust and fair assessment system.

The challenge in finding a highly effective title for 'expert teachers'

One of Shakespeare's best known lines is 'What's in a name' and continuing 'a rose by any other name would smell as sweet' (*Romeo and Juliet*). However, the world of education has not been so confident about what to call a 'very good' teacher, and certainly, that term 'very good', however much used popularly and informally, has not been seen as providing the right status for what is being described. It is worth reflecting that this stems partly from many other factors (professionalism, unionisation, materiality) covered earlier in the chapter that bear down on this descriptor, once it becomes a status with a title. When the term 'advanced skills teacher' was first imported to England from Australia in 1997, and became a formal term, it was highly controversial. The popular press published cartoon images of 'super teachers', dressed in Superman costumes, flying through the windows of classrooms (Goodwyn 1997). Although this was largely humorous, it nevertheless symbolises the popular view that, given that teaching is seen as a rather ordinary activity, then any extraordinary claim about it is rather ludicrous. It is immediately clear then that the title and/or descriptive term matters very much and may well reflect a very determining view of what the title bearer is also to do with their expertise. For example, why does England have the advanced skills teacher and also the excellent teacher? Ultimately, it is difficult to decide on the best term because what is being captured is in itself very complex.

Advanced skills teacher

The current use of the term AST in England was derived from an attempt in several Australian states to both identify and reward the best teachers and to retain them; this development has had its own controversies (Ingvarson and Chadbourne 1997; Kleinhenz and Ingvarson 2004; Ingvarson 2008). These definitions appeared first in 1994 and have been revised, but they capture what is also now current in South Australia (see Government of South Australia website).

The AST was introduced in 1994, and the AST2 level was added in 2006. The characteristics of these ASTs are a very simple model:

An AST1 must be able to demonstrate the possession of high-level skills which enable them to show that they can:

a. apply a range of effective teaching approaches and methods of evaluating and reporting students'/children's progress;
b. generate positive relationships with individual students/children, class groups and groups of children;
c. develop ideas gained from their own teaching practice and apply ideas gained from professional development activities to enhance students'/children's learning;
d. apply to their teaching the knowledge of current trends and developments in education;
e. work collaboratively with other teachers;
f. communicate and work effectively with other teachers, parents and the wider site community;
g. contribute to the organisation, planning and development of the site's curriculum;
h. assist other teachers in their professional development and supervise, instruct and counsel beginning and student teachers;
i. provide professional and personal support to less experienced staff and poorly performing staff to facilitate performance improvements.

Government of South Australia website

These are recognisable as related to Hattie or the chartered teacher model, but it seems their rather modest expectations led to a revamped AST2 model from 2006:

An AST 2 will be able to provide evidence of their sustained role as a teacher leader and the impact that their work has had in challenging, changing and improving the practice of, at least, 4–6 colleagues at a team, site, district or systemic level.

All criteria should be interpreted with these ideas as the underpinning premise.

1. Demonstrated ability to teach students in an exemplary manner using current learning theories and innovative methodologies.
2. Demonstrated ability to model, develop and positively influence the professional reflection and practice of colleagues.
3. Demonstrated positive collaboration with colleagues and contribution to their professional support and growth.
4. Demonstrated involvement in the critical evaluation of professional practice to challenge, change and improve the quality of teaching of colleagues and the learning outcomes for students.
5. Demonstrated contribution, as a leading practitioner, in the development, implementation and evaluation of a learning area, subject area, program, or a new teaching and learning initiative.
6. Demonstrated ability to effectively influence and expand knowledge and practice of colleagues through mentoring or conducting professional learning opportunities.
7. Demonstrated effective contribution to school/site improvement planning, identification of priorities and to formal school/site decision-making processes.

Government of South Australia website

What is interesting here is the emphasis on the extended professional concept, but also on being a leading practitioner who influences and develops others, something implied in the AST model in England and now stated in the excellent teacher definition. This 'second stage' is also something missing from the original idea of the AST in both Australia and England, i.e. how you keep developing a highly developed teacher (see Chapter 8).

In England, the AST has its own longevity, having been in operation for over a decade. After an early period of uncertainty and considerable opposition, the role has become widely accepted and now accounts for 1 per cent of the teaching workforce. There have been two Ofsted reports (Ofsted 2001, 2003), both broadly favourable, and a review sponsored by CfBT (Taylor and Jennings 2004). However, there has been no substantive review or research to determine evidence upon which to build future policy. The arrival of the 'excellent teacher' role has not clarified any policy intentions. The standards for the AST, which have been in use since 1998, have been essentially subsumed into those for the excellent teacher, leaving just three that are specific to the AST. The excellent teacher standards can be clustered as follows:

•   Be willing to take a leading role in developing workplace policies and practice and in promoting collective responsibility for their implementation.

- Research and evaluate innovative curricular practices and draw on research outcomes and other sources of external evidence to inform their own practice and that of colleagues.
- Have a critical understanding of the most effective teaching, learning and behaviour management strategies, including how to select and use approaches that personalise learning to provide opportunities for all learners to achieve their potential.

DCSF website

These standards focus on teaching and learning and give the excellent teacher a leading role in teaching and learning and also a degree of criticality, although nothing like as strong or autonomous as the Scottish chartered teachers. The next group focuses on assessment and curriculum:

- Know how to improve the effectiveness of assessment practice in the workplace, including how to analyse statistical information to evaluate the effectiveness of teaching and learning across the school.
- Have an extensive and deep knowledge and understanding of their subjects/curriculum areas and related pedagogy gained, for example, through involvement in wider professional networks associated with their subjects/curriculum areas.
- Have an extensive knowledge on matters concerning equality, inclusion and diversity in teaching.
- Take a lead in planning collaboratively with colleagues in order to promote effective practice.
- Identify and explore links within and between subjects/curriculum areas in their planning.

DCSF website

It is notable that the Hattie-style word 'deep' only appears once; otherwise, the rather vague term 'extensive' is much used. The next three are about being exemplary:

- Have teaching skills which lead to excellent results and outcomes.
- Demonstrate excellent and innovative pedagogical practice.
- Demonstrate excellent ability to assess and evaluate.

DCSF website

There is something very reductive here about merely repeating the word 'excellent' as if it is self-evident what that means. It is an interesting question how far expert teachers are exemplary in all respects; clearly, the extended professional communicates to a range of audiences, so the standard that teachers should:

Have an excellent ability to provide learners, colleagues, parents and carers with timely, accurate and constructive feedback on learners' attainment, progress and areas for development that promotes pupil progress.

DCSF website

is highly appropriate. Equally, and rather like technology, an addition to teachers' knowledge base can now come from data-rich school environments:

Use local and national statistical data and other information in order to provide:

- a comparative baseline for evaluating learners' progress and attainment;
- a means of judging the effectiveness of their teaching, and a basis for improving teaching and learning.

DCSF website

Finally, there is a section about working outside the classroom and collaborating with and developing others:

- Work closely with leadership teams, taking a leading role in developing, implementing and evaluating policies and practice that contribute to school improvement.
- Contribute to the professional development of colleagues using a broad range of techniques and skills appropriate to their needs so that they demonstrate enhanced and effective practice.
- Make well-founded appraisals of situations upon which they are asked to advise, applying high-level skills in classroom observation to evaluate and advise colleagues on their work and devising and implementing effective strategies to meet the learning needs of children and young people leading to improvements in pupil outcomes.

DCSF website

These standards are very much a mixture of discourses. Some are literally pedagogical, e.g. 'demonstrate excellent and innovative pedagogical practice'. However, compared with, say, Hattie's definition of what characterises excellent teachers, we are left with only a guess as to what such pedagogy might look like. The discourse of managerialism is evident throughout: 'be willing to take a leading role in developing workplace policies and practice and in promoting collective responsibility for their implementation'. This implies that such policies are simply morally and educationally neutral; in summary, you should do what the management tell you to do as they know best. The word 'critical' appears once, reflection is never mentioned, and affective terms such as 'enthusiasm' and 'passion' are entirely missing. Do they appear in the final section on standards for ASTs?

- Be willing to take on a strategic leadership role in developing work-place policies and practice and in promoting collective responsibility for their implementation in their own and other workplaces.
- Be part of or work closely with leadership teams, taking a leader-ship role in developing, implementing and evaluating policies and practice in their own and other workplaces that contribute to school improvement.
- Possess the analytical, interpersonal and organisational skills neces-sary to work effectively with staff and leadership teams beyond their own school.

DCSF website

These standards are even more explicitly managerial and implementational than those for the excellent teacher. The only interesting aspect to them is that they make explicit the operational distinction between the excellent teacher's focus on their school (inreach) and the ASTs focus on other schools (out-reach). Outreach was one of the most imaginative and generative aspects of the AST role, essentially requiring them to spend a day a week in other schools or settings. Early research (Sutton et al 2000; Goodwyn and Fidler 2002) sug-gested that this was highly valued and could be very effective. However, there has been little research in any depth to evaluate these early positive findings.

It is seems reasonable to say, then, that the AST role is significant within the English system; what the excellent teacher role will add is unclear. This is especially the case as the scheme is three years old at the time of writing, and the sole review of the role, sponsored by the DCSF, concludes:

The Excellent Teacher Scheme (ETS) came into being in September 2006 to provide a new career route for experienced teachers as an alternative to management and leadership posts. It was envisaged that over time, some 20% of eligible teachers would be employed as Excellent Teachers (ETs). However, by December 2008, only 59 teachers in England and Wales had undergone assessment and fully met the ET Standards.

Hutchings et al. (2009)

The review is a thorough one and gathered data widely and principally from head teachers and teachers who had not taken up the role in their schools as well as undertaking case studies of excellent teachers (ETs). One of their striking findings is how much the ETs themselves disliked the title:

The vast majority of ETs strongly disliked the title Excellent Teacher; only one positively liked it. Most of them told of being teased by colleagues.

While much of this was 'jokey', the cumulative effect of this had made some of them miserable. They felt the title placed an onus on them to be excellent in all aspects of their work, and this was hard to live up to. They were also aware that there were many other excellent teachers in their schools. In two schools, the title was not used at all, and in others, the ET discouraged its use. All this contributes to the invisibility of the scheme. But they also complained that in some public contexts and research contexts, ET is not included as an option, and this also tends to make he whole scheme invisible.

Ibid.: 12

Other teachers were also negative:

While most interviewees identified at least some positive aspects of the ETS, the majority gave much more emphasis to negative aspects, and in particular to concerns that the scheme, and the title ET, are potentially divisive.

Ibid.: 10

So clearly, although AST has become accepted, 'excellent' has not. The introduction of the ET role, the report concludes, has been a hugely wasted opportunity. Most teachers know little about it, and those who do are completely confused by its relationship to other roles and especially to the AST role. It might be argued that the role just needs time, as the AST role certainly did (Goodwyn and Fidler 2002), to become 'normal' and credible. The review team suggest a clearer relationship with the AST role:

Many of the schools also employed ASTs. While the key difference between the two roles was generally identified as the AST doing outreach work while the ET did not, this was not always the case; a number of the schools employed 'inreach' ASTs. In these circumstances, there was little difference between ET and AST roles. Generally, however, ASTs were perceived as being better paid and having higher status. They were also seen as more likely than ETs to move into management roles, while ET was described by some as a *'dead end'* in terms of career progression.

Ibid.: 4

In order to achieve this clarity, they suggest:

bringing together AST and ET into one route under the AST title (this being more familiar and accepted); this route could then include 'AST outreach' and 'AST inreach'.

Ibid.: 5

This would certainly be a pragmatic solution, but it also elides the question of a culture in which the term excellent teacher is rejected; presumably expert teacher would be even more unpopular? The teaching profession will need to come to terms with its own expertise at some point soon!

With only fifty-seven teachers, the ET scheme cannot yet have had any significant impact, but surely the AST role after ten years must have an evidence base? In fact, there is very little evidence upon which to evaluate the importance of the AST role at any level. For example, has it added any status to the profession in the eyes of the public, the media or politicians? Do pupils have any positive awareness of the role? Do great numbers of teachers aspire to the role? Has it produced any identifiable 'gains' to the school system? Has the role itself inspired and/or developed expert teaching? Do we now know more about expert teachers through this particular characterisation of advanced skills teacher? Has it been money well spent?

We do not have clear answers, but we do know, if we trust Ofsted, that there are many excellent teachers who, for whatever reasons, do not have a designation as such, but who have been recognised through inspection.

Models of expert English teachers

It is worth reviewing two more models, one from the USA and one from Australia, before focusing very directly on English teachers in England, and this is partly because these models have developed subject-specific standards. In the USA, two terms have some salience: one is 'master teacher', which is a designation given at district level and usually follows from some professional development work. However, it tends to be very parochial in scope, and definitions of such teachers are formulated in relation often just to one institution, typically a university.

However, nationally much more significant has been the establishment of the National Board for Professional Teaching Standards (NBPTS) in 1987 and its adoption of the term 'highly accomplished'. First, it is worth noting that the idea of a National Board partly stems from the USA issue of teachers only being certified in one state. The NBPTS was partly created to certify teachers who could become employable anywhere. Second, and more significantly, the NBPTS has been notable for its attempt to develop a highly sophisticated set of standards that are far more precisely calibrated than broadly generic notions such as 'excellent teacher'. NBPTS states as its mission (see website):

> The world-class schools the United States requires cannot exist without a world-class teaching force; the two go hand in hand. Many accomplished teachers already work in the nation's schools, but their knowledge and skills are often unacknowledged and underutilized. Delineating outstanding practice and recognizing those who achieve it

are important first steps in shaping the kind of teaching profession the nation needs. This is the core challenge embraced by the National Board for Professional Teaching Standards® (NBPTS).

Their mission echoes a key theme of this book: that the teacher is the absolutely key factor in improving schools, not national strategies or inspections.

The NBPTS is also now the most developed model in the world; 74,000 teachers are now 'Board certified'. As further evidence of the Board's tried and tested approach, in 2008, the NBPTS was given a very thorough review by the National Research Council of America whose substantial report runs to 323 pages (National Research Council 2008); it examines the benefits and claims of the scheme in rigorous detail. The NBPTS model focuses on teachers who put themselves forward for a year-long period of professional development designed to produce evidence against quite specific either age-related or subject-related criteria, sometimes both. The assessment involves teachers creating a portfolio of evidence, including a video of their teaching, undertaking certain written assignments and attending an assessment centre for further written tasks designed to assess the depth and complexity of their knowledge. Candidates typically pay for themselves (about $2,500) and receive reimbursement from their school or their district if they pass (a large number fail) and then possibly a pay increase; the certificate is valid for ten years and then must be renewed. There are twenty-five certificates including English Language Arts (essentially secondary English) and Literacy: reading – language arts (essentially primary English).

The NBPTS is one of the only organisations to develop very detailed subject-specific standards; this is an example of one of the standards for secondary English:

> Accomplished Adolescence and Young Adulthood/English Language Arts teachers have a thorough command of the various domains of knowledge that compose the English language arts.
>
> NBPTS website

What makes these standards so valuable is that the 'elaborations' are in great and precise detail; here is a brief extract of what elaborates the standard above:

> Accomplished English language arts teachers operate with a sense of purpose in the classroom. They have an impressive command of the various domains of knowledge that comprise the English language arts, and, as lifelong learners, they deepen their content knowledge through continual study and accumulated practical experience in the classroom. In this way, their command of the theory, research, and practice in the various domains of the field are all brought to bear for the benefit of

student learning. Accomplished teachers ground instruction in their knowledge of the various domains of English language arts: (a) literature, including traditional and contemporary fiction, nonfiction, poetry, and drama; and other print and nonprint texts; (b) reading processes and how students learn to read; (c) writing processes and how students learn to write; (d) speaking and listening and the conventions of oral communication; (e) viewing and producing media texts; (f) language, its conventions, and the role it plays in shaping all forms of communication; (g) the cognitive and social development of adolescents and young adults; (h) current research on effective instruction in the English language arts; and (i) assessment in the English language arts. These domains are informed by what students are expected to know and be able to do in English language arts.

These descriptions are further evidenced by ascribing real characteristics to the actual teachers, making them recognisable:

Accomplished teachers themselves are well-read, and they know how to read thoughtfully and strategically. They understand literature as an expression of human creativity that has evolved over time, and they can describe the key intellectual currents, social forces, innovations, individuals, and groups that have contributed to this evolution. They appreciate the intellectual growth that can flourish through reading literature, know the main traditions of literary criticism and theory, and know how theory and criticism enrich interactions with that text. Teachers understand the distinctive features of literary genres and how those features influence audiences.

They are skilled in responding to particular literary texts, and can interpret and discuss literary texts from different critical perspectives or lenses. Teachers know how literary elements and terminology help readers construct meaning from texts, and they appreciate the artistry of how an author orchestrates these elements to create a text, and, ultimately, to deepen the enjoyment of the reading experience. Accomplished teachers know how to judge the literary merit of what they read.

See Standard VIII—*Reading* (NBPTS website)

This is a small section of one standard; the document covering the English Language Arts runs to a hundred dense pages. The 'candidate' has to generate evidence over the assessment year to demonstrate that they meet these standards through their teaching and professional work. The standards were put together by genuine experts from the domain of English teaching and have been updated twice since 1993. I was so impressed with this system that I visited the University of New Mexico to interview the first ten candidates for the English qualification. I then led a small-scale research project in

England with some local expert English teachers to generate something similar. We came up with ACE (the Advanced Certificate in English Teaching); this was written up in *Developing English Teachers* (Goodwyn 1997). This project is now a veritable footnote in history as it was overtaken by the AST initiative and so only ran for two years. However, the descriptors we devised remain the only such 'standards' produced in England, specifically designed by English teachers for English teachers (see Goodwyn 1997: 123–27).

NBPTS is not without many issues and challenges; there is, for example, no actual classroom observation by any peer or 'expert', only a candidate's presentation of a video diary and accompanying evidence. The system has also been criticised for being very bureaucratic and overly dependent on psychometric models of teacher assessment. However, the National Research Council report is very clear that this model is a strong and significant one. The report expresses disappointment that they could find little research evidence that 'proved' the impact of these highly accomplished teachers on test outcomes.

However, much more importantly, the report raises the crucial point that simplistically measuring teacher effectiveness through the outcomes of students on standardised tests may entirely miss the impact of such teachers on real learning. 'Standardized tests of student achievement are not designed to assess the sorts of higher order critical thinking skills that teachers following the board's recommendations would be encouraged to focus on....This kind of teaching demands thoughtful decision making, which depends, in turn, on a teacher's ability to reflect on his or her practice. This approach to teaching may be very effective and yet not be reflected in higher scores on tests designed to measure basic math and reading skills (ibid.: 253). The report goes on to recommend research that genuinely investigates the effectiveness of these 'expert' teachers, 'such as student motivation, breadth of achievement, attendance rates, and promotion rates' (ibid.: 254). This is a powerful message to policy-makers about the need to shift attention away from their obsession with standardised tests to much more appropriately sophisticated, but much more accurate and meaningful, assessments of teachers' relationships to student achievement. In England, the VITAE study (see above) is a start in this direction.

A final model, and one very worthy of consideration, is the Australian STELLA project (Standards for Teachers of English Language and Literacy in Australia). (All references are from the Australian Association for the Teaching of English (AATE) website.) The claim for STELLA is:

> As it stands STELLA demonstrates the ability of the profession to identify its own 'best practice' in a language that reflects a shared professional identity and a commitment to achieving professional recognition. STELLA is also an exemplary professional development program which, if used judiciously by teachers, faculties, schools and tertiary

education institutions, can up the ante enormously in terms of the profession's understanding of, and commitment to, professional teaching standards. It has the capacity to enhance teacher professionalism, both within the education and the wider community.

This is quite a claim, but well justified. What makes STELLA unique is that it is a dynamic environment that is constantly developing. There was an initial phase (rather like the ACE project), led by a research grant and the input of many teachers and academics, during which the standards were drafted and made public. The second, and ongoing, phase is dominated by 'teacher narratives'. This allows teachers to put forward a 'narrative' illustrating what they think is best practice and to offer it as exemplification of a standard or standards. Such an approach stems from the STELLA 'principles':

- professional standards only have validity when grounded in teachers' own knowledge, experience, skills and values;
- teachers' knowledge, experience, skills and values are, in important respects, discipline-specific. For example, the depth of knowledge and the range of skills an English or Literacy teacher needs in order to teach well are different from the knowledge and skills required to teach Physics or Physical Education.

STELLA attempts to capture the depth and range of accomplished English/Literacy teaching.

STELLA website

Essentially these standards both 'belong' to the profession and are in a dynamic relationship with practice, as expressed here:

The STELLA materials identify current best principles and practice for English Literacy teaching but they are not intended to be definitive statements that sign off on behalf of future members of the profession. They encourage continuing reflection, review and dialogue about what 'good' English Literacy teachers believe, know and are able to do. Teachers around Australia have used the materials individually and in workshops as a platform for professional development in English/Literacy.

Inevitably, the validity of such an open approach can be contrasted with the scientific psychometrics of NBPTS, but a real gain has to be the engagement of teachers in the notion of best practice; something, I would argue, that is much closer to an art form than a scientific paradigm.

These last two models are predicated, as is this book, on the fundamental point that expert teaching has some generic components, but that real expertise in teaching English is very situated and specific. So an excellent

English teacher in England can certainly qualify to become characterised as 'excellent', but the generic standards are relatively crude indicators. Looking back at Dreyfus also reminds us that one can be expert in a number of aspects within a domain but at quite different levels in other aspects. In English, this can easily be evidenced in relation to the interface of technology and language, for example with texting. Texting is demonstrably part of the literacy of many social groups in the way that letter writing once was, and texting is having a clear impact on the English language and is, in many ironic ways, highly conventionalised. The highly accomplished English teacher is likely to see texting as an exciting development and one that brings students' emergent literacy into the classroom in a valuable way; they are likely to need to acquire some knowledge of 'how it works' and of how best to make use of it pedagogically. This process would be chiefly one of developing new content knowledge. The 'expert' teacher enjoys these challenges; they are part of the process of constant renewal.

Chapter 3

What is English teaching?

Belonging to a subject community

Pam, Interview 3: *Well, I always did love English – from secondary school onwards – and especially when I had some great, really inspirational teachers – and English just keeps changing, evolving, there is always something new ....*

How 'well made' are teachers? Initial training

Does an excellent teacher of English necessarily need to know the origins, history and formative influences of 'English'? There is no concrete evidence to suggest this is so, but then there has been no serious research to investigate the matter. Robert Protherough's two books, *The Making of English Teachers* (1991) and *Students of English* (1989), explore some of the issues associated with this territory and make a case for such knowledge; with Judith Atkinson, he also explored this in a chapter called 'Shaping the image of an English Teacher' (1994); Grossman offers a valuable US perspective (Grossman 1990). The argument throughout this book is that the expert teacher is an extended professional who is a model for, and influential upon, others and their development. Standards, like notions of competence, can be dominantly narrow and reductive, although they need not be; there can be a message that one simply 'reaches the standard'. The expert teacher makes good use of standards where they have validity, but is not controlled or positioned by them. Deep knowledge of a school subject by a good teacher is a key part of understanding the nature of that subject and also of being a source of such knowledge to novices and peers. The emphases of the last twenty years, and to some extent much longer, have been on 'subject knowledge', i.e. of the academic subject, and this has often obscured the importance of both contextual knowledge and of the history of the school subject itself.

Perhaps the oldest bit of folk wisdom about teaching, not held by many teachers, is that some form of pure love of, and deep knowledge about, a subject is really all one needs to be a good teacher. At one level, as Hattie makes clear, this element is important in being an expert teacher. However, the best teachers, as Hattie also makes clear, have a deep understanding of the need to represent the subject to students and to contextualise that representation to particular groups and individuals. Expert teachers make their subject meaningful to students, recognising that deep knowledge is potentially a barrier to communication, not automatically an advantage. A crucial element in this knowledge is a perspective on how 'English' as a school subject has been shaped and developed over time.

Certainly initial teacher training (ITT) courses make no serious attempt to cover subject history or the history of education itself. There was a time when postgraduate certificate of education (PGCE) courses were much more formally academic and covered not only the history of education but the philosophy and the sociology of education as well. That model of teacher education (and the use of the term education *not training*, was, and is, significant) disappeared in the 1970s. It has been replaced by a competency model.

It is worth noting that this change began very positively, through a recognition of the inadequacy of the formal academic model by its providers, the universities themselves. The Oxford 'internship' model is widely acknowledged as a prime mover in this genuine reform. A key principle was to enable student teachers to learn about best practice in the setting itself; broadly conceptualised, it was more like the well-established model in other professions such as medicine and law of participating increasingly in practice through working with living models of that practice. These other disciplines, however, have never reduced their attention to deep academic subject knowledge or ongoing professional development; we will return to the latter in Chapter 8.

The principled developments of the Oxford internship model, and those of the many other programmes that evolved in the 1970s, greatly improved teacher preparation. Many professions provide intensive periods of initial training and recognise that their 'novices' must rapidly meet basic standards of performance in order to undertake qualified practice. However, arguably no other profession is under quite such pressure as teaching; its novices are expected to perform at a high level within months of entering the profession. This is perhaps best illustrated with the example of the first year of qualified teaching. For the majority of the twentieth century, initial training was all the training a teacher received; therefore, the first year was 'make or break'. In the last part of the twentieth century, a modest recognition of the needs of newly qualified teachers (NQTs) developed; even the use of that term was a breakthrough. However, it was not until 1999 that an NQT was offered even a modestly reduced timetable and the support of a trained mentor. Compared with other professions, this is an extraordinarily primitive model.

It is crucially important to reflect on the point that one of the drivers for changing initial teacher education (ITE) was to make beginning teachers ready to cope with the extraordinary demands of the first year of teaching; the previous model had not achieved this aim. Equally, the new model was designed to make schools and teachers feel much more directly involved in teacher development and much more understanding of how teachers do, and do not, develop. At that point, the late 1970s, many teachers in the profession had not had training at all, or very basic training, and those who had experienced the academic PGCE model were often fiercely critical of it as far too 'theoretical' and not practically helpful towards the urgent demands of the classroom. Essentially, then there was almost an anti-training culture in schools, which demonstrated itself in common parlance with comments such as 'forget what they tell you in the university'.

There are two issues here that remain significant for the contemporary teacher. The first is that models of initial training are vitally important, and that relatively speaking the current model in England works reasonably well in balancing time in the practice setting and time out from it, to learn in different ways and to reflect on that learning (Goodwyn 1997). The second is that no serious profession thinks initial training is enough, least of all to produce the highly accomplished practitioner (Eraut 1994). There is plenty of evidence to suggest that the dominant, one-year model of ITT is both woefully inadequate in itself and vastly overloaded. It is highly significant that the development of the standards for ITT preceded any other standards. It is equally significant that the Teacher Training Agency (now the Training and Development Agency for schools) was originally conceptualised purely to regulate and control teacher training.

A deep problem in all this apparent emphasis on ITT is in the folklore of teaching itself. There is always a current of thinking that does believe teachers are born and not made, that 'you can either do it or you can't' and that you have to 'sink or swim'. Such a stance is fundamentally a kind of faith in the innate and the experiential; if you have a talent for teaching then, over time, you will become at least effective. This view, the so-called common sense view of teaching, is often echoed by politicians and parents (see Chapter 1). It is a view frequently voiced by student teachers themselves who want to plunge into the action. One of the striking features of Schon's early work on the reflective practitioner was to acknowledge and analyse this need. He coined the terms 'reflection in action' and 'reflection on action' to help us understand this powerful tension between *doing* and thinking about what we *have done* and how we might *do it better*. This combination is the essential model for good ITT.

What the common sense view of teaching does to the profession is make it prejudiced about both 'theory' and subsequent training. For example, very few teachers undertake substantial in-service training, and even fewer follow Master's-level study; this will be reviewed in more depth in Chapter 8. Teachers who want to develop to a high level should reflect deeply on what ITT could realistically do for them and what it can do for others in the future. They should probably have an influential role in the development of beginning teachers, but they should be wary of any automatic assumptions about their ability to be a mentor or even a role model (Goodwyn 1997). The debate about whether teachers are born or made is utterly sterile. Inevitably, some teachers are more apt when it comes to learning how to teach.

Inevitably, some individuals who are highly motivated to become teachers prove themselves relatively inept very quickly; they then 'fail' their teaching practice. This process seeks to be fair and transparent, but always struggles to be seen to be so. Such gatekeeping is essential in the profession of teaching, but it is partly driven by the highly pressured and stressful nature of ITT. It may well be that some individuals are lost who would have benefited from a different model of training; although there are other models of training, none of them is substantially different in essence. For example, it might be argued that the graduate teacher route is even more immediately intensive than the PGCE and certainly offers less opportunity for 'reflection on action'. That some individuals, especially 'career changers', prefer it is not in any way proof that it is better than or equal to the PGCE; it would need a really robust longitudinal study to evaluate the two routes in any meaningful way.

These contextual points help any teacher to reflect on the nature of teacher development. Put crudely, it does not matter how innately talented Miss Smith is to be a teacher, she still has to become one – once she has entered the profession, she ought to get progressively better; how do we make sure this happens? We want her to acquire knowledge and deep understanding of her teaching; does it seem likely that forty years of 'doing it' will be sufficient? And, even if they were, is it best to wait forty years or could we accelerate that development, starting in Year 1?

The 'quicksilver' subject of English

The school subject of English will always be contested territory; even its name is problematic (Goodson and Medway 1990). This chapter will not adopt a fully historical perspective, but some reference to the origin and development of the subject will be pertinent throughout, starting with the vexed name. As 'English' first emerged as a university discipline in the late nineteenth century and then as a school subject in the early twentieth century, it has a very short history compared with the 'Classics', mathematics, science, etc. However, it has long shed any minority status, coming into the spotlight as *the* major school subject by the time of the Newbolt Report of 1921 (Departmental Committee of the Board of Education 1921). There remains a genuine contemporary relevance for its best practitioners in the following ways.

One of the members of the Newbolt Committee, the first official review of English, was George Sampson, whose book *English for the English* (1921) immediately illustrates a powerful and ongoing issue. The subject name 'English' evolved to give the vernacular language, the language of the people, and the vernacular literature equal status with the Classics. It was formulated during the days of the British Empire and carries with it a potentially nationalistic agenda, reflected in the text of the existing National Curriculum for English and its preceding versions back to 1988. Indeed, it goes back to

Sampson himself, who argued for English to be the social glue of the nation, holding everything together. Throughout the twentieth century, many have debated the purpose of studying English, and some have put forward this nationalistic agenda argument. As English is also the name of a globally powerful language, arguably the most 'valued' language of all, then to study 'English' in school is, inevitably, to encounter some of its power and to consider its 'dominance'. This issue is equally present in 'English Literature', where claims for the 'greatness' of this literature resound loudly from critics and politicians alike.

The subject 'English' therefore is contested at a historical and political level that is unusually high profile. All subjects attract such attention at times, but English was notably the first subject to be defined within a National Curriculum in 1988. Taking that year as a starting point, no other subject has received such relentless political attention and interference as English has. Paradoxically, it receives this attention because of its consensually accepted importance, although this importance leads to endless interference about what its content should be. For the teacher, this can be an intensely frustrating irritation, and the period 1997–2008 was especially marked by prescription and interference (Goodwyn 2008). However, one benefit of some historical perspective is that it reveals this latter period as a phase, and phases come to an end; teacher autonomy is more or less subject to external pressures as is the 'control' of the actual curriculum. Some historical perspective also enables critique of contemporary formulations of a subject. School subjects necessarily need to adapt as society changes, but they may also need to resist attempts to distort what is important; some changes may involve returning to earlier formulations that offer a more generative way of working. These variations might be termed the affordances of the subject's history; knowledge of them is not merely archival, it is regenerative. Much has been done unto English that its practitioners do not agree with, that is, many changes have been made, especially in the late twentieth century, that were regressive not progressive. Knowledge of a subject's history is a powerful asset to any teacher but, in English, I would argue, there is a greater need and a greater value to such knowledge because of the subject's contestable condition.

This consideration leads on to first a consideration of the notion of a community of practice, i.e. what shared knowledge do English teachers have of the subject, and then to a review of some notions of English as a school subject.

Some formulations of the subject are written down, an increasing trend in all school systems. There are obvious national documents with official 'status', such as a National Curriculum, Examination Board Specifications, Ofsted reports and so on. More recently, there have been pseudo official documents produced by 'The Strategies' as in *The National Literacy Strategy* and *The Framework for English*, technically non-statutory but hugely powerful (Goodwyn 2004a, 2004b). The latter documents have huge impact on a publishing industry that generates text books and resources. One mark of the effective professional is knowledge of these materials and discrimination in their use (Shulman 1986; see discussion below). But, however powerful, they are not the enacted subject in the classroom. Equally, school-level policies and schemes of work, although much closer to actual practice, are not the enacted subject. English 'happens' in classrooms, and its existence is 'in the heads' of teachers and students. What is then the nature of the enacted subject, and what kind of knowledge enables it to 'happen'?

The specialist knowledge that teachers have and how they use it is the subject of many excellent books, and these texts themselves are part of our long struggle to define what we mean by such knowledge. For our purposes, it is important to stress that there is now a recognition that teachers do have very specialist knowledge, and that such knowledge puts teaching on a par with many other highly regarded professions (although not quite yet, see Chapter 1). To some extent, the introduction of the advanced skills teacher (AST) and the excellent teacher is part of that recognition, although their conceptualisation somewhat elides this fundamental point.

I would argue that the evidence is now overwhelming that highly accomplished teachers have a deep form of specialist knowledge; some of it is nevertheless broadly generic, in that English and maths teachers have much in common. The most specialist knowledge is unquestionably within a more specific domain. Such knowledge can be partially represented in forms such as texts or presentations, but it is important to accept that much of it exists 'in practice'. Observation (see Chapter 7) of teaching is, therefore, another powerful, although still partial, way to understand excellent teaching.

English teaching as a community of practice?

Perhaps the most valuable concept for the developing teacher is 'community of practice'. Lave and Wenger's seminal work (1991) provides a very valuable means to understand how particular sets of practitioners work and insights into how individuals can understand what is happening 'to them' as they become part of such a community. Lave and Wenger's model can be applied to many groups of specialist practitioners; their original study examined midwives, tailors, quartermasters, butchers and non-drinking alcoholics. Essentially, Lave and Wenger explored notions of 'apprenticeship', not as ritualised training models but as a conceptual period for an individual coming to terms with entering a practitioner community. Such a community will have some definition, 'a set of relations among persons, activity, and the world, over time and in relation with other tangential and overlapping communities of practice' (ibid.: 24). The notion of overlapping communities is valuable, as it might extend to distinct, but comparable, professions such as nursing or social work but, more importantly, it helps with considering teaching expertise in, say, primary and secondary teachers. 'Expert' secondary teachers and their primary equivalents should be able to acknowledge both their overlap and their distinctiveness. This is an especially important point for teachers such as ASTs moving between phase settings or for schools trying to improve transition.

Lave and Wenger's argument is that specialist knowledge and practice are inextricably linked, 'a community of practice is an intrinsic condition for the existence of knowledge' (ibid.: 24). That knowledge, then, exists in the community of practice; it is not somehow acquired from somewhere else. This is a powerful message for ITT and for professional development. However, it does not at all imply that the community of practice is merely in existence when the bell goes; the practitioners might well be sitting together, seminar style, in any place, it is their shared sense of activity that makes them a community.

A key concept for Lave and Wenger is 'legitimate peripheral participation' (ibid.: 34), 'far more than just a process of learning on the part of newcomers. It is a reciprocal relation between persons and practice. This means that the move of learners toward full participation in a community of practice does not take place in a static context. The practice itself is in motion'. They describe newcomers as caught in a dilemma, because they must engage with practice as it exists, 'as they find it', and they are very keen to belong to this established community and to understand it. At the same time, they are creating their own identity within the community and, as a unique individual, they immediately bring something distinctive and so enter into an active and change-oriented relationship with the community and its practice. That community offers them this 'peripheral' role while they form their initial identity. Lave and Wenger call this 'the continuity–displacement contradiction'. Therefore, a community of practice is one where knowledge already exists but is in a dynamic condition; practice is moving and newcomers are immediately producers of new knowledge, not just passive recipients.

Whether these are the exact ways that all communities of practice operate is not 'proven'; some experienced teachers might feel that, after the prescriptions and inspections of the last twenty years, this model seems innocent of external interference and control. However, my research over that period certainly attests to teachers' continual efforts to work in the positive way that Lave and Wenger describe. Experienced teachers, in particular, have been adamant that their best practice has survived and evolved, not just as a coping strategy but particularly in areas such as the new technologies and media where innovation has been more at teacher level.

The implications for the English teacher, novice or expert, are clear: one must join the community, be not just part of its activity but actively part of its development. We will consider some of the wider implications, for example membership of professional associations and bodies, in Chapter 8.

As Lave and Wenger indicated through their research, communities of practice come in many forms, quartermasters and butchers for example. However, English teachers have two other fundamental and interlinked commonalities that relate to their professional identities. The first is their formative identity as students of English who then become its teachers; the second is the subject of 'English' itself as they become 'legitimate participants' in its development.

It was made clear in the 'Introduction' that this book is not a manual; there is no single or simple way to become an expert teacher however much we improve our knowledge of how expertise is acquired. One obvious factor is that individuals come differently formed and shaped, principally by experience. It is worth noting that teaching is also a 'late development' compared with chess players or swimming champions (Ericsson et al. 2007). In these fields, prodigies can be very young; equally in music, players can be highly precocious. In all these fields, such emergent talent is not only common, but it is understood by other practitioners, and models of development have been established and tried and tested. It is not that teachers (or say doctors or lawyers) are unable to be prodigies or precocious talents, it is just that they are professions and so we approach the whole notion of capability very differently. Individuals may have been noted as 'good at teaching' long before they are trained, and people do say 'I have always wanted to be a teacher' but, rightly or wrongly, we, and almost all comparable education systems, do not offer the chance to be a teacher until adulthood. In the UK, this is typically at the age of about twenty-two. One important feature of teaching as a career is also that many individuals join the profession much later and that a significant element of its workforce are 'mid-career' changers. This is well understood in teaching and is one reason why having alternative qualification routes may be justified. The original graduate teacher programme (GTP) required trainees to be at least twenty-six, although this requirement was later dropped for pragmatic reasons. What marks teacher training, however, is its move to a consistent model that is competence based not experience or maturity based. As discussed earlier, at least one reason for this is to raise its professional status, making it much more comparable to, for example, 'top professions' such as law or medicine.

Indeed, a scheme in England called 'Subject Knowledge Enhancement' (SKE), introduced piecemeal over about ten years, but made nationally available from 2008, is worth a brief consideration in relation to expertise (see the TDA website). It is predicated on the well-recognised problem of attracting good graduates into teaching in subject areas such as maths and science. In England, these subjects saw a long-term decline in popularity at 'A' level and university. As student numbers declined, so did the number going into teaching. There has been a marked effect, over time, in the quality of teaching in these subject areas, leading to a downward spiral. Successive governments attempted some intervention by giving trainee teachers in these, and some other, subjects enhanced bursaries and even 'golden hellos' with some modest effect. However, the SKE programmes are a more systemic intervention to stop the downward spiral. Their premise is that career changers may need to 'boost' their subject knowledge in order to benefit much more from the conventional PGCE or GTP one-year teacher training programmes. Such trainees may need this enhancement because they have not used their degree-level knowledge in, say, physics for many years because they had been, for example, a manager. Equally, they might have a degree in engineering and have worked in that domain using lots of mathematical concepts in their work but now need a more formal study of 'pure' mathematics in order to teach the subject at 'A' level. These programmes can be anything from two-week intensive-style courses to a whole year; applicants have to secure a teacher training place in order to be accepted for SKE.

What has all this to do with expert teaching and especially English teaching? From the former point of view, it is an interesting development, highlighting, as it does, the importance of specific forms of 'subject' knowledge. Its starting point is clearly not the common sense view of teaching but the view that subject knowledge is one crucial form that a secondary teacher certainly needs, and that undertaking a PGCE is so demanding as a training year that 'weak' subject knowledge may lead to failure. There might be much to debate in all this but, practically, it is clearly a recognition of the absolute importance of teacher quality.

'English' is often seen as a 'shortage' subject, that is that there are not enough practising teachers available, but it is rarely seen as a quality issue. This is chiefly because English is a strong and popular 'A' level subject, equally so as a university subject; plenty of its 'top graduates' go into teaching, and there is competition for places on training programmes. There is a very different problem as regards retention, which actually accounts for shortages in English; this will be discussed in more depth in Chapter 7. The implication in all this is that trainee English teachers are well qualified and have good subject knowledge; therefore they do not need SKE.

In practice, teacher trainers do not make such a naive assumption. At the simplest level, no two English degrees are the same even from the same university. All degrees offer options and choices and so, for example, a student might not study any Shakespeare at university. There is, quite rightly, no attempt to match university English degrees to the needs of the school curriculum. Some courses, especially combined English and education courses, do have a relationship with the school curriculum, but there is no hard evidence that this is especially beneficial. Teacher trainers have long recognised that this diversity is the reality and, especially in the long term, has many advantages. In the short term, it raises some issues that are explicitly dealt with and do raise some particularly interesting issues about knowledge of 'English'.

One practice that has emerged is that of 'the subject knowledge audit'; it began as a voluntary activity but is now essentially a requirement and inspected by Ofsted. It is decidedly a mixed blessing. It is clearly valuable for both the trainee and his/her tutor to review what 'knowledge' is being brought to the training year, and it is especially valuable for the trainee to reflect on areas of particular strength and relative lack of knowledge, particularly in relation to Key Stage 4 and 'A' level. Trainees also need to reflect on the breadth of English as a subject and its emphasis on language, media and drama. A lack of confidence about teaching formal aspects of language, especially 'grammar', is a very typical concern for trainees. However, the rather sterile ticking of boxes can be a superficial and mechanistic exercise and lead to very little genuine reflection. Such exercises can also send the wrong message that very particular content knowledge can be a guarantee of good teaching. Expert teachers are especially aware of what they 'don't know' and typically comment on the value of the ongoing acquisition of new knowledge about their subject. Even the term 'audit' is problematic with its emphasis on an accounting model of knowledge (Ellis 2007). Expert teachers know that knowledge is dynamic and that much of the most valuable knowledge about teaching a subject exists in the community of practice to which the novice brings a new perspective and helps to generate new knowledge.

There is an important caveat to consider about the concept of a community of practice. Its value is that it stresses that notion of community and of shared understanding, but the lived experience of joining such a community involves much more stress, confusion and debate. All communities have internal debates and disagreements, they would be static without them; at times, these turn into real conflicts. So it is also important to reflect on school subjects as arenas. Lave (1988: 1) defines an arena primarily as a setting of activity 'physically, economically and socially organised space-in-time', which individuals enter and have some influence over but soon recognise that this arena is highly structured and formative. The individual then has a dialectal relationship with the setting, acting in and on the arena. Goodson (Goodson and Ball 1984: ch. 2) adds an important dimension when he states that subject communities are also 'arenas of conflict'. Inside the subject arena, there is an ongoing debate about the subject itself, and the participants have every right to engage in that debate; outsiders such as politicians may well have views about the subject, but these usually lack credibility and authenticity to the practitioners. The expert participants expect to argue and disagree while still maintaining the community; they know that argument is necessary as a dynamic part of change and the creation of new knowledge. However, when outsiders impose change within the arena, such changes, however powerfully enforced, have no intellectual or moral authority and they are resisted at different levels; this resistance marks the period in English from about 1990 to 2009. Such resistance is emotionally damaging as it is also a distraction from the real business of the arena, and it displaces the internal discussion, highly valued by experts, and the subject suffers attrition.

Models of English?

The expert teacher is very familiar with the official documents of the subject at macro level (national curriculum) and micro level (lesson plans/worksheets), what Shulman has defined as 'curriculum knowledge' (1987). Such teachers are also highly aware of how these official materials are both subject to end-less change and always needful of local interpretation and implementation. They also have a sense, although it is harder to articulate, about how closely these materials fit with or express the deeper mission of the subject. English, being a politically high-profile and contestable subject, has endured much opinionated commentary on what its mission should be; there has been rela-tively little empirical work on what it actually does, but what there is offers some fascinating insights into 'what is English teaching'.

As outlined above, 'subjects' are much debated and discussed among their communities, and many books and articles are written about how to define them, very often with the writer, or writers, arguing for some change to the subject's 'boundaries'. However, it is in the realm of schooling that this process actually leads to very formal definition; for example, the National Curriculum for English (in England) is a legal, a statutory text. What rela-tionship exists between such a fixed, formal definition and the dynamic entity as it exists in the community of practice? Another important dimension to any committed practitioner's thinking is the consideration of the 'subject paradigm'; this is the conceptualisation of the subject along two dimensions. One dimension is its knowledge, what is it 'about'?; the other is essentially its purpose 'what is it for?' Although English still counts (see above) as a rela-tively new subject, it has certainly attracted, proportionally, a huge amount of debate, which I will not attempt to summarise fully here. Instead, I will con-sider a significant historical moment when the official version and the lived version met in real creative tension. This key moment will then be used to illustrate some fundamental concerns for all English teachers, but especially for those who are leaders within the profession.

One significant moment in the history of English occurred in 1989 when the very first National Curriculum for English was published, carrying with it the legal apparatus of being 'statutory'. The story of how this version of Eng-lish came into being is a story in itself, one version of which has been written by Brian Cox, the committee chair and lead author of the Cox Report (see Cox 1991, 1992). One very striking claim of Cox and his committee was that there were 'five models of English'. They claimed that these 'models' were understood and used by all English teachers. This was a bold claim, based as it was on no real research but on much conversation and consultation with the profession. The models were:

A "personal growth" view focuses on the child: it emphasises the relation-ship between language and learning in the individual child, and the role of literature in developing children's imaginative and aesthetic lives.
   A "cross-curricular" view focuses on the school: it emphasises that all teachers (of English and of other subjects) have a responsibility to help children with the language demands of different subjects on the school

curriculum: otherwise areas of the curriculum may be closed to them. In England, English is different from other school subjects, in that it is both a subject and a medium of instruction for other subjects.

An "adult needs" view focuses on communication outside the school: it emphasises the responsibility of English teachers to prepare children for the language demands of adult life, including the workplace, in a fast-changing world. Children need to learn to deal with the day-to-day demands of spoken language and of print; they also need to be able to write clearly, appropriately and effectively.

A "cultural heritage" view emphasises the responsibility of schools to lead children to an appreciation of those works of literature that have been widely regarded as amongst the finest in the language.

A "cultural analysis" view emphasises the role of English in helping children towards a critical understanding of the world and cultural environment in which they live. Children should know about the processes by which meanings are conveyed, and about the ways in which print and other media carry values.

Cox (1991)

The section outlining the models was just a few paragraphs in a very lengthy document, but it was a rare attempt to 'capture' the subject paradigm succinctly. It seemed to me that these 'Cox models' deserved some acknowledgement and also some challenge.

The work of the previous decade had generated some other versions; indeed, one of the most well known was Barnes et al.'s *Versions of English*, published in 1984. It was especially important because it was based on a three-year study in six schools and four further education colleges, focusing essentially on 15- to 17-year-olds. It, in turn, owed much to Dixon's *Growth through English*, first published in 1967. That text is a perfect illustration of how debate and discussion lead to new knowledge, as it followed on from the 'Dartmouth' seminar held in the USA. At this seminar, leading figures from around the English-speaking world met to debate the nature and purpose of the subject. Dixon's seminal book was the outcome as it attempted to capture how the subject English was conceptualised in England.

He identified three dominant approaches to English in the 1960s. First, there was 'skills'; this approach was about 'drills' and exercises undertaken to improve basic literacy and was marked by decontextualised use of language. Second came 'cultural heritage', the notion that there was a well-defined high culture and that, by passing on knowledge of this culture, students would become more civilised and unified nationally through an appreciation of their great heritage. However, Dixon's own proposal, based on the work of James Britton in particular, was for a 'personal growth' model. Dixon's emphasis was much more on processes than on content. Central to his model was the placing of the individual learner at the heart of English and, through various processes involving language use, developing that individual. His approach was essentially a constructivist theory of learning, arguing that individuals create new knowledge and then order and consolidate this knowledge. Dixon did not reject literature or high culture, but he saw them as having a negative impact as the students were too passive and the teaching too transmissive. He thus took a stand against the Leavisite tradition (usually categorised as the Cambridge school), which fundamentally viewed high culture as a form of literary salvation. He very much rejected the skills model because it was decontextualised, and he placed a very strong emphasis on students using their own writing and local language. He was much concerned with the nature of city schools and drew many of his examples from London where he taught, giving rise to the tag of the 'London', as opposed to the Cambridge, school of English.

The personal growth model, I would certainly argue, has remained the most quietly influential force in the community of practice itself. There has been much critique of Dixon's text and of the personal growth model, but it has not been displaced and was identified by Cox and his committee as central to English teaching in the late 1980s, twenty years after *Growth through English* first appeared. Dixon's achievement was to bring together much of the best thinking of the 1960s and to challenge the grammar school orthodoxy; his text was essentially a manifesto for change and provided a real catalyst that energised English teaching and still does.

Between Dixon and Cox, there was much debate, and Barnes et al.'s *Versions of English* was especially important because it was much more research based. Dixon's evidence was almost exclusively of students' work; Barnes and his team focused on teaching through observation. There were also more sociological studies of English, for example Mathieson's influential *The Preachers of Culture* (1975).

The Cox models capture a shift in the subject paradigm that is still reflected in practice today. The full report contains a short, but very important, chapter on information technology and on media education. This chapter is eminently uncertain quite 'what to do' with these new areas, but it is emphatic about their growing importance to society and to its young people. The Cox curriculum itself includes media education in English, and this was its first real recognition (in England) as a part of formal schooling (Goodwyn 1992b).

Cox started with personal growth because he had come to realise that this was at the heart of English teachers' beliefs. However, Cox and his committee also recognised that cultural heritage remained a real force in English and that most teachers related to it, often critically, but nevertheless it had a certain dominance and also a loyal following. The adult needs model is partly the skills model and partly what came to be the great literacy paradigm of the late 1990s and beyond. The most important model was cultural analysis, as it signalled the paradigm shift towards accepting the study of media, popular culture and to developing a critical approach to all texts. Clearly, these 'models' are both complementary and contradictory, but this is their collective strength, and Cox was quite right to set them out in this way. He was wrong about 'cross curricular'. Although he was essentially right in recognising the powerful influence of the 1975 Bullock Report, *A Language for Life* (DES 1975), he was mistaken in thinking this was part of the English paradigm. My surveys of teachers and student teachers over fifteen years are quite consistent in their findings. English teachers state that 'Language across the Curriculum' is a whole-school approach and is chiefly important to teachers of other subjects who need to recognise their responsibility (as Bullock actually proposed) to monitor their own use of language in their teaching and to pay attention to helping their students develop as language users (Goodwyn 1992a, 2004a; Goodwyn and Findlay 1999).

The other major finding of my surveys is that personal growth remains the most important model for English teachers regardless of age and experience. They generally put cultural heritage last and cultural analysis and adult needs close together, but they do 'recognise' that these models capture what goes on in the community of their practice. When asked to identify what the official curriculum demands, they often put cultural heritage first, perfectly illustrating the difference between the prescribed form of English and its lived reality in practice. Surveys are, of course, self-report and might well reflect espoused models rather than realities; nevertheless, their consistency is remarkable, and there has been no major empirical study to challenge these findings. An interesting critique is contained in Marshall's *English Teachers – The Unofficial Guide: Researching the Philosophies of English Teachers* (2000). One recent observation-based study, *English in Urban Classrooms* (Kress et al. 2005), brings a valuable multimodal perspective to understanding how English teachers carry out their practice.

The final concern of this chapter for any teacher who wishes to improve as an English teacher relates to what might best be called 'professional identity'. There is a very valuable body of work that has examined how becoming a professional, such as a teacher, impacts on identity (for a recent overview, see Rodgers and Scott 2008). English teachers generally have strong subject-oriented identities (Ellis 2007) as, indeed, do many other subject teachers. In that sense, every subject teacher needs to adopt the principles of reflective practice and to consciously examine their developing professional identity. This identity is never fixed, however long a teacher has been teaching, although there is a danger of becoming stagnant or plateauing as a professional. The study of teachers' lives and career phases is very clear about this (see Day et al. 2007). Part of the formation of that emergent identity comes as the teacher or future teacher creates their own 'personal subject construct'. That personal construct of English has been forming throughout their student years and will be one of a number of such subject constructs. Inevitably, as the pressure of forming a professional and pedagogical identity intensifies, the personal subject construct will be revised. The question of importance as regards developing expertise is how 'knowingly' will this revision take place?

In considering how teachers become expert, we have already observed how important is some automaticity, to free up mental space. However, there is no paradox in saying that such automaticity should allow the expert teacher more capacity for self-awareness in the classroom or any professional setting. Inevitably, the novice finds it very difficult to manage this emergent knowledge, and there is much evidence that a very typical reaction to classroom pressure is for student teachers, certainly initially, to 'fall back' on how they were taught the subject. In that way, accessing the personal subject construct is much more as a student than as an effective teacher. Possibly this is a necessary stage, a means of breaking down the 'old' construct as pedagogical knowledge is created and as the novice truly enters the community of practice.

It can be reasonably argued that English teachers should be especially self-aware because the practices that they are teaching have an illusory 'ordinariness' or 'everydayness' about them, i.e. reading, writing, speaking and listening. Inevitably, successful English teachers often acquired these capacities easily and continue to develop them as teachers. This is by no means universal; others who struggled to acquire them or who have a particular challenge, such as dyslexia, can make excellent teachers partly because of the insights that they have gained. It is notable that the best teachers have deep insights into what makes their subject difficult (see Hattie 2003) and how to represent those difficulties in a meaningful way to students (and sometimes also to novice teachers).

What stands out as especially formative for English teachers is the act of reading. Whether this is desirable or not is a question we will return to below, but its significance is very powerful. One of the most striking things about interviewing applicants for a place on an English teacher training programme is how insistent they are that 'I have always loved reading'. It might be argued that they think this is what they are supposed to say to please their interviewer, but there is a good deal more evidence to demonstrate how 'formative' their reading experiences have been. One of the things most frequently expressed by serving English teachers is how little time they now have for their own reading. I am arguing that the act of reading is highly affected for English teachers by their formative personal and professional identities.

My own research suggests these important points (Goodwyn 2003b, 2003c). First, that the dominant reason for becoming an English teacher is some kind of 'love of reading'. This might merely be seen as stating the obvious given that the great majority of such individuals took an English degree, which consisted principally of reading literary texts. Of course, as discussed above, English degrees are hugely varied, and PGCE programmes will sometimes accept applicants with drama, language or media studies degrees. However, the need to convey this 'love of reading' goes very deep in the profession. It can be argued, therefore, that literary reading is something of a dominating paradigm. This is partly evidenced because, when student teachers do reflect deeply on their own reading, they 'go through' their pasts and often comment with guilt on periods when they did not read or, even worse, read mere magazines or even 'trash'. One point of this reflection is to help them see that their reading patterns were often normal adolescent ones and that they now need to understand adolescent reading as a phenomenon.

A second point is that the study at 'A' level is very decisive as this led to a university choice. During the 'A' level period, occasionally earlier, these future teachers encountered an English teacher who themselves embodied that love of reading and whose enthusiasm and inspiration are vividly remembered. So much so that that teacher is very often cited as the most important influence on the future teacher and one major reason why they think English teaching will be rewarding and exciting (Goodwyn 2008). University study is rarely as influential, and university tutors are rarely cited as inspirations. Equally, a deep paradox is expressed about English at university as simultaneously crucial and valuable while also being negatively analytical; some future teachers comment that they could not pick up a poem or a novel for some time after university.

The key point in considering this formative influence is that expert teachers may very well be expert teachers of literature, something discussed in Chapters 4 and 5. However, they also need to be expert teachers of writing, and of speaking and listening, certainly in England where English is taught as an integrated 'whole'. In the US, for example, reading and writing in high school are often taught separately and by different teachers, with acknowledged differences in expertise. Future English teachers very rarely say 'I have always loved writing', and very few have undertaken any 'creative' writing since the age of about fourteen. In terms of expertise, this needs some serious reflection and arguably suggests that the dominant influence of a love of reading may, at times, severely limit the development of expertise unless teachers consciously address this as an issue. It certainly suggests that the overcrowded training year will not be sufficient to address this potential imbalance. It is quite striking that one of the most successful in-service programmes for English teachers has been the National Writing project in the US.

It might also be argued that their nostalgic memories of an inspirational English teacher need some deep reflection. Was that enthusiasm for literature, which so impressed them, having the same effect on all their peers? Might it not have been as offputting for the less favoured students as it was exciting for the chosen? Whether such influence was fully beneficial or in fact distorting is in no way provable. The point is that, in wanting to be a very good teacher, one element is being able to recognise the needs of all students, one very consistent characteristic of expertise in teaching. Therefore, very good teachers will reflect on the dangers of allowing merely personal preferences to distort their otherwise fair and even approach. There is no paradox here with that other consistent characteristic of the expert teacher, enthusiasm for the subject; the key point is that this enthusiasm is for the whole subject and reaches all students, perhaps especially those who find the subject difficult and hard to enjoy.

Overall then, the expert teacher is aware of having a personal subject construct and that it is a dynamic entity when taken seriously. They can also recognise that for novices this construct can be a severe limitation, and that they may experience real difficulty as their previous construct breaks down under pressure. The expert mentor, then, takes care to understand and work with this scenario. The expert teacher, whether a trained mentor or not, should be able to empathise also, because they have a deep capacity to reflect on the difficulties of their subject as experienced by each student.

A final reflection on the subject of English is that it is not just like 'quicksilver' in being hard to define at any given time, it is also incessantly changing. Of course, all subjects are developing and changing in their community of practice and at some official level. However, English draws very deeply on two simple sources. One is the language itself, something that by its nature is changing at the point of utterance all over the globe on every single day. The other source is texts, whether high culture or not, whether verbal or not, and texts are equally being produced in vast numbers every second. These dimensions combine in many ways, but a simple example is genre or even 'form'. To take an obvious example, there are serving teachers who were novices before email and the internet existed, who experienced websites and texting as novices, like the rest of the population. What extraordinary changes those teachers have seen as they affect the language and its communicative affordances. And certainly this is what very effective teachers of subject English remark upon, that the subject can never be anything but exciting because, in its direct relationship with the real world, it is in perpetual and visible development. It keeps its teachers on their intellectual toes and always facing new possibilities; it remains a source of new inspiration, not reliant on ossified models from the past.

Chapter 4

Teaching English

Jane, Interview 4: *Well it has been a long journey but an exciting one and I do feel genuinely thrilled after a really good English lesson...some lessons I feel I 'have to do', for the tests for example – but even then you can make them enjoyable and challenging...but some lessons you just think 'why did I do that' and you go away and it nags at you to re-think...and that is why it is very rarely dull, at least in English...and I do observe other subjects and sometimes think, how do these kids put up with this...I am not being arrogant, these are competent lessons but there is so little there for these lively young people...English, I hope, is always alive.*

In this and the next chapter, we will focus on the theory and practice of teaching English and will view the classroom through the eyes of some very accomplished teachers of English with some attention to the Cox models of English (see Chapter 3). We will explore their thinking using Hattie's dimensions (see Chapter 1):

Expert teachers
- A: can identify essential representations of their subject;
- B: can guide learning through classroom interactions;
- C: can monitor learning and provide feedback;
- D: can attend to affective attributes; and
- E: can influence student outcomes.

and we will examine the detail of their reflections using Hattie's characteristics (simplified version, see Chapter 1):

- Deep understanding of teaching and learning;
- Problem-solving approach;
- Anticipate, plan and improvise;
- Excellent decision-makers – prioritise decisions;
- Optimal classroom climate for learning;
- Recognise the multidimensional nature of the classroom;

- They recognise that teaching is context dependent and highly situated;
- Constantly monitoring student progress and providing valuable feedback;
- Testing 'hypotheses', i.e. is this working?;
- More automatic, i.e. they keep plenty of 'mental space' available;
- High respect for all students;
- Passionate about teaching and learning;
- Highly motivating – building students self-regulation, self-efficacy, self-esteem;
- Set appropriate but challenging goals and tasks;
- Positively impact on achievement;
- Enhance surface and deep learning.

For a period of two years between 1999 and 2001, I worked with six such teachers, observing their teaching and discussing it with them and interviewing them about their lives, their careers and their evolving views of the subject of English. The National Curriculum was then ten years old and a new curriculum was launched in 2000, debates raged about the nature of the subject, the high stakes testing regime and the possible impact of the National Literacy Strategy on secondary schools and English in particular (see Chapter 8). However, the data from the period, now several years old, are not dated by these topical issues. As Chapter 3 has explored, the nature of the subject will remain contested and politically high profile for the foreseeable future; therefore, there is always some debate ongoing and some kind of change is on the way or working through.

The six teachers were not selected scientifically because of their results or through careful consultation with their peers. They were selected because they all worked in a school that had a partnership with my university and in an English department that had consistently taken PGCE students over many years. Each of them took an active interest in student teachers and either was, or had been, a mentor, usually for a number of trainees. In each department, although this was not a selection factor, there were several other teachers who had trained at the university. What united them was an enthusiasm for the subject and strong belief that English teachers had a very important job to do; this was very clear from many conversations with them over several years. Four of them were now heads of department, two were second in department; four were female and two were male. Their managerial roles and the gender proportions were deliberate as the project needed to achieve some representative quality and to consider the tensions between management and remaining an excellent teacher.

The other key contextual factor was the introduction of the advanced skills teacher (AST) role the year before the research began. At that time, the AST role could not be combined with being a head of department (or equivalent), so the case study teachers would have had to 'give up' managerial responsibility to take on that role. This limitation was removed after three years as the number of applications (as later with the excellent teacher scheme, see Chapter 2) had been disappointing. It might be argued that the original concept of identifying outstanding classroom teachers and maintaining their focus on teaching, not managing, was compromised by this change. The introduction of the AST role was the subject of discussions as one element of the research.

It was remarkable that the chosen six all agreed to take part; they were the 'first choice' in every sense. They shared, with some variation, a generational factor in that they had passed through schooling before the comprehensive reform of the 1970s, but they now all taught in a comprehensive and were determined that this form of state schooling was best for children and society. This must be recognised as both very typical of English teachers in the state system but also as a potentially defining, it might be argued, limiting factor in their perspective. Over the research period, each participant was observed five times and interviewed five times. Each interview involved discussion of the observed lesson and then a semi-structured set of questions exploring aspects of the subject, for example a discussion of the 'Cox models' (see Chapter 3). Lessons were not recorded using any technology, just notes; this avoided all problematics related to technology, with the obvious limitation of individual observation and both its biases and its reliance then on memory. On balance, this approach was highly suited to the project. All the teachers were used to the observer, and it meant lessons did not require any adaption to fit with the project because of, for example, being filmed. To the observer, lessons seemed absolutely authentic and part of the normal work of the class. The teachers often apologised that the lesson was just routine or highly inflected by an external influence such as impending tests, but this was a benefit for the observer. They were all asked not to do anything different from normal, and such teachers were also so busy and under pressure that they had no time for special preparation. Nevertheless, an observer has some impact and this must be acknowledged (see Chapter 7 for a detailed discussion of observation). The total number of lessons observed was therefore thirty, a modest sample. However, the teachers were reflecting on well-established careers giving the project access to many thousands of lessons. These teachers were also trained and experienced observers, partly of student teachers and newly qualified teachers (NQTs, i.e. novices) but also of their experienced peers. None of them, see above, was an AST (this role had only just come in to the profession in 1998; see Chapters 2 and 8) and at that stage no one aspired to become an AST.

At that stage, I had observed teachers at all stages of their careers for a variety of reasons and interviewed many for research projects. However, the majority of my extensive observational experience for the previous ten years had been of student teachers. What was very striking during this project was that all the predicted differences between novices and experts were borne out. The participants' teaching was always highly impressive; by no means does that mean 'charismatic' or teacher-dominated teaching, all lessons were very student centred and highly personalised. As a real appreciator of how challenging teaching is by its nature, and of how even more demanding teaching becomes when an observer is present, the quality of teaching was consistently very good. Expressed simply, it was the difference between watching an amateur performance of Shakespeare and seeing an outstanding one performed by the Royal Shakespeare Company. You attend with very different expectations, but the latter one has to be exceptional because you have other great performances with which to compare it. However, the performance metaphor should not be over emphasised. The teaching was a fascinating pleasure to observe and always concerned with student success, it felt a privilege to be present; as far as I could tell, for the students, it was just their normal English teacher on a normal day, they never expressed surprise at what happened or reacted as though the lesson was somehow made different for the observer's benefit.

In introducing the teachers, care has been taken to disguise identity and, methodologically, to anonymise more than just names. These case studies of real people are here to be illustrative not to pretend that these complex, sophisticated professionals can be somehow 'captured' in a few words. Some of their distinctiveness will be lost through the act of mediation and also for the purpose of the book, which is to consider expert teaching of English in broad terms. What remains is their own words as quotations whenever possible. These voices are then used throughout this and the next chapter to illustrate general points about very good English teaching. Each quotation is linked to a specific point, but they often illustrate simultaneously several dimensions of expertise, for example reflecting on helping a novice may generate several key points about their own teaching. Quotations are often paragraph length because English teachers can really talk about their subject and, when they do, they reveal an underlying enthusiasm and commitment that demonstrates their passion for teaching. This does not make the quotations 'text book' comments; they are the genuine and unedited views of very busy teachers, sometimes revealing the pressure they feel as well as their passion for teaching. The only editing is of pauses and 'uhm' type sounds as they merely distract the reader.

Lucas was head of a large English department in a girls' school, where he had been for many years; he was a grammar school boy who attended an elite university and had taught in grammar schools before deciding on working within the comprehensive system. Pam was second in department in a large, mixed comprehensive. She had also been a grammar school pupil and then attended a red brick university going straight into teaching. Sally had attended a private school (unhappily) and had rather drifted into secretarial work and having children, but had then undertaken some part-time teaching. This motivated her to take her degree, part time, and to become a qualified teacher; she had then risen rapidly to head of department. She was then in her second post as head of department in a mixed, 11–16 school. Charlie was head of department in a very large, mixed comprehensive. He had attended a grammar school, an elite university and had considered a research/university career before deciding that teaching was more meaningful. Jane was head of department in a large, mixed comprehensive; this was her second role as head of department. She had attended grammar school, a red brick university and gone straight into teaching. Polly attended a grammar school, a red brick university and had gone straight into teaching; she was second in department in an 11–16 school where she had been for some time having also had a career break for children.

As classroom teachers, they had many differences in style and character, but their similarities were far more striking. The overarching commonality was professionalism. Even if it must be accepted that being interviewed about being a teacher might lead the interviewee to present their 'best side', this also had to be borne out over every observed lesson. I was also a frequent visitor to their department and often saw them interacting with colleagues and student teachers. This mode of professionalism was multidimensional. In each case, it stemmed from a sense of duty. It is interesting that Hattie does not directly include this in his characteristics nor does he discuss professionalism in any depth. However, professionalism as an attitude and as a set of values underpins not only his characteristics but is very evident in every way in the case study teachers. They all entered teaching with the belief that it was more important intrinsically than extrinsically and that becoming a promoted teacher was more about accepting more responsibility than about career progression or material benefit.

Professionalism was combined both in discussion and very visibly in the classroom, with a passion for teaching and learning. In the classroom, this was evident in both spoken and body language and in a discourse of encouraging challenge for each class and all students. They frequently praised students but equally often identified difficulties that 'we' have to face with a challenging new topic or new text. The great majority of the time, that enthusiasm was reflected back by their classes, who demonstrated both self-belief and engagement. However, there were many challenging students in their groups and many situations arose that came from the normal dissonance of school life. What typified their conduct on those occasions was first that they maintained a fluid performance with the rest of the class; they were neither distracted nor irritated by individual behaviours, dealing with them often in what appeared a light touch way, i.e. a glance, a word, using a name, standing close to a student or sitting next to them, encouraging a student to decide what they wanted to do next and giving them time to think about it, etc. Lessons were frequently interrupted by the appearance of other students 'at the door', sometimes sent on an errand by another teacher but often sent by another teacher to be 'dealt with'. On such occasions, the student was either incorporated quietly into the class or given a few moments' attention and then was either sent or taken to an appropriate environment. The students in the class itself were accustomed to their teacher dealing with these situations and typically took no notice, and certainly did not see these awkward moments as opportunities to cause other problems. A marked feature of these situations, and of each classroom all of the time, was a combination of a very serious attitude towards 'the importance of the work' and also a capacity to display both deep enjoyment and to engage in what is best described as 'light humour'. Of the six teachers, two might be characterised as quietly serious, two as serious with a good sense of timing and wit, two as serious with a real ability to cajole students through humour. It is clear that these characterisations are not very scientific and certainly mostly impressionistic; no attempt was made while observing to count when students laughed or smiled or when the teacher spoke 'humorously'. What is evident about these six teachers is that seriousness, enthusiasm and enjoyment (not humour) are the marked characteristics of their expertise as teachers of English. The very great majority of their students took their teacher very seriously and their work equally so, and these teachers commanded respect without fear. One of the teachers could certainly be intimidating, and her style was to be more openly critical of a class (although never publically of individuals), and her demeanour was certainly 'stern' on occasion. There is no one model for the demeanour of the expert teacher, commonality need not be uniformity; each of the teachers was highly respected by students and by colleagues.

Indeed, their conduct with staff and students was exemplary, and they were considered as role models by numerous colleagues. They all felt that it was a duty to support the future of the profession by volunteering their departments to work with student teachers and by undertaking this commitment continuously year on year. This approach did not make them merely supportive of any student teacher; indeed, they were often highly critical of students who did not aspire to reach high professional standards. They were fierce gatekeepers for the profession and determined to support any student teacher who demonstrated commitment and hard work, but equally determined to challenge novices who they felt were clearly not potential professionals.

Although they demonstrated all the 'automatic' qualities that go with expertise, they were unquestionably reflective practitioners and they reflected in action and on the action. The former is not simplistically provable but is evidenced through comments such as these as they recall their decision making during lessons:

> Lucas, Interview 3: *Well it is a familiar situation but each student really is different, what he needed was the right working partner, as soon as he was moved away from Gary and with Linda, he was working well for the rest of the lesson.*

> Polly, Interview 1: *It is difficult material for them* (A Christmas Carol *by* Dickens) *and I immediately realised that I was losing them, so I changed tack and did that pair work while I went round and spoke to each pair,*

then put them in fours for the next few minutes... after that speaking to the whole class helped to reassure them and then they really could work individually... that definitely did the trick.

What this demonstrates is very much what both Schon and Hattie argue, that experts solve problems. Because of their deep reservoirs of knowledge (not just experience), their attention is drawn to the problematic and they apply solutions. It is notable that they distinguish themselves (unprompted by the interviewer) from novices and even competent teachers

Jane, Interview 2: *It's usually when you come into this problem of, you know, children crossing, talking over each other and you have to be very experienced and skilful to do those things, and so I would say, you know, if it's an afternoon lesson particularly she knows they are going to be unsettled so go in and read something to them, settle them down and then go from 'what have we read' you know, give them a focus to talk about...*

Charlie, Interview 2: *When I first became a teacher I couldn't believe in all discipline stuff, and didn't tell people to tuck their shirts in and stop tapping... and stop chewing I just didn't, just didn't interest me. But, now it interests me incredibly, not because I have any, you know, problem with someone chewing or having a shirt untucked or wearing a grey coat with a black fur collar or whatever, but it's that establishes your personality with them and then any real problems say with actual learning can be your focus – for example, the real problem might be quite an interesting one, so you should come and see my Year 10 at the moment 'cos what's happened with Year 10 is I've got or had inherited two difficult students from other classes, one of whom has since been expelled and I allow them into the class over the course of half term, they're out, told off, the class are allied against them because I've got nowhere else to send the other kids so, and then they come into the class on our terms, rather than theirs and this is how you can learn from experience and particular situations...*

This point seems to relate to them recognising, first, how situated teaching is. This situatedness has many elements and they link to the developing dynamics of a group:

Polly, Interview 1: *They are a very nice class, I mean they are lively I think they are not a difficult class I think anybody would get on well with them actually... yeah, delightful group of very enthusiastic youngsters whose...*

AG: *How are they constituted?*

P: *It's mixed ability, totally mixed ability, yeah, so that's actually a tutor group, yeah, including the children who would normally be withdrawn for learning support, they were all there today, which has been another problem*

I have to overcome with watching the film because several of them have been withdrawn and so they have to watch it in another lesson.

Jane, Interview 2: *So the lesson, the lesson wasn't bad for a Tuesday afternoon, I have to say, I've had a lot worse, a lot more fractious Tuesday afternoons … they are a very talkative group, I have never really cracked that but I have learnt not to be confrontational about it because it doesn't get them anywhere and it doesn't get me anywhere, so we sort of battle through with a certain amount of good humour and on the whole it works but they don't, you know, work with the rigour that I would like them to work with and sometimes they are exasperating because of that. I feel sometimes I am taking the exam more than them …*

Charlie, Interview 2: *So, as the lesson went, I was reasonably pleased with it because I think it's a very distinct group in that it isn't, hasn't been cohesive, it's been a group where there are a number of students, maybe four who are significantly either more verbal or brighter than the other students, who tend to lead and what was nice today was some of the quieter students who speak less were not having to be asked to speak, but were very, very happy to volunteer and discuss and posit ideas and I thought the level of thinking that they were doing was more advanced than I thought, my plan was to get them to begin the chart and we'd continue the chart next lesson but the rate at which they grasped that just meant that I felt it was appropriate for them to do that for homework – that group really achieved a great deal today, they really moved on …*

And the particular characteristics of an individual student on a particular day:

Polly, Interview 2: *I think you … it is a constant balancing act for getting relationships with those kind of children right … and it depends which way the wind is blowing quite often if they come in a mood you know, one of the girls was in a really bad mood yesterday because she had just chucked her boyfriend the night before and somebody else's parents had just split up last week and you never actually know what you are going to hit when you come into those classes and you have to give them a little time to do the human being bit before you can do the teaching.*

Jane, Interview 1: *It was nice when Chris actually made that spontaneous comment about, you know what you are going to say because he's, he's a very weak student and it, it's really nice to find an opportunity to, to praise him and bring him out in front of the class as having said something that, you know, is very worthwhile.*

Charlie, Interview 2: *She is hugely lacking in confidence and she, I've taught her now for three years, and that's always been the case and you'll often get a 'oh just can't do this' but she can, she does need boosting and it's a trick that we I think in Year 10 at the end of Year 10 actually instigated because her complaint often was that things were moving too quickly. She was in, she was in a top set, but by the skin of her teeth sort of thing but it really was this sort of lack of confidence and therefore that lack of sort of psychological comfortableness with what you are doing and then you close down rather than feeling 'yeah I'm on top of this' and so it was very much something that we talked about together, saying if you don't understand something clarify, clarify, clarify and she always does it now which is so good for her learning and I believe her confidence is just beginning to develop and that is a joy to see.*

The second dimension is the affective; they are monitoring the class and the collective atmosphere and mood, but also the feeling of individuals, very often anticipating what an individual is about to do:

Polly, Interview 4: *H is a very male dominant force in there, it intimidates the boys so that they feel bad about working with the girls I think so it's a difficult class from that point of view in trying to get them to be comfortable with each other's differences which I would say you don't normally get at Year 10, had you come to my Year 11 class that is quite different although they sit equally split it's perfectly easy to get them to work together because there is a more comfortable group of boys... H is a very dominating influence and boys are intimidated by appearing to seem willing, the only boy who will work very willingly with the girls is L who was sitting next to H, he's equally comfortable with boys and girls, you have to know what they are thinking and feeling to get the best out of them...*

Jane, Interview 2: *He's a very complex character. He wants to do well, he is very disappointed when he doesn't do well, but he hasn't yet reached a stage where he can see the link between his behaviour and his achievements. He's incredibly competitive and he has quite a bit of success in sporting subjects, in sports and PE and things, but even there he's got this phenomenal temper and it just causes him lots of problems. In fact, the reason he wasn't in my lesson last week when the folder and the marks had been given out was because he'd had a bust up with another teacher... you have to treat him individually, not just on his own terms mind you, but establishing a really direct relationship with him...*

The third element here is the optimal learning environment. This environment is as much emotional as physical or cognitive:

Charlie, Interview 2: *But there are other classes who, if you look at the list of individuals they are not a difficult class but the chemistry in the room, the time that they are taught, the work that they're asked to do, the teachers that they have, the dominance of a particular individual makes that a difficult class and I think that the classes who are difficult with some people aren't necessarily difficult with others. You need to create a special space for each class, challenging but caring, demanding but safe to take risks as a learner, not to feel anxious about what other kids say…*

All these comments show that they are expert teachers and also that they reflect in action, that they are very actively thinking in the lesson and that certain 'problems' are noticed, attended to and then remembered. Their reflection on the action is best demonstrated, I would argue, more by their comments about the long term. It is almost inevitable that a lesson in which they are observed and then this action is almost immediately followed by an interview will prompt a form of reflection and an accessing of short-term memory. However, comments like these below demonstrate that individual lessons are viewed through a longer perspective and that each teacher has an 'ongoing dialogue with the situation':

Pam, Interview 2: *That was one example of a type of lesson that I do every few weeks to refresh their thinking and engage them with their own longer term development.*

Sally, Interview 3: *That was quite typical of what you do when you are working with their immediate needs, here writing an essay, and trying to develop them as individuals and as writers.*

It is clear from these teachers that reflection helps to keep them expert rather than competent; it is also clear that they see interaction with colleagues as part of that process and that they 'know' they might slip into automatic pilot if they do not reflect deeply.

Polly Interview 2: AG: *You mention your own interaction with student teachers, has that been an element at all in your development?*

P: *I have enjoyed it very much and yes I think it has been important, it's made me … it certainly makes you reflect on your own practice and about all your teaching … but I think the business of watching them … makes you realise what a long way you have come and it also makes you break down the elementary skills you don't realise how much you take for granted I think … I mean just the business of standing in front of a class, just the business of timing when you speak … being able to read well aloud in class you know all the things … and have your eyes on the class … all the things that you absolutely take for granted you realise that students can't take for granted and I think that's very salutary and it's also very heartening to think that you have got all these amazing skills and that you must keep thinking about them, never become complacent…*

Charlie, Interview 3: *Being a mentor was a very formative experience because really it was the first time since teaching practice in a way that I'd fundamentally questioned my own practice to explain it to somebody else, which is good because it helps you to undertake some real reflection.*

Another connection with reflection is innovation. In the lesson, reflection in the action typically leads to solving an immediate problem. The reflection on action triggers a need to change, to try something new. This can be entirely driven by the teacher's often intuitive sense that something new is needed:

Polly, Interview 1: *So I shall do a bit of media studies, a bit of creative writing, the film throws up lots of issues as well about two points of view of things so the exercise is partly to look at those two points of view and partly to lead in to some creative work and also trying to preserve the idea of different images I suppose, so it was all those things I suppose. They have just been doing a piece of creative writing which was in prose so I thought it would be nice to look at some poetry, and …, its actually … I changed, I've done, I taught some last year but that lesson I haven't done before like that. We did something on just looking at the words that might be used for different groups but I hadn't actually done it with the still pictures and I thought that would just give it a focus the idea of the art gallery which is actually something I have done in Year 7 with a completely different exercise but I just moved it.*

Polly, Interview 1: *Yes, so, yeah I mean again, because we have new people coming in with new ideas, we go on courses quite a lot, I would think that every year I do something in the classroom that I haven't done before that's a new challenge.*

Charlie, Interview 2: *Hamlet is our focus, so I think it's quite good to do this one as a coursework looking at heroism, Hamlet as Renaissance Man, full hero, and all the rest of it. Where it came off from me was one of those sort of more inspired moments when you are sitting watching a film and you suddenly think, 'yeah I could use that' which is part of I suppose creativity isn't it, teaching, people come into it for that feeling and also you must keep trying new approaches to keep yourself fresh as well improving your teaching…*

Lucas, Interview 2: *… I am always trying to avoid falling into a rut of routing out your old favourites, doing the same thing so, seeking out new material, trying to, trying to maintain that kind of vibrant enthusiasm, because many at my stage of career can walk into a lesson having not prepared it, having nothing, you know apart from the materials that the kids are already working on and teach, teach what would be deemed a satisfactory lesson with the minimum of pupil disruption …you have constantly to try new approaches.…*

It can be a response to external demands:

> Polly, Interview 3: *There have been some positive things about the new curriculum in that it has encouraged us to explore other avenues that we might not have done otherwise like media perhaps…and I think it has not been a bad thing, I think the whole move towards making Shakespeare accessible to all children has been a good thing and certainly because it has been on the syllabus for everyone we have had to find ways of doing that I…in many ways that has been positive and has helped me and colleagues to try really new approaches…*

> Sally, Interview 4: *So it was clear we were stuck with these tests on Shakespeare, so we decided as a department to rethink all our schemes and try some really challenging lessons, not to let the dullness of the test dominate our teaching.*

It can be a response to a colleague's ideas:

> Pam, Interview 2: *And my colleague said 'I use soap opera for that kind of work', and I thought, well I never used soap opera, so I asked to watch one of her lessons and immediately I could see what I could do now…it was so stimulating.*

This dialogue with the situation includes the philosophical dimensions of the subject, i.e. what English is as a subject and all the curricular context and its endless changes. They very much demonstrate Schulman's notion of the teacher with deep subject pedagogical knowledge including that wide view of the various forces bearing down on the classroom.

At the philosophical level, this is evident through their comments on the Cox models. They are all using personal growth as their starting point:

> Jane, Interview 1: *Certainly the 'personal growth' view, everything starts from there…*

> Lucas, Interview 1: *'Personal growth' is crucially important and, and development can't happen without that.*

> Pam, Interview 1: *It must be about the individual child, personal growth is the crucial approach.*

That this is a thoughtful position not a status quo is evidenced by the way they feel this model is always fragile because of external impositions:

> Lucas, Interview 2: *It seems child-centred is now a dirty word…it is all about 'Literacy', that is nonsense, it is still about the personal growth of each child, what is the point otherwise?*

Equally they discussed the other models in depth, all of them acknowledging their importance:

> Charlie, Interview 4: *Attention to all these models, I think is very, very important in terms of the approach that we take with our students towards English. This idea of making critical engages in their cultural context, I think it is vital. In terms of the others, the personal growths, the adult needs, yes those two things have to go side by side with what we do and where I still feel I have a weakness in my own professional practice I think is probably with the students who are in terms of threshold are really just accessing language and reading skills are sort of threshold level, they are the areas I still you know need to sort of develop my expertise.*

> Lucas, Interview 1: *I think Cox was completely right to say that there are a number of models that will work. It is, sort of conceptually plural.*

But all cluster towards cultural analysis as a key aspect of English in a media- and technology-soaked society:

> Jane, Interview 1: *Certainly media in terms of feeling that it's an influence on their lives which has a huge force and impact and I feel that they should be equipped to deal with it, and you know, understand it and use it rather than it use them...*

> *When thinking about the child, and the child's needs, well 'cultural analysis' and 'personal growth' can be seen as sort of similar things, can't they. You know, if they are to grow as an individual and understand their lives then they understand the influences on it as well.*

In discussing both cultural heritage and adult needs, they reflected on these as real elements of the English subject but also as models often distorted by political or cultural pressures:

> Polly, Interview 1: *Certainly personal growth, I think we would certainly use that...uh...(pause) well I think we have an awareness of the cross-curricular but it is not something that would...instruct our teaching necessarily...(long pause)...in that...the Adult Needs again we are aware of it and obviously you are trying to develop children to...but its more to do with personal growth than Adult Needs I think...(pause)...we are aware of the cultural heritage and we do...and we are talking about Year 8 now you see with this, well you've...do you want me to concentrate on this class?*

> AG: *I would talk about you, now as opposed to that particular group.*

> P: *Well we have been forced to take note of the cultural heritage because you cannot do GCSE without it...And I think we've...we've found ways*

of doing that well…but I think it's also meant that in some ways it's narrowed the kind of range of reading that we've done in the past, because you are forced to do something which is pre-twentieth century, but I think we've always been happy to teach books that have been…I think it's been, you know, we have followed the personal choice of the teachers the ones that the teachers want to teach more than being aware of it being good for their souls or whatever…

Here, they clearly would have liked more genuine autonomy to engage with these aspects of curriculum and children's learning but with much more freedom to design and develop a coherent but also situated approach:

Charlie, Interview 5: *All teachers need much more flexibility but English especially can be so responsive to students, prescription and restriction do not enable good teaching or learning.*

Neither Schon or Hattie say very much about expert teachers in relation to each other or as collaborators; to be fair, this was not their focus. However, the standards for the AST, the excellent teacher and the chartered teacher stress the very important role that outstanding teachers both can, and should, play with their colleagues. It must be said that there is little 'hard' evidence of the benefits of collaborations, partly because so much emphasis is on individual teacher performance and also because little real research has been conducted. However, these teachers see collaboration as essential to their work, although some were more driven by this than others.

As discussed above, all were committed to student teachers and all also had a firm view about supporting and inducting NQTS. They were clearly very aware of their novice status but were also firm in their beliefs that they should be treated as far as possible more like a peer so that such a relationship felt collaborative not hierarchical.

Polly, Interview 2: *I mean I actually quite like team teaching anyway and it helps beginning teachers so much, I mean we have been doing it regularly up to now we have done it some times so she has read one lesson and I have read the next…we have the wider reading lesson which is when the special needs children are withdrawn so we do something different on Thursdays, she's been effectively leading Friday's lesson because we can talk about it, what she's going to do, we've…but we've shared the reading aloud, the yeah we've shared bits of it, anything that lends itself to sharing between us we've done it. It helps her confidence and makes her feel part of the team…*

The essential point is that they all recognised that teaching could be isolating and that mere repetition, however effective the teaching, was reductive, and they saw collaboration, whether in planning (see Chapter 5) or in resource design or actual teaching, as a way to keep fresh and be challenged.

Polly, Interview 1: *We have a very good department and we are always having new people in and because I mentor new staff I think those kind of challenges are building on the strengths and I think that what my HOD is very keen to do is to get people to work as a team and that's something we have to constantly work at and that is one of my roles really is to help the team work and the sharing to take place so for example last year, working with my HOD you can never stand still anyway I have to say (laughing) you are never allowed to rest so I find that there lots of challenges within the department and last year we suddenly decided that we had all become terribly classroom bound because of the National Curriculum so we said well why don't we do across the year activities again, we have got this new block that is an opportunity which we haven't used and so we decided, I took charge of Year 8 and we decided to do an across the year activity with Year 8 and so we had everybody doing a political campaign in the summer, it was absolutely wonderful you know it really ... they are a very difficult year group last year and uh it was just an amazingly positive end to the year and things like that ... are really ... those are the challenges that we have now and I think this year my challenge is to try to get that working in all the year groups, Year 7 and 9 as well, so that we have some sort of ... we get back to the idea of celebrating and enjoying rather than sticking to the National Curriculum grindstone I think (laughing).*

Jane, Interview 2: *I think people would say 'Jane will know a short story or a poem about that' you know, so if somebody said 'oh I want a poem about, or I want a short story' or you know 'what class reader shall we have', I think, you know, they would probably say 'oh Jane will know something and she will always share her ideas with you'. I mean, I don't read as much as I used to do, but you know there was a time when I was totally up-to-date with children's fiction and everything and it was just so useful, really, really useful and I still like library lessons now if I can you know, just catch on something that a child likes and give them some recommendations and, you know, be able to just, they ask you for something and you can just say 'try this, that's great'. So I feel that I am a resource for my colleagues and all my students...*

They also saw such work as developmental for their colleagues:

Polly, Interview 2: *I am the biggest sharer in the department actually, I am the person who, by my own admission, I find it difficult to do things on my own and I therefore I like to work with other people, so I've worked a lot with our NQT with this ... we both had the same kinds of groups in Year 10 and we actually developed this course for the bottom set Year 10 jointly, a lot of shared ideas there, so I think people might come to me just to bounce ideas off, just as I go to them, I think, I am the person who likes to share most in the department, this is really important to me and, I believe, really makes us all better teachers. ... no, I don't do them for other people, I like to work with other people to develop things, that's probably what I do best. ... That it is a sharing thing? Oh yes, yes I think so, that is the joy of it for me.*

One of the most striking elements of their practice and their thinking was their attention to what Hattie summarises as the multidimensional nature of the classroom. This might be simplified into these elements:

- The teacher (the self);
- The class (and its history);
- Each individual student (and their histories);
- The long time frame (the year/Key Stage);
- The short time frame (this lesson in relation to the previous one and the next one).

The interview transcripts consistently illustrate this multilevel thinking.

The above typology might well be evident in competent to good teaching, as any 'effective' teaching can only really take place within this multidimensionality. However, a very distinctive feature of the observed lessons was the absolute attention to individual students and the depth of knowledge of each student. Given that all these teachers had significant managerial responsibility within English and often also in the school as a whole, this was especially remarkable. Their relationship with students was individual, and it was a mixture of the affective, demonstrating a caring concern and also of the 'high respect', as Hattie puts it, taking their learning absolutely seriously. They did not discount students' personal lives and difficulties; instead, they saw their task as a caring adult with a responsibility towards the student *as a person*.

> Lucas, Interview 3: *I have known him over several years, from a little boy to a troubled teenager, he is essentially a good kid from a messy life, you have to acknowledge what he goes through every day, we are both real people.*

As discussed in earlier chapters, English is a subject in which the personal is part of the subject domain and where identity formation is a dynamic in the classroom. This is not to downplay the work all teachers accomplish, it is to highlight the foregrounded nature of the personal in English and to demonstrate that it is part of the expertise of English teachers to understand how the subject enables students to work with their forming identities. Here are some comments that illustrate this knowledge of individuals and how it is expressed within the paradigm of Hattie's 'high respect', being 'highly motivating' and having a 'positive effect on achievement':

> Polly, Interview 2: *But uh the boy here, this one, on the end, is quite a difficult child and A and I both spent quite a lot of time with him last*

week establishing some ground rules about what he was going to … what was going to be tolerated and what wasn't and actually A spent quite a lot of time with him after school and he talked about how he plays the class clown because he's lacking in ability and I have spent some time with him re-assuring him that he will never have to read aloud in class which was apparently upsetting him and he was really misbehaving very badly last week and he seems to have settled so we've got a, we have got a settling down, then there's the boy in the corner that causes a lot of trouble with the other kids really needs moving but I don't know where to move him to but I think the class have got to the point in Year 7 where they are beginning to know the relationships within the tutor groups because they are mixed ability tutor groups so I think a lot of them know each other from primary school which actually is a problem with these particular characters, they are tired of them already and they are now in the same class with them so there's been quite a lot of settling down for them and for establishing ground rules of what's tolerable and what's not tolerable so I think it's becoming more comfortable and more relaxed now but they weren't a particularly easy class.

These teachers feel that respect is vital to all students and the less able students especially need to feel this from their teacher:

Polly, Interview 2: *I mean I have still got … I have got a bottom set Year 10 here and … my way of handling them is amused tolerance I guess … I tend to have a very relaxed manner with them but again that is very difficult to suggest that a student teacher does that, being a student is very difficult from being an established member of staff … they need clear structures I think, they need tasks which they can do quickly and easily to get them settled and reasonable … they need to have things broken down into a lot of variety of things a bit of speaking bit of listening bit of reading bit of writing quite quickly, they need to feel that they are not being patronised, that's very important I think, to feel that they are achieving so I have for example very little problem teaching Shakespeare to a bottom set Year 10 because they think they are being treated like everybody else in the school and I did a bit of Ted Hughes with them last week and their responses were superb you know but it was based … I started with their experience, I think that is the way in to start with, the way in is to start with what they know and to move away from it that's certainly something but its much easier … its much easier in this school because children are on the whole treated like human beings and that to me is the difference.*

These comments all come from post-lesson interviews, but they were all generated by discussions of actual moments in the lessons and are examples of the individual teacher reflecting on the student viewed in Schon's terms as a 'problem', i.e. not something in itself negative, but something that requires attention and potential solutions. Again 'solution' is not a simplistic term implying complete closure for the teacher or the student. A solution in this sense is a much more elastic and flexible stance, one based on a deep understanding of learning that does not take the novice stance that if 'x' was changed then the student would also be changed.

> Charlie, Interview 4: *So I realised after a few years in teaching that you get difficult moments with classes or individuals… and great moments… and you need to learn from both… they really help you think through how to work with groups over a whole year and to put highs and lows in a true perspective… you have to get it wrong some times in order to get it right most times.*

It is evident from these comments on individuals that the concept of the 'case' is one thing that differentiates expert teachers from others. As has been argued throughout this text, a good deal of this understanding comes from experience of many, many students in many, many classroom situations, but equally, experience is not enough. The comments illustrate the capacity to see both typicality through patterns of student learning and behaviour but also atypicality and individuality. A case, therefore, is not a fixed category; it remains dynamic and capable of constant revision; and individuals students both add to the case and change its nature. This openness seems to be a very important feature in both the development of expertise and maintaining it over time. A striking absence from all the interviews is any comments of the 'kids these days' type. Despite very many years of teaching, the individual teachers did not 'lump' students into categories or generations, and they certainly did not make observations about declining standards. They occasionally commented on how society's changes, e.g. the prevalence of the internet, were affecting student's interests, but these changes were seen as interesting and offering a new challenge rather than as a sign of prevailing decline in students' attitudes or concentration. There was much criticism of prevailing governmental policy and its restrictive impact on teacher autonomy and student engagement (see Chapter 5), but this was often perceived as much more of a problem for less experienced teachers who struggled to cope with both prescription and immense pressure to cover content and teach to ensure good test results.

The chapter concludes with some general comments about the importance of English to these teachers.

> Polly, Interview 1: *I was in (a big city) at the time, and the more I saw was that if you went into Social Work, you were dealing with children's lives after they were broken, and it seemed to me it would be much more worthwhile to get in at the end where you might have some influence over helping them changing their lives for the better even influencing to the extent that you might keep them away from the worst things that might happen to them,*

I know that this is all terribly idealistic but at the time I was … and I love my subject so it just seemed to me that the way in was through teaching English and it also was because it is a personal growth subject you could touch areas of children's lives that seemed to me important and better than going in as Social Worker and mending things 'what were broke' and having less influence over them….

Jane, Interview 2: *I like dealing with literature, I like teaching poetry, I like short stories, I like reading to kids and having them all wanting to know, you know, hanging on your every word. I still find that's a great thrill, and I still find it so satisfying that they, they are prepared to do that and most children are, if you get a good story and you give them a good reading of it, they are there, they're with you, they want to know and there is still that, it doesn't matter how 20th century the rest, or 21st century the rest of the world is, they are still there, so I love doing that…*

Lucas, Interview 5: *Absolutely no regrets, English is still fascinating every day.*

Charlie, Interview 5: *Most of my University friends are accountants and drive big cars (laughing). I feel I have a hugely valuable experience every day teaching English and learning from my students.*

Chapter 5

Curriculum and assessment

Polly, Interview 4: *It is really hard to write English down isn't it? All these documents and frameworks and guidelines are all meant to help ... and some times they do, mind you often they don't! And I think a department has to articulate what matters to it, that is properly professional ... but I quite like the fact that you cannot pin English down, it keeps escaping!*

In Chapter 4, we examined the philosophical stance of the case study teachers using the Cox models as a point of reference. They all espoused a personal growth model as a way of developing each individual student, and this was visibly borne out in their lessons; they also valued cultural analysis as a powerful means of developing students' critical understanding in a complex, media-dominated society. They acknowledged the importance of adult needs and cultural heritage, although both were seen as too narrowly defined by the then curriculum strictures. The 'Language across the Curriculum' model was also valued but seen as a whole-school issue with a place in English but not a model that any English department should be saddled with. At that time the literacy strategy was having its first impact on secondary schools, and they had mixed views about its proposed benefits (see below). Fifteen years of research (for example, Goodwyn 1992a, 2008) has suggested that these broadly conceptualised models of English do persist, and neither the literacy strategy nor the Framework for English have fundamentally changed their importance or their usefulness to teachers in thinking about teaching and learning in English.

In working with a National Curriculum for English since 1988, it might seem that the job of teaching English has become easier. The introduction of the much more prescribed Framework for English (2001), which was also accompanied by much in-service training, could also be seen as helping teachers plan every lesson. This period, 1997–2008, is also marked by the production of masses of materials to support teaching, some of these for classroom use but equally as many for use by English departments (and ITT trainers) as aids to improving teaching and, therefore, raising standards. To understand the scale of this at primary level, Stannard and Huxford's account (2007) of the literacy strategy is very revealing, as is its title *The Literacy Game: The Story of the National Literacy Strategy.* 'It was and remains the biggest educational reform programme of its kind in the world' (p. 1) (see Chapter 8 for a more detailed analysis). It was also, despite their rationalisation, a political 'reform' and one based on neither a sound pilot nor substantial research evidence (Wyse 2003); useful accounts of research were produced later (Harrison 2002; Beard 2000, 2003); for a critique, see Goodwyn (2003b).

My research throughout this period demonstrated that experienced English teachers did not feel very differently about the ideas contained within the Framework from the way they felt about the original National Curriculum.

> Lucas, Interview 2: *The thing is that there is plenty of good stuff in there but mainly because it is not new, we have always taught structured lessons with a beginning, a middle and an end – although we are far too capable to think that every lesson should follow such a simplistic approach – and starters, what is this, a restaurant? And 'plenaries' – it is all so patronising – and the so called training – how many manuals do we need? At least the National Curriculum started off well – there was literature and language and it was great to see the media in there, something we had been doing for years but now recognised properly – there was space to really develop ideas – Key Stage 3 is becoming a kind of motorway that we are all rushing along just to crash into the wall of the test – oh dear, I do sound disheartened.*

Lucas' mention of the 'original' National Curriculum makes a salutary point about the affordances of that period (see also below in relation to the grand design concept). As discussed in Chapter 3, English is almost always the highest profile and more contested subject and therefore the one that receives the most attention and the highest priority; this can be traced back to the Newbolt Report (1921) and the fact that it was the first subject to be defined within the National Curriculum (Cox 1992). It is worth recalling that the National Curriculum for English overtook another major report, the Kingman Report, even before its recommendations were implemented (see Chapter 8 for a fuller discussion).

It seems essential then to accept that English will always suffer from what its own experts see as interference, and that these attempts to control it will be articulated through a curriculum, structured by an assessment regime and policed by some sort of inspection force (see Chapter 8 on Ofsted). These external forces will vary in terms of which dominates and the degree to which all three interact or counteract each other. The best English teachers will subvert or get around these forces when they are at their most negative and restrictive:

> Jane, Interview 5: *In the end I put the students first and their experience of English. Once you have the confidence and experience you know that you can get the right grades and do some good English, though it is more difficult now than ever before, I hope things will eventually get more sensible again.*

There is no point in this chapter in discussing any particular English curriculum as better or worse; each one is of its time and will change. It is important to consider the notion that change is related to teacher expertise; change can be designed by the teacher or implemented to make the best of external demands. The expert teacher is looking for that 'optimal learning environment' for her students. Equally, there are more glacial changes under way that are the interactions with social, cultural and technological change. I have devoted a good deal of research and writing to both the place of media education (for example Goodwyn 1992a, 2004c) and that of digital technologies in English (Goodwyn 1998, 2000a, 2000b), and there is an extensive discussion of the latter in Chapter 6.

In other words, exactly what English will contain and how its proportions of attention will be defined will ceaselessly change. I am a strong advocate for a mixture of personal growth and cultural analysis and would subsume adult needs and cultural heritage within their framing perspectives. Equally, I would advocate a balance between attention to language and to particular texts, some of which would be Literature, some would be literature and many would come from all kinds of media and also ephemeral sources. I would also argue that English belongs more in the arts than in the linguistic disciplines, but that it absolutely belongs to both. All this leads to a recognition that both curriculum design and assessment principles will be discussed below without reference to any detailed existing or previous curriculum or assessment documents, with the exception of considering how one period of time (the mid-1980s) illustrates a period of relative autonomy when teachers' expertise could really be used and developed (see below).

> Pam, Interview 3: *Your attention should be on that particular group of students, on what they need ... I find guidance valuable and am happy to draw on the best ideas from other people, whether the QCA or my colleagues ... we all find maps helpful but, you know, they need to be understood, interpreted and the teacher is a kind of guide, deciding which is the best route for these kids, this child.*

Curriculum and curriculum design

In Shulman's view (Shulman 1987, 2004), good teachers are very knowledgeable about the curriculum and its related materials. Hattie (2003) only uses the word 'plan' once, 'Expert teachers can anticipate, plan, and improvise as required by the situation', but it is very evident in his stress on an 'optimal learning environment' that such teachers design every detail of the learning programme and are constantly assessing and monitoring levels.

There is a very marked difference between novices and accomplished teachers when it comes to planning at any level, and it is clear that novices take time to acquire that knowledge and that the current structures of induction in England recognise that, i.e. both postgraduate certificate of education (PGCE) and graduate teacher programme (GTP) models allow for a gradual assumption of responsibility for students' learning, and the newly qualified teacher (NQT) year offers a modest recognition of novice status with a 10 per cent reduced timetable. Experienced teachers, having become familiar with whatever the current curriculum specifies, frequently express weariness with endless changes to curriculum and examination specifications (Goodwyn 2004a). However, this latter point should not be confused with how very good teachers value and implement curriculum design.

It is important to distinguish here between lesson planning and curriculum design. As teachers become more experienced, they appear to devote much less time to planning and, in a literal sense, this is true. Novices can spend much more time planning a single lesson than is occupied in teaching the lesson itself; this is a necessary learning stage, again well recognized in initial teacher training (ITT). Experienced teachers only devote this amount of time when they face a truly novel situation or an unusually difficult one (this is the problem-solving stance discussed in Chapters 2 and 4). However, there is an important balance between necessary automaticity in everyday teaching and more strategic thinking.

There is ample evidence (Goodwyn 2004a, 2004b) that experienced English teachers' frustrations with the national strategies are chiefly at the curriculum design level. It is not just the issue of professional autonomy, fundamental though that is (see Chapter 1); it is also about planning expertise and the satisfactions of accomplished design. The frustrations expressed above were not expressed about the National Curriculum as first conceived; there was a broad consensus that an overarching, what might be considered 'grand design' was both welcome and valuable (Goodwyn 1992a, 1992b). However, from about 1993 (Goodwyn 2004a), English teachers felt increasingly hemmed in by the prescriptions of the Framework for English and by the very heavy pressure of high stakes testing. This was equally true of primary teachers, especially in Key Stage 2 and after the introduction of the literacy hour (English et al. 2002; English 2003). All the case study teachers were apprehensive about the impact on English of the National Literacy Strategy, as indeed were the great majority of English teachers (Brookes and Goodwyn 1999; Beverton 2000, 2003). The case study teachers had all visited primary schools to observe the literacy hour and were all very impressed by what they saw and remarked on the great skill of the teachers involved. However, they felt that much of what they saw was 'not English' even when it involved teaching about poetry and stories. They all felt that the children were learning about language in a functional and often mechanistic way:

Polly, Interview 2: *The Literacy Hour really reminded me of my grammar school, all the kids in rows picking out metaphors ... it was done in quite a fun way and the teacher was really enthusiastic but it seemed more like Maths or something. . . .*

One outcome of the National Literacy Strategy and the follow-on Framework for English is that English teachers disassociate themselves from the term 'literacy' (Goodwyn 2004a) because of its conceptualisation within these prescriptive curriculum designs. This contrasts interestingly with other countries, notably Australia, where English teachers are comfortable with the title of teacher of English and literacy. The STELLA website (see Chapter 2) illustrates this well, STELLA standing for 'Standards for Teachers of English Language and Literacy in Australia'. The case study teachers, with one exception (Charlie), had been teaching long enough to remember periods of much more autonomy in both curriculum design and planning for assessment. Their view of the previous few years was that it was a period of prescription and overtesting; they anticipated an increase in both and they were right. However, their 'longer view' is valuable in allowing this chapter to look at what best practice can be in curriculum design and assessment in English but also to be very grounded in the ever changing compromise between what the expert teachers feel is best and what external forces are demanding and imposing.

All teachers work with the narrative of the school year and its distinctive features, certainly in England, of the year, the term, then the half-term, with assessment typically coming towards the end of that year; there is more variety than this, but these rhythms are formative and structuring. English departments tend to work within the half-term period for a 'scheme of work' (SOW); I prefer scheme to unit, as scheme implies a planned sequence, a unit just 'fits in'. Again, the half-term is an envelope in which much shorter SOWs can be taught and work can go over much longer periods. However, partly to facilitate curriculum coverage and also to allow sharing of resources, i.e. not everyone can teach a novel at the same time otherwise the department would have to own hundreds of copies (which of course has happened with Shakespeare because of the standard assessment tests or SATs).

At the macro level, there is clearly a role for grand design within a Key Stage or an individual year. One of the indicators of expert teachers is this deeper understanding of the longer term structure of both curriculum design and the logistics of resources and timing. In times of relative autonomy (the late 1970s and early 1980s), this led to innovation at the macro level. For example, some departments took the opportunity for extended reading course work at GCSE to design SOWs led by student choice, i.e. students could choose from a range of options with each teacher offering something they really wanted to teach. In the last fifteen years, changes to planning have almost all come in response to increasingly prescriptive external demands, and planning has therefore been dominated by logistics rather than design.

However, experienced teachers, such as the case study teachers, maintained design at the level of the SOW. Their comments suggest that they do not think in lessons but more in episodes of learning with the emphasis on flow and momentum. An episode can be a SOW but is more often a subsection, perhaps a component, necessary to be accomplished before the next episode can be undertaken. They maintain a balance between the overall momentum of the whole class and the individual trajectory of individual students.

Polly, Interview 1: *Well the long term aim for each year group is to make sure they have an experience of all the different elements of English I suppose and this will be their media bit but not too heavy at this stage in Year 8 I think just introducing them to some media ideas ... and I suppose a lot of the units I do in Year 8 cover, they are not just media or just creative writing they cover lots of different elements so ... we have done some work on the short story and we have looked at presentational technique in writing, article writing, we have done quite a bit, quite a bit of non-fiction work so this is creative and we have viewed images ... it's yeah it's mostly to cover the media, the media idea and a shared text that happens to be a film, so that's, film is one element we cover next term I will probably go on to do some more work on story, we have got some ... last year I did pre-twentieth century, now that's another element that comes in so it's just one of the many elements we fit in, do some story, do some poetry, do some creative writing, do some media work, do some non-fiction, do prose study, bit of drama play work, cover all the elements throughout the year.*

The key point is that expert teachers do plan but not in easy ways for others to interpret. The written form of SOW will be interpretable and is meant to be accessible to the novice or the experienced teacher; to the former, it may be like the plan of a building, very defining and to be followed closely, to the latter more like a simple tune upon which they will improvise extensively while retaining a recognisable tune throughout. For novice and expert alike, ownership of planning is very important and developmental; certainly this is the opinion they express. Novices need lots of help with planning, but they do need to have a plan that is authentic to them. Rather like the notion that it takes 5,000 hours of practice to master a skill (Ericsson et al. 2007), there is a similar relationship between time spent learning to plan and becoming both adept at it and developing that deep understanding of teaching and learning.

It can be argued that, without that opportunity for design, some key elements in the development of true expertise are missing. It can also be argued that lack of early planning experience and the use of 'scripted teaching' may permanently reduce the capacity of an English teacher to develop deeper understandings of English teaching. These deeper understandings seem to come from the reflective cycle inherent in good planning, whether at the macro or the micro level. This cycle is very like the action research model discussed in Chapter 8, in which a teacher designs a teaching episode and carries it through, often making many adjustments during the cycle, and then coming to a time of reflective evaluation. Novices are expected to demonstrate their evaluations in written form and evidence their capacity to learn from experience and to revise accordingly; as with planning, this is both a necessary learning stage and part of developing a standards-focused portfolio. For the expert teacher, evaluation is best conceptualised along Schon's lines as a dialogue with the situation. During the teaching episode, the dialogue is continuous; at the conclusion to a more major episode, the dialogue becomes more like an interview of the situation with more major questions being asked about the value and quality of the learning period.

> Jane, Interview 3: *Well I think about each lesson as it goes along and afterwards but I really take stock of everything from time to time, I then consider whether I have really achieved what we needed and whether individuals have genuinely improved ... I often recognise that some things just were not successful enough and need re-thinking.*

What appears to be the case is that expert teachers' reflections and evaluations are expressed in the next design rather than in a retrospective account of 'what went well'. At a practical level, this is both efficacious and time efficient, as the design is improved and the time is spent in both designing and becoming better at such design. However, this is another case where we have little research and little means of sharing this expertise. Typically, more experienced teachers (whether expert or not) recognise the need to literally help novices plan at both the micro and the macro level. This help can mean sitting together and working through a teaching episode, reviewing plans and offering advice and guidance or feeding back on how the plan was carried out and how the teaching experience can now be used to improve planning. There is evidence that expert teachers, as with the case study teachers, share their design expertise at the departmental level. There is evidence that they can work collaboratively with individual and experienced colleagues:

> Polly, Interview 2: *We are always a sharing department, especially important for old timers like me to learn from everyone, student teachers as well as my Head of Department.*
>
> Pam, Interview 4: *You have to make a conscious effort to share planning, not just stick a work sheet in the resources filing cabinet, but sit down with colleagues and thrash out some real ideas about what the point is of a plan.*

However, there is very little evidence of how their qualitatively deeper planning expertise might be accessed by less effective teachers. There is even some evidence that the idiosyncrasy of teaching (Eraut 1994) may make such sharing problematic. Given earlier points about authenticity and the need for every English teacher, even the novice, to feel they 'own' their planning and teaching, an implication may be that, to feel 'right', each teacher's plan is somehow unique. We do not have enough research evidence to prove this or to discount it. What we have is a concern that real curriculum design expertise does exist in expert teachers and that we need to understand it better before we know how it might be best disseminated to other effective and developing teachers. It is also clear that the curriculum environment of the last fifteen years has proved inhibiting for English teachers at all career stages; there has been far less opportunity for design at any level with a markedly decreased emphasis on innovation (Goodwyn 2004a, 2008). The latest version of the standards, including those for initial teacher education, actually includes the word 'innovation', but this is mere rhetoric without actual and authentic opportunity. In a best case scenario, the failures of prescription and scripted teaching over that fifteen-year period may lead to a more devolved form of curriculum, with a consensual 'grand design' and a real degree of autonomy, encouraging teacher-led innovation. It is noticeable that the chartered teacher model in Scotland (see Chapter 2) is far more explicit (than the advanced skills teacher (AST) or excellent teacher) about the concept of both the extended professional and their influence on curriculum evaluation and change.

Assessment and monitoring

Charlie, Interview 2: *Assessment in English is relentless but crucial, it would be so easy just to skim work and say 'well done', you get to realise that not only is that pretty lazy it is also counter productive, you have to devote time and energy to it and then the kids get serious about your assessment and really improve.*

It is important to note that the methodology of the case studies of the expert English teachers was strong on classroom observation and interview and, much less so, on their assessment practices. The quotations below are still valuable, but the research cannot claim to have studied how expert teachers of English conduct assessment for the majority of the time. What the interviews reveal (see Chapter 4) is a deep knowledge of individual students; much of this understanding comes from assessment as well as classroom interaction. Indeed, it seems evident that one feature of expert teaching, perhaps especially in English where speaking and listening are part of the assessment paradigm, is that, in the act of classroom monitoring, these teachers are also assessing student progress.

Polly, Interview 3: *What do I do? ... I have felt that when I have asked them to do something based on the book I need to direct them in what to look at I hoped ... what I hoped was ... I would give them a few ideas and leave it open enough so that if they wanted and in fact, when I was going round today, a lot of them have used their own ideas, they have not necessarily used it, the weaker ones have definitely used that structure and there's enough weak kids in the class that need it I think, so that's why I did it, and Mark, who is the weakest of all was really getting down to it, I checked several times and he did not need any actual help today.*

Unquestionably, for all teachers of English, the assessment load feels burdensome at best, overwhelming at worst. There is a strong professional argument for English teachers to have either smaller class sizes or one less class a week than other colleagues; these colleagues are most unlikely to agree with that view, and schools are not resourced to support such a difference. Therefore, most English teachers quite rapidly develop a form of competence with assessment that is logistically driven and highly pragmatic. This is not essentially desirable but it is a fact of school life for most teachers. The principal burden is the volume of writing that students produce over the week with the ironic side-effect that the more stimulating the teaching, the more they write! As has been regularly stated, this book is not a manual, it is an exploration of expertise. English teachers have many coping strategies for dealing with assessment, and especially with writing, but coping is not expertise; in fact, however understandable at a pragmatic level, it is almost certainly a block to its development. This section will reflect on assessment in English at the level of its deeper purpose and genuine benefits; some of this may seem couched in what may sound like ideal terms.

The best English teaching is holistic on a number of dimensions, for example speaking and listening and reading and writing are not treated most of the time as separate 'skills' but as language modes that are in constant interaction with each other.

> Pam, Interview 3: *The challenge for me is keeping it all together, of course you have to focus on different things in different lessons, but they should experience English as a whole thing, that is partly why this literacy label is not helpful, English is about connecting all your language uses together ... so I make sure every lesson has something of everything and over a few weeks they have really made use of speaking and listening and reading and writing.*

They can be treated distinctly when this is fit for purpose:

> Charlie, Interview 4: *English is best thought of as a holistic enterprise and I do not think any aspect of language should dominate, of course, in some lessons you really focus down, as you saw today, you have to really teach skills like formal and informal speech styles and I think that worked well, several of the boys literally improved during that lesson, you could see their skill and confidence growing.*

Another way in which English is holistic is that curriculum design is also assessment design. Expert teachers are not thinking 'how can I test that discrete skill?', they are thinking 'what powerful learning experiences can I generate that will also provide me with ways of enabling student progress?' They are thinking 'what is an exciting and challenging task for my students?' 'How can it be differentiated so that all students can succeed and learn something about both the content and also their own development?'

The best assessment in English can be described as informed by these characteristics:

- authenticity;
- integrity;
- interest;
- satisfaction with outcomes.

Authenticity has several dimensions; they are both complementary and overlapping. The first is that the assessment, whether diagnostic, formative or summative, is intrinsically worth doing, i.e. it is valuable to the students and their learning, and it will provide the teacher with important knowledge about the students and their progress. The second is that it is organic to the work. Although all curriculum and all assessment tasks are designed, many of the tests teachers have been expected to work towards are felt to be a distortion or, as it were, unnatural; rather than designed, they seem contrived. This somewhat metaphoric use of the notion of what is 'natural' fits closely with how teachers talk about the purpose and significance of assessment.

> Lucas, Interview 2: *That is what is so depressing about these endless tests: they just are no real use as assessments and my staff are jumping through ridiculous hoops all the time.*

> Sally, Interview 3: *No, I really think the testing policy is crazy now, the teacher should be always thinking about how assessment supports learning and gives kids feedback. It is fine having agreed guidelines and criteria, like GCSE used to be, but then you have constantly to look for real opportunities that go with the work and the progress of the class.*

The final key dimension with authenticity relates to teacher autonomy. As Hattie (2003) points out, expert teaching is 'situated' and so is assessment. The teacher needs to believe in and 'own' the assessment task or process and feel both responsible for it but also to take some pride in its effectiveness for that particular class or individual student.

The element of integrity comes from the teacher's views about the subject of English and may relate to the Cox models and other value-oriented beliefs. In this sense, the assessment is not only authentic in the terms outlined above, but it aligns with the deeper purpose of English. For example, it helps an individual student improve self-expression and reflect on real life experience (personal growth); it enables students to articulate their critical views of the way young people are stereotyped in the media (cultural analysis); it enables students to show their understanding of the power of evil as manifested in *Macbeth* (cultural heritage); it helps students produce a pamphlet they might write in later life as part of a local campaign (adult needs).

> Polly, Interview 2: *I have just got more and more child-centred over the years – how out of step am I!!! ... English is about who you are as well as what you are ... these kids have lots to say, they need real opportunities to talk about life and try and communicate how they are doing in the real world, all these tests just muzzle them and make them say what happens to get a Grade C or something.*

> Jane, Interview 3: *That lesson really had nothing to do with the Shakespeare test did it? I really wanted them to get into the play and find something about the real world in there, then they want to write a decent response and argue with the other kids about what really matters to the characters, that is what assessment should help with, not hinder.*

Another revealing example relates to assessing reading. Teachers need to understand how well individual students are understanding a particular text but also how their reading is developing more broadly. Very good English teachers do not ask their students to do comprehension 'exercises' in a decontextualised way, even though pragmatically that might be a quick and apparently reliable approach. They will design a task that has a real context and a longer term purpose than a 'test'. They might well use the technique of close procedure, but the text being used will be from a text that the class is already studying, leading to a deepening of understanding of the text as well as how language is working. They may ask the students in groups to design some questions about a difficult poem after some initial reading and discussion; then, after further reading and discussion, ask them to try answering those questions themselves. These tasks are both authentic and have integrity.

> Pam, Interview 5: *It was important today for them to stand back from the book and think about what they know about it having spent several weeks on it – that is why they did these role play interviews – to find out what the questions are that the book asks us as readers ... I was really impressed by the standard of some of the role plays, it cheers you up when you see them really 'getting it'.*

It may seem initially banal to suggest that assessment should have 'interest', given that it has many purposes and there is always time pressure. However, the best assessment tasks in English produce work that has a real interest to the teacher, to some extent regardless of the quality of the product. This seems a paradox at first. Good assessment allows students to demonstrate what they 'can do' and also to experience some sense of achievement. It also reveals what they are struggling to do and what they need to try next to continue to improve; in that way all assessment tasks can be diagnostic. 'Interest' then is not whether the work produced is itself 'interesting' (although that helps), it is whether the task's design has produced work of interest to the teacher's understanding of the student and of the class; and at a deeper level of the nature of teaching and learning for all students of English, Hattie's deep learning characteristic. Ultimately, the teacher is interested in the feedback that the students' outcomes provide about the teaching. At this level, the teacher not only owns (autonomy) the task and believes it was worth doing (integrity), but evaluates whether the quality of the task design was really effective (interest, partly in the teaching self).

> Charlie, Interview 4: *That's the thing though, the way they produced those essays helps me know what they know, and also what I do and don't know about them…I hope that makes sense?…we are all getting some kind of understanding of how we have all done with this unit and what we have got out of it…and I really learn about my teaching and how to improve longer term.*

Satisfaction for the teacher is a highly important element in all aspects of teaching but, in relation to assessment, it is strongly foregrounded. Satisfaction, like authenticity, has several elements. One is very simple and pragmatically oriented, best described as 'it worked', it produced what was needed. Experienced teachers are more tolerant of a rough and ready outcome if other circumstances have been impacting on the situation, e.g. not the right amount of time, the physical conditions were not ideal and so on.

> Sally, Interview 2: *Well that was very so, so I must say, but the way the criteria work you just have to run lessons like that and you have to get them to produce about each poem something that fits the boxes, it is not what I would choose but I have enough experience to recognise it for what it is.*

However, 'it worked' is a default situation not the desirable one. A higher, deeper level comes from student achievement; if the task has produced good outcomes and really demonstrated that some students are now making real progress, then this is extremely pleasing to the teacher. It is both celebratory of the students and motivating for the future and also a positive piece of feedback for the teacher's self-esteem and self-efficacy; it is a sustaining outcome for the teacher, especially in an era of high stakes and distorting testing which is externally imposed.

> Lucas, Interview 3: *Well I am really pleased, that was bit of a risk really, setting it up with the drama activity first and then the writing and then another drama activity but I have to say they were great all the way through and what a work rate…and it was so enjoyable, great atmosphere.*

An assessment task is also a very deliberated part of teaching. Whereas expert performance is marked by degrees of automaticity, fluidity and improvisation, assessment design is carefully deliberated and quite precisely executed. The outcomes are then literally assessed and are a powerful tool for deep reflection on student progress and the effectiveness of the teacher. As well as being very rationally and deliberately planned, assessment tasks, given their importance, have a higher risk factor: they may not work well, they may let down and even 'fail' the students. Therefore, assessment design also has both an aesthetic and an emotional dimension, i.e. it is deeply satisfying when it succeeds and is perhaps especially emotional in a climate of externally imposed testing of a kind that lacks both authenticity and integrity; the teacher has 'more to lose'.

> Polly, Interview 2: *That just felt right for them and I did enjoy the speeches, we have worked so hard together and I really think they kind of grew up in that lesson.*

English teachers always face a dilemma when it comes to assessment, and that derives from the assessment framework within which they have to operate. This framework is subject to constant change, from minor tinkering to complete overhaul. It is, to some extent, linked to curriculum change, but the relationship is by no means as logically close as might be desirable. Expert teachers are extremely good at both working with the prevailing testing model, so that their students 'succeed' and also working around it, so that their students are enjoying a good experience of English. However, research has shown (Goodwyn 2004a) that, since the introduction of the National Curriculum for English, there has been a steep increase in the amount of testing in English (see Chapter 3). In England in the first part of the twenty-first century, it is undeniable that much of English, from Key Stage 1 to 5, has been affected by 'teaching to the test'. That teachers have coped with this might be evidenced through the year on year improvement in grades at 'A level' where, it might be argued, teachers are teaching using their most specialised knowledge. This 'coping', as argued at the opening of the chapter, is not best practice and does not develop genuine expertise. As the assessment regime will continue to change perpetually, it is worth a brief reflection on when things were different and how they benefited the development of expertise; this example offers some kind of model for the future. This example also illustrates how more teacher autonomy with curriculum design intertwines with expertise in assessment.

> Polly, Interview 2: *It is so disappointing now I have to say because I have been a course work moderator for years and that was important to me but because course work is being treated in such a cavalier way now ... it's really*

not very interesting, you are just not as important as you used to be as a professional English teacher ... I don't like the work very much but I shall keep doing that because I ought to be prepared to do examining but I am not. I just can't face hours and hours of marking of work that is so much less successful and interesting than it used to be.

The introduction of the first GCSEs in English in the 1980s demonstrates a number of key points. These examinations were brought in after a reasonable consensus was reached that the traditional 'O' (ordinary) levels in English Language and also English Literature were no longer suitable for the comprehensive school system, created principally in the 1970s. They had been designed to test only the 'top' 20 per cent of students. Equally, the CSE (Certificate of Secondary Education), which had evolved in the secondary modern schools, was only designed for the next 60 per cent but lacked status with employers and universities. It was, however, a much more dynamic qualification where a good deal of innovation had been encouraged, and many of its elements (speaking and listening, coursework) were considered best practice among English teachers.

The key point is that the GCSE gave English teachers a great deal of freedom and also a high degree of responsibility. A department could choose to assess both curriculum areas, i.e. English (which had both language and literature components) and Literature by 100 per cent coursework or by 50 per cent coursework and 50 per cent examination. English contained a major element of speaking and listening that had to be assessed continuously. For those choosing 100 per cent coursework, there was almost total freedom to select texts and, as 'wider reading' was a compulsory element, students were also actively encouraged to choose their own texts.

Polly, Interview 4: *That was such a challenging time, for all of us, teachers and students, I mean it was so varied and engaging, kids were reading all kinds of things and really felt excited about them and bringing them into school ... I know that some people ... these Literacy consultants for example ... keep telling us that it was all haphazard and kind of indulgent ... that is so unfair and untrue ... we worked incredibly hard and ... yes ... it was less controlled and kind of uniform ... but that was because it was so creative and exciting ... that is not something that can be said of the three part lesson every day formula!*

The implications of this radical change were far reaching. English teachers had the opportunity and the responsibility to design a secondary curriculum that was suited to their students. They were working within an assessment framework that emphasised continuous assessment and was never dominated by tests or examinations. This assessment framework demanded teacher-designed tasks whose outputs were externally moderated but not externally driven. An external moderator could lower the grades of all students if the department had been too generous and might raise them if there had been insufficient recognition of student achievement. The coursework folder of writing had to cover a wide range of genres, but the teacher and student were able to choose the student's best work. This meant that every piece of writing could be important, but that experiments that did not 'work' were not going to distort final achievement. Some coursework had to be completed in 'controlled conditions', ensuring that the teacher could see what the student could produce in the classroom and then compare this outcome with others produced at home.

Finally, all this meant that English teachers had to discuss their assessment practices constantly, relate them to their own curriculum and revise and improve them whenever possible. These discussions happened in every school and at meetings involving groups of schools. Despite the workload and the challenge of new areas such as speaking and listening, the professional atmosphere was extraordinarily creative and productive. There were some very difficult questions to address such as, 'What about student plagiarism or parental help?', 'Can you really assess speaking and listening in a crowded classroom?', 'Can a teacher accept written work about a text they have not read?' and so on. It is not, therefore, that there were not many assessment issues to address and some problems that could not readily be solved, it was that English teachers had to be increasingly expert in assessment and in curriculum design.

Assessment has a rather more technical vocabulary than most aspects of teaching and also a tendency for terms to become outdated quite rapidly as another wave of 'reform' comes roaring in. These two aspects tend to hide what has been consistent in assessment over longer periods of time and also what has been lost by political interference. For example, the 'Assessment for Learning' (Black and Wiliam 1998) movement in England has been an excellent corrective to the obsession with national standards and persistent testing. It has certainly helped teachers to look on assessment as at least as much formative as summative. However, many of its best features were present in the period exemplified above. Equally, the period dominated by teaching to the test seems to have reduced teacher confidence in being an assessor and in curriculum design.

Just as the act of teaching needs hundreds of hours of practice to become competent, never mind expert, so does assessment. Assessment in English must also have those features outlined above, authenticity, integrity, interest and satisfaction, if it is to be developmental for the teacher. It is ironic that a period dominated by testing should be one in which assessment becomes less expert, but that clearly is an outcome. It is also clear that a period dominated by a prescribed curriculum will reduce the curriculum design expertise of all teachers. The case study teachers all, in different ways, reflected on the impact of these external and negative pressures.

Polly, Interview 1: *Oh, well I have been aware that change has been forced upon us, I think, but I think in this department certainly and in this school we have been allowed to retain our professional ... intuition if you like ... just our professional beliefs, we are still allowed to teach in the way that we wish to but at the same time obviously the National Curriculum has come in, but I don't think we ever saw it as a straightjacket. I think we have been able to adapt within it to retain the things that we think are important ... but you can't ignore things like the changing of the GCSE syllabus which has changed dramatically. I think the way that we teach from when we did one hundred per cent course work to what we are doing now ... I mean some things within it I still think that we haven't we probably haven't changed very much we still feel very strongly that with response for example and we try to retain that within the way that we teach literature but at the same time we have got an exam which is being forced upon us and we have to teach children in a different way in order to prepare them for that exam and in terms of exploring the text I will still take the reader response approach to it and then have to impose something else at the end ... no it isn't just imposed at the end it's, but you have to be more aware of that I suppose so it does change the way that you teach to some extent without necessarily betraying all your principles and how you teach, we try to retain that I think ... a sense of personal growth I think.*

Jane, Interview 3: *Well GCSE had just come in when I came back into work and I actually welcomed that, I actually liked GCSE very much. I thought it was a tremendous improvement on what we had had before and the sort of divisions between CSE and GCSE which GCE ... which of course we are getting back now in tiers so everything seems to be going full circle again which is unfortunate but I've particularly enjoyed the years when we had one hundred per cent course work when I first came to this school and there seemed to be much more freedom on the curriculum where we could ... do things ... certainly within the department we shared much more we put classes together and you had celebratory things because the curriculum was less packed and you did not have to get through so much so I think there has definitely been a change now into pushing you back into your own classroom and having to get through an enormous amount of material in order to prepare them for the exams so I think we have lost some of our freedom but I don't think we have lost all our responsibility for the way we teach so I think we can still teach the things that we think are important in terms of how you teach a book or how you explore an idea.*

Charlie, Interview 2: *The pressures on, on GCSE results, target settings and so on force us to take a responsibility for it actually .... Reducing the curriculum, dare I say it, I think now we did what we didn't used to, which was what we used to do was look at the National Curriculum and teach it and then by default you'd hit GCSE, so GCSE criteria, now we actually invent assignments to meet the benchmarks which is the wrong way round of doing it because it does limit, but it gets them good grades and then that hits us at 'A' level because we've done it for them or they've had a very limited experience at GCSE and it affects 'A' level when they ought to think for themselves.*

Equally, they were resilient and remained positive about the enduring value of their subject and their own passion for teaching it.

Polly, Interview 1: *And ... certainly, I mean I suppose I always believed that English was the most important thing and the idea of personal growth goes right through it ...so that probably it did inform my early teaching ... but the way I was taught was completely different in a grammar school and I think I have become much more child-centred than I was, that's unfashion-able isn't it, we are not allowed to be child-centred now, I don't know, but I would say I have become more child-centred and I certainly teach English in a much more active way than I used to you know it used to be much more instructional well I'd have done it through discussion but basically sort of lit crit approach to whereas I have learned about reader response ... and now I have the balance right I hope, so that English is challenging to my classes but still full of life and enjoyment.*

Charlie, Interview 3: *I enjoy everything about English really, then the other things that I enjoy doing but, which I suppose are more difficult to control are things like the more creative side of, rather than analytical sides of things, media where you are getting the students to maybe run their own newspaper or run an advertising project, something like that I enjoy as well, ... where your own creativity can have some sort of play. I think that those are the sorts of things I enjoy teaching most. Even teaching sen-tences by making the kids words and have them running round the room getting sentences, that's, that's quite enjoyable but that sentences on the board approach ... terrible.*

You know it is important in English to being something to do with releas-ing people to be creative, communicators, lovers of literature, there is an issue about also teaching them to write in sentences so they, you know, they pass their exams, so yeah it's changed it and I, I don't completely resent the change, I think it's changed because the times are changing anyway. So my view's adapted but I think looking back over the last 5 years that that's, it's inevitable because my role has changed, but also the priorities in educa-tion have changed too ... but English can handle all this because it has an integrity beyond external tests and interference.

Chapter 6

English teachers and digital technologies

Polly, Interview 3: *I think the use of computers can be fantastic and the kids do love using them. I am still learning my way and mostly enjoying that but I really need more time and at least some training, but I think the potential is tremendous.*

A little context

The point was made in Chapter 3 that novice teachers of the late 1960s, teachers who may well now be highly expert teachers, began working in the classroom before the creation of the internet, the mobile phone and even the personal computer. As for the media, television, for example, was a mere three channels, had to be watched in real time and was yet to be either recognized or demonized in relation to children; colour broadcasting only began in 1967. The general point is clear: that teaching exists in a world experiencing fast paced technological change and with very direct impact on the classroom (Goodwyn 2000a, 2000b). At the same time, it is often remarked that schooling itself (see Chapter 1) still operates a somewhat primitive, almost nineteenth century, factory model; quite simply, technological change has not transformed education. How truly different is a whiteboard from a chalk board? I was involved in a piece of research that examined teachers' use of information and communication technology (ICT) in relation to pupil literacy (Goodwyn and Findlay 2004). A school identified a subject teacher (not English) as an outstanding user of ICT. On investigation it turned out that he had taken all his notes, etc., and put them, more or less unchanged, on to PowerPoint, using it in every lesson, every day. The point is well made: extensive use is not better use; in fact, it may well be much worse for the experience of students.

This rather striking, almost comic example does not diminish the seriousness of the challenge to teachers or underplay the stressful effects of changes on the teaching force. As discussed in Chapter 2, the Dreyfus model is clear that expertise in a broad domain may well be inconsistent and that a practitioner can even be a 'novice' in a particular area. Equally, as Schon pointed out many years ago, learning a new skill can be frightening and highly distressing as we realise just how incompetent we are. This has been the experience of many otherwise confident teachers over the last thirty years, specifically in relation to ICT, and English teachers have been no exception. But some of this uncertainty was productive. Many of the claims made for the transformative impact of technology were naive at best and simply absurd at worst. Some professional suspicion about such claims was highly justified, and one example (the Lottery fund) will be considered. Much more important than mere suspicion has been the critical treatment of both the claims and the hard sell of the latest products. For the vast sums spent on ICT equipment in schools, the benefits have been relatively small and very hard to prove. Very good teachers focus on students and on pedagogy, as will be discussed in detail below; the chalk board was a very effective technology in its time.

Teaching and technology in intellectual and physical spaces

For the developing teacher, the point about chalk boards is salutary and aids some reflection. As the compulsory school model emerged in the latter half of the nineteenth century, so did the classroom and the school as purpose-built environments. It inherited certain technologies such as the slate and the ink pen. It also inherited certain architectural and furniture typicalities, for example the positioning of high windows and the use of pupil and teacher desks. The windows tend to be lower now and bigger (often inappropriately so) and the desks (or tables) more portable, but the classroom has remained very consistent over at least 150 years. It must be stressed that this is not in itself a problem. The comparison often made that hospitals are now transformed compared with schools, particularly the operating theatre, is neither especially accurate nor helpful. First of all, since 1870, our medical knowledge has been transformed but, it might more usefully be argued, we knew so little at that time. Second, we did know a great deal then about educating people; schools in that sense came from a more tried and tested pedagogical model. Third, hospitals are really not that different for patients, unless you are very wealthy, as the experience of lying in a bed in a ward is in essence at least similar to what it was in the nineteenth century. So, hospitals and schools are much more comparable in the way they reveal their traditional origins, and particularly how they illustrate the scaling up of both medical treatment for a whole population and the equivalent for education, than anything else. The difference that I would accept between the institutions, in their contemporary form, is that the expert in the room is probably more knowledgeable and up to date if a doctor than a teacher; the reasons for this have been discussed in Chapter 2. All this leads to the simple but powerful conclusion that it is the knowledge of the expert user that makes the technology worth having. Certainly some equipment in hospitals is far more specialist and extraordinarily complex than that found in schools, but its users have been offered the necessary training to optimise its use. It would be fair to say that, during the period of the emergent 'new technologies', the same cannot be said for teachers generally or for specialist teachers either. However, it can be said with absolute certainty that schools in developed education systems now contain much larger amounts of technology, and teachers use a great deal more equipment in their teaching; most of it with a reliably short life and 'built-in' redundancy. This last point creates a paradox for all teachers. Is it worth learning how to use 'x', if 'x' will be replaced by the much better 'y' next year, leading to the thought is it worth learning 'x' at all? Finally, and most importantly, is 'x' actually going to improve teaching and learning? Power-Point, that most beloved presentational device, was designed very much for the corporate world and not for schools. The phrase 'death by PowerPoint' is worth noting and has followed on from 'death by work sheets', something that was a very specific technological invention of mass schooling.

The use of technology therefore exists in a curious intellectual and physical space and interface. Schools have not changed very much, and this provides a well-known and understood set of physical environments that both enable and limit good teaching. Classrooms are, very typically, crowded and uncomfortable spaces, dominated by either intense movement or 'sitting still'. The envelope of the school is equally dominated by those extremes, and the peculiarities of other spaces such as corridors, schools halls and even the 'playground' are both well understood and yet still uncomfortable environments for many or all children and young people.

For the individual teacher, it is inevitably the classroom that dominates and predominates, although this is not an absolute fit with the 'learning environment' that an individual teacher can establish. This is clear from the point that certain teachers can enter almost any classroom, with a class that they already know, and still engage their students within a version of the learning environment that they have already established.

To reiterate, schools and classrooms are both highly enabling and highly constraining for teaching and learning, and they certainly make radical experiments with physical structuring at the macro or micro level very difficult. What very good teachers do is recognise this challenge as a factor; what distinguishes them is that they think hard about the limitations as they affect their students and also think carefully about the maximum enablement that can be made for quality learning. They also treat the classroom as a three-dimensional and highly embodied space in which technology plays a key role. As they have a deep understanding of how students learn, they are constantly concerned to maximise the attention of their students and to work with the limitations of the classroom, which frequently work against supporting sustained attention. Much technology is focused on generating attention; this can be as distracting as it is engaging, but essentially this is what good teachers are looking for.

It must be said the 'new technologies' are substantially different within the right learning environments and with the appropriate degree of teacher expertise; note that the latter need not be particularly technical as will be discussed below. The claims for the new technologies have been hugely over-inflated, not least because the physical environment of schools is a great limitation to changes in pedagogy or models of learning. The early versions of the computer 'lab', for example, epitomize some truly terrible classroom design. The inflated claims were also not good for teacher morale as they implied 'if only teachers knew how to use the technology', then learning would be transformed, i.e. teachers were somehow a problem (Goodwyn et al. 1997). This latter problem persists and can certainly affect even very good and experienced teachers. However, adopting a critical view of the claims of 'impact' of these technologies has not prevented many teachers from recognising that they are potentially transformative for young people and that they do represent the beginning of a paradigm shift in teaching and learning. For more detailed considerations of that shift, see Lankshear and Knobel (2006) and for implications for English, see Adams and Brindley (2007).

Policy and practice

As this paradigm shift has been having both a positive and a disturbing effect on schools for nearly thirty years, it is worth considering how expert teachers of English have developed during this time; this will be illustrated through two contrasting approaches to change. The first concerns the 'New Opportunities Fund' (NOF) training and the follow-up evaluation; the second concerns a research project conducted to investigate the actual practice of teachers.

As has been argued throughout this book, very good teachers are highly 'competent', but they are not technicians who simply carry out the policies or instructions of others. They are open to and they value training opportunities; training in clearly defined skills is especially acceptable. Learning how to make more of word processing software or better use of a spreadsheet are simply useful additions to a skill set. No activity is ideologically neutral but, in relative terms, such training is mostly value free for the individual trainee. But such an activity may be embedded within a policy that is deserving of much more critical attention per se.

The NOF project is certainly worth a critical discussion in relation to both the topic of this chapter and the general aim of the book to aid reflection on the professional context of teaching. A very good question is to ask whether the NOF project aided the development of expertise in teaching? I worked within the project as the evaluator of one consortium for four years. For three years after the project, I worked as an evaluator of its impact, specifically on English teaching and English departments. Both these roles were part time and relatively 'independent', that is, I was being asked to provide evaluative insight based on my knowledge and experience. Inevitably, I learned a very great deal from this rich experience, and it was something of a privilege to visit schools and to be invited in to observe and review their practices and their policies.

NOF itself lasted from 1999 to 2003 and was funded to the tune of £230 million; a further £50 million was used to generate materials and a separate £20 million was available for school and college librarians. I shall draw initially from the evaluation report produced in 2004, produced long before the evaluation in which I was involved was concluded. The report begins:

> The New Opportunities Fund's (NOF) programme on Information and Communications Technology (ICT) was intended to bring all full time classroom teachers up to the ICT standard of a newly qualified teacher. The training programme was a bold step to use innovative teaching methods like elearning and to emphasis pedagogy rather than ICT skills. The aim – to provide training opportunities to all teachers who require them – was certainly ambitious. Few training programmes in any sector had ever been on a similar scale. The programme was underpinned by the investment of £1.9 billion in the National Grid for Learning (NGfL). The focus was ICT in the classroom and much of the training was expected to be online. £230 million was spent on this initiative in the UK (£180 million in England) by the New Opportunities Fund (NOF), the lottery distribution body responsible for education, health and environment initiatives. In England training for 395,000 teachers was undertaken by forty-seven English approved training providers (ATPs) at a cost of £450 million. The Teacher Training Agency was responsible for quality assurance.
>
> Preston (2004: 5)

This is factually accurate and its comment about scale is also appropriate; this really was an attempt to help an experienced workforce to 'catch up' with the ICT skills that most novices brought with them into the profession; the 'digital natives' as they are often described. It is also accurate that it stresses 'much of the training was expected to be online'. It is barely credible that all the evidence about how teachers learn should have been so absurdly ignored. If teachers could have found a way to learn ICT 'online', they would have done so, who would have needed NOF. What teachers needed was time in groups to be taught skills and then time to adapt them into their pedagogy. The consortium with which I worked adopted exactly this model and it was a terrific success. The report goes on:

> However, the programme had a difficult start. The intention that schools would update their ICT skills before the start of the programme was not realised. The idea that schools would receive their Government funded ICT equipment and broadband connections before they started their training was over-ambitious – teachers needed time to familiarise themselves with the equipment and the on-line learning environments were not sufficiently reliable when large numbers engaged. Trainers, particularly those

skilled in online teaching had to be trained and it took time before there were enough of them to deliver the training programmes. In addition, most heads and senior managers were not trained in the management of ICT in schools at the start of the programme. Schools too frequently chose training providers who were good at marketing themselves rather than one that was most suitable for their own school. The concerns of the unions over the lack of supply cover had to be considered and as a result a programme that was a critical part of Government policy had to be treated as if it was optional training for the individual teacher.

Ibid.: 6

Again, these comments are relatively accurate although they are too moderate in their judgements. The expectations were simply absurd and took no genuine account of the realities of teachers' lives. Everything about the project at the national level was badly timed and poorly executed. The passing point about most senior managers not being trained is quite extraordinary given that the other comment is that 'schools frequently chose training providers who were good at marketing themselves rather than one that was most suitable to their own school'. These comments really are double think. The fault lay not with the senior managers but with a wildly ridiculous competitive tender system that allowed a number of big players in the ICT business to make a great deal of money by offering a very poor programme. Early in my evaluative work, I entered a staff room where all the staff (110 teachers) had piled up their huge training manuals in a corner as a visible protest against the way they had been treated. Teachers in that school were extremely angry with their experience, and it has disastrously affected morale and caused some severe internal tensions with and within the management team.

The report summary concludes:

In response to these concerns, which were also being articulated in the press, NOF and the TTA decided to strengthen the quality assurance process. Rather than keeping rigidly to the original plan, the ATPs were advised to make effective modifications as the programme progressed based on the schools' returns. For example, ATPs were encouraged to address the lack of basic ICT skills where this was proving to be a barrier to learning about the use of ICT in the classroom. The quantitative findings in this report suggest that this strategy of modification and adaptation to local conditions had been largely successful by the end of 2002. The teachers who completed their training, and the schools that supported them, have made significant efforts to raise their standards in ICT.

Ibid.: 5

There is again some reality in these remarks, but the judgement is far too moderate. What happened was that there was a recognition that, in the majority of schools, NOF was a disaster; this is almost admitted in the comment 'the lack of basic ICT skills ... was proving to be a barrier to learning about the use of ICT in the classroom'. It is almost like suggesting that you might need a bit of basic French to teach French in the classroom.

The remark about 'quantitative findings' elides the whole disaster of the project. Many schools, in frustration, signed off their teachers as having 'completed the training', and this was meant to be based on evidence of their new ICT competence; it tended to be more loosely based on the number of hours that each teacher reported they had spent on their NOF 'learning'. This 'signing off' process allowed for claims to be made about how many schools and teachers had benefited from the project.

My experience of the next three years was very much qualitative, and I visited over twenty-five schools and spent a great deal of time in each English department. The selection of the schools was also on a mainly quantitative basis and hopelessly inaccurate. The schools selected were all meant to be effective users of ICT at subject level, hence my involvement as an English specialist. However, I was almost always able to meet the head teacher to get the leadership and financial perspective, the head of ICT and/or ICT co-ordinator to learn about ICT policies, basic levels of equipment and technical support and learning environments and overall their post-NOF strategy and vision for the future. What was a very valuable feature of this evaluation was that I was actively encouraged to feed back at the end of the day to all the above participants with my comments and to hold a discussion. This allowed the school and English department in particular some real opportunities for professional reflection and developmental review. Nothing I said had any 'authority' in terms of compliance; none of my suggestions or critical comments required action. However, I was able, partly on that basis of having no power, to engage in really frank discussion with other professionals who could take me seriously without having to pretend that they agreed with my views. In education, this has been all too rare an opportunity over the last twenty years in particular.

What I 'found' was that these schools and departments had reached very different levels of ICT competence. Some, who had supposedly completed NOF very well, were actually literally incompetent, although this was not their fault. They had given up on their training, in any meaningful sense, quite early on, having become utterly frustrated and, as a result, were now resentful and very cynical about any claims for ICT and these 'new technologies'. But what was much more remarkable was the number of departments who had soon recognised that NOF was not going to benefit them because it was a poorly conceived model. This is a tremendous tribute to their professional judgement and their real capacity to exercise critical reflection on a faulted policy which they articulated to me with real passion. Their reaction, however dissatisfied with NOF per se, was neither negative nor cynical. They had recognised that their young people's world was changing rapidly, and they wanted to engage with it and with all the excitements of the affordances of the new technologies. So, with an irony of which they were very self-aware, they recognised that the failings of NOF were part of the inflated claims of the new technology evangelists' that simply engaging with the technology (as young people seem to do) was transformative. They recognised that there was hard work involved and that training needed to be provided in a way that teachers could manage and value. As a result, many of the schools had developed their own training programmes post NOF or even during NOF and, in time-honoured fashion, just 'got on with it'. The piles of manuals in the school staff room were an ironic tribute to the fact that the teachers rejected, as good teachers, the failed pedagogies of NOF.

As a result, I encountered English departments full of exciting developments and full of exciting new competences. I inevitably saw quite a few lessons that were more about impressing me than teaching the children, but they were the exception and not the rule. I met English teachers very close to retirement who now, for the first time in their lives, had their own laptop and internet access and who were bubbling with enthusiasm about how this would change their teaching in the future. I met many novices who had found themselves informally promoted to expert status because of their ICT knowledge and understanding.

I also met a whole range of English teachers now engaged with a new level of thinking about pedagogy. In a simple way, this was about what the content of the lesson could become. Was it still a true English lesson if they were teaching the finer points of drafting using a word processing package and therefore teaching about the package itself? Should that kind of teaching belong with the ICT teachers? At a more conceptual level, the discussion was more about how English was changing and what its contribution might be to the new 'literacies' emerging in the twenty-first century?

I put forward three brief lesson summaries that illustrate this point very effectively and which I have found productive as a stimulus for discussion with both novices and experienced teachers about this developing area. (NB These are simply lesson observation notes and therefore not published formally so have no 'reference'.)

Example 1: An example of an ICT and English lesson

The HOD had a top Year 10 group, studying To Kill a Mocking Bird. *The lesson was put on in the library with pupils paired at machines. The task was to produce an imagined radio interview between Atticus and an interviewer.*

The teacher began with a thorough Q&A session about a chapter in the book, pushing pupils to back up their comments with textual knowledge. She then defined the task and talked through how they should ensure that the speech style of the South should be used and the group offered examples. A pupil asked 'Why are we doing this on the word processor miss?', to which the reply was 'It should help you with layout'.

For the rest of the lesson, she monitored and prompted pairs with one exception. After about twenty minutes, she stopped the group and went through the way they should lay out what is essentially a script and rebuked them for having forgotten what a play looks like on the page.

My observation and discussion with pupils revealed that they do not usually do this kind of thing in English. Many of the class spent as much as twenty minutes creating a heading using Word Art and then managing only a few lines of dialogue. Some of the dialogues were beginning to develop well by the end of the lesson showing good use of language with some excellent discussions of choices of vocabulary.

When the teacher concluded the lesson, she praised the class but expressed her surprise that they would now need another lesson to complete the work.

This demonstrates very clearly an ineffective lesson where the experienced teacher lacks expertise both with technology but even more with pedagogical content knowledge. The students become caught up in fiddling with a detail that is of no significance and the lesson has not been conceptualised. It is easy to see that the task in itself could be worth undertaking.

Example 2: An example of an ICT and English lesson

Lesson in the ICT suite (not their normal room) with LCD and laptop available – twenty PCs spaced round the room – lesson is part of a sequence – class have been taught about designing web pages and have completed hand drawn designs and some text in note form – NB work sheet is scanned and attached as additional evidence. Purpose of the lesson is to begin design of a site about a horror home page – see the work sheet.

The class teacher reminds the class about previous work on web page design and hyperlinks – quizzes pupils to see that they are clear, refers to work sheet and to her ability to demo using the LCD if needed. Establishes through Q&A that audience and purpose come first and that the hyperlinks are to aid the reader.

The class start working, mostly indidividual – there are five pairs (NB the pairs tended to develop passive partner syndrome, i.e. the key board operator doing all the work, the partner just adding the occasional idea).

The pupils were well briefed and skillful – they employed Word Art, Publisher and Word, used graphics including some grabbed from the web – they showed good knowledge of graphic design and of how websites 'really look'. They were highly motivated and worked briskly – the teacher went around monitoring and troubleshooting.

She stopped the class once for a couple of minutes just to go over the use of hyperlinks and to remind the class about saving work, suggesting that discs would be helpful so that they could have individual access to their work.

With five minutes to go, she focused the class on finishing off, saving and logging off – saving two minutes for a brief plenary about 'what have we learned' – pupil responses were chiefly at the level of skills but confidently so – the teacher will be assessing all the pages and therefore will have evidence of learning outcomes.

This is a well-run lesson, but English teachers argue about whether it has now become an ICT lesson.

Example 3: An example of an ICT and English lesson

The class had just completed Year 10 exams and the lesson began with some feedback and discussion. The class were then introduced to the idea of a 'fresh look' at the anthology (NEAB GCSE poetry from other cultures section). They are to work in groups of five or six and to visit various identified websites in order to create two A4 pages, one 'the background' to their given poem, the other to offer the poem in a new way. Teacher asks for suggestions and pupils offer ideas about font, bold, italics, colour, size of text, using graphics, etc., as ways of enhancing/showing meaning. The teacher adds some other ideas about cut and paste, changing to prose, picking out sections, etc. Pupils are encouraged to work hard this lesson and next as they will be presenting their ideas at the end of lesson two.

Pupils discuss their approach in groups and then move to the English and library PCs, each with an agreed brief. Pupils begin by typing out their poems, establishing access to the agreed websites, undertaking web searches about authors, key places, etc.

After forty minutes, the class moves back into the normal room and the teacher asks for feedback from each group for a minute. Each group comments on the websites, info gathered so far and what they have left to do.

This lesson is always considered to demonstrate the right balance between effective use of ICT but with a strong English focus.

I partly include these scenarios because they are very valuable reflective tools for English teachers, especially when they come in a manageable size and offer different outcomes to analyse. This approach will be discussed in the chapter on professional development.

Digi-teachers?

NOF is an example of a poorly conceived policy. The National Literacy Strategy (NLS) and the Framework for English were better conceptualised, but they also created immense problems for good primary teachers and English teachers. They will be considered, especially as models of developing teacher expertise, in the final chapter. Their relevance here relates to how very little they had to offer on the topic of new technologies. Indeed, the 'Strategies' singularly failed to engage with the new technologies, and it has been well argued (Goodwyn 2003a) that they were peculiarly regressive in their nineteenth-century obsessions with print. Even if they paid occasional lip service to technology on paper, their impact on practice was decidedly to emphasise 'pen and paper'. One of the ultimate ironies of the strategy was that many teachers tried using one of its pedagogical recommendations, which was to use A4-size wipe boards. The premise, in itself reasonable, was that students could write rapidly on these boards and so the teacher could gain immediate feedback on 'pupil understanding'. It was most peculiar in the early twenty-first century to see whole classes essentially using the same method as slates and chalk! As I observed many lessons when this practice was used I was genuinely impressed by what the children could write, but I was usually seeing the side of the boards that the teacher did not see; what they often wrote was colourful and rich, and quite often rather amusing, but it is not printable here. Overall, I would argue that the NLS and the Framework not only repressed teacher expertise generally (see Chapter 8) but also severely limited the kinds of flexible and experimental approaches to teaching needed to develop the affordances of the new technologies. The research on the use of electronic whiteboards currently shows that many teachers not only overuse them but now teach in a more didactic way than previously (Andrews 2004).

To return briefly to policy, post NOF there has been no real developmental policy in this area. BECTA (British Educational Communications and Technology Agency) has done a great deal to support teachers, but many teachers do not even know of their existence (see below). They have conducted some major projects seeking to establish a clear relationship between the use of ICT and raising standards; the most extensive of these are the 'Impact Reports' (Watson 1993; Harrison et al 2002). Ultimately, there is a basic epistemological but also practical problem in this somewhat vain pursuit. The pen is a technology, and better pens produce clearer writing and may make the act of writing easier to do; this is not likely, in itself, to improve the content of the writing. Good teaching and motivated students together improve writing. Schools are also not trying to produce the kinds of knowledge in their students that would demonstrate the positive impact of the new technologies. This is the practical problem: the children are being tested on traditional knowledge and almost always using the most old-fashioned methods – sitting in a big hall writing with pen and paper. If anything, schools have been made hugely anxious about the 'bad effects' of the new technologies, viewing the internet as a giant source of cheating. Overall then, BECTA has not been able to find this causal relationship and, under current circumstances, never will. Much research (Lankshear and Knobel 2006; Livingstone 2009) is demonstrating that the nature of learning outside school is changing, perhaps fundamentally, and that many students feel they can 'do more' outside school than when in a classroom, and that what they can do is more creative, more engaging and personally more important than most of their activities in school. This point does not elide that, in material terms, many young people do not have access to the new technologies and that school retains a vital role in this and many other respects.

Despite all these difficulties for teachers, many have continued to acquire ICT skills and to improve their teaching. Everyone now takes for granted the simple affordance of being able to generate high-quality materials for the classroom and to be able to update and improve them. The benefits for all pupils is vast and is especially effective for individual children with special needs making 'personalised learning', something very good teachers are extremely good at, an authentic possibility. This aspect of the new technologies really does enhance effective pedagogy.

This recognition that policy was not developing practice, and that simply devoting huge amounts of funding to provide hardware and software was not necessarily improving learning, has led researchers to seek classroom-based evidence of good teaching. The project I was involved in was not focused on English teaching per se but did include a number of English teachers, and has led to an understanding of how some English teachers have refined their pedagogy (Goodwyn et al. 2009; Goodwyn 2009).

The project sought to find teachers who were good teachers first and recognised as such by their schools and their peers, but who were also enthusiastic and effective users of at least some aspects of ICT. Therefore, these were not going to be the ICT teachers or the 'extensive' users; these should be the selective but more intensive users. As this was a peer nomination method of identification, it was not going to be perfect. However, what the project generated was seventy telephone interviews with a real range of teachers explaining their current practice, how they felt about teaching and how they made use of ICT as a part of their pedagogy. A number of teachers volunteered to be case studies, and twelve were selected to be observed and to engage in more in-depth discussions.

The research team considered various titles to distinguish this group and felt that 'digi-teachers' was the most useful, partly because they share with 'digi-kids' a pragmatic and personal approach to technology; it is a simple and distinctive term to cover this emergent group of expert practitioners. These teachers fit well with current views of expert teaching, but they are not usually ICT specialists and a distinguishing feature is their capacity to integrate ICT into everyday teaching.

They recognise that ICT both engages and motivates students and therefore has benefits for classroom management and learning. For them, technology is just one more element in their expert domain of teaching, yet is a medium that allows for innovation. 'Digi-teachers' are not determined by their age, although the newer generations of teachers have more such teachers. Nor are they characterised by the attractions of gadgetry or the 'whizz bang' factor of ICT per se; they are concerned chiefly with the learning of their students and have a strong motivation to connect with their students' lives using the media that students recognise and engage with. In that everyday sense, 'digi-teachers' have normalised the use of digital and other technologies in the classroom and they use every kind of technology.

The vast majority of these expert teachers are self-taught, although they fully recognise the importance of in-service support and training as well as opportunities to experiment through 'trial and error'. Digi-teachers are very much expert teachers, not technicians and accept the need for strong technical support and expertise of that kind as essential in any school. They are adamant that developing ICT expertise requires a high level of reliability and technical support, so as to minimise problems when they occur. Their teaching is almost never about ICT itself and is often done by the students who contribute content ideas much more consistently than in other lessons. They feel that what they principally do is 'adapt' the technology to fit the needs of the lesson and of the students. Some of these ideas are as much about a change of use. For example, one sports teacher has started to use his digital images of his students (originally taken to help them) to show to their parents to 'illustrate' his parental meetings. He found parents much more engaged when they could see their children 'in action'.

All these characteristics are broadly generic and can be found in any subject area and in different ways in both primary and secondary settings. There does seem to be an English model with more precise characteristics, although the sample was very small. Some of its elements are the typical approach of the best English teachers in any lesson, but they are highlighted by the use of the new technologies and this is exemplified through some quotations from the English teachers.

The English 'digi-teachers' were consistently and powerfully student centred, as one teacher expressed it: 'Personal interest as well – I recognise myself in the students of today – sites like YouTube, which are influential in producing innovation and creativity'. Another commented, '…using technologies for example that students are using and understand, keeping up to date with the way that young people are interacting in the world'. This stance included the notion of the individual and the personal. One teacher said 'you should really know the individuals you teach – inside and outside the school – have personal conversations – ICT is part of their personal world'. The individual was also placed within a strong social environment that was highly inclusive, 'they can come and write on the whiteboard, it's a sense of real belonging, they are really involved in the lesson, it's now a two way thing and we learn together…it's important for them to see we learn together'. Ultimately, this might be summed as an 'affective pedagogy', an approach that is full of emotion and engagement. The English teachers were themselves so engaged with the benefits of the ICT they used that they described the learning experiences using terms such as enjoyable, exciting, motivating, delightful, enthralling, never boring, vivid and enthusing.

Future policy and practice

It is clear that the workforce contains a number of very good teachers who are effective and enthusiastic users of ICT (digi-teachers). The proportion of those teachers within the profession in England is not known; more such teachers should be identified and their innovative practice should be disseminated. Identifying and supporting those teachers would lead to many benefits to students and other teachers. These 'digi-teachers' make more difference than the number of computers in a school; therefore, measuring the number of such teachers per school would be valuable.

Most of these teachers are 'self-taught'; they provide excellent role models for their colleagues and should have more recognition. They should be given release time to further improve their practice and to help others. Many teachers would value teaching assistants who are very competent with ICT; teaching assistants need more ICT training. Most teachers do not know the ICT capabilities of their teaching assistants; there is a need to audit the ICT competence of teaching assistants.

The key point and most relevant to this book is that policy should shift towards developing and supporting teacher expertise rather than an obsession with technology itself. The developing pedagogies using ICT need research focusing on defining expert use, rather than extensive use. Such research should seek to produce more qualitative insights, e.g. case studies of digi-teachers, and at least some research should be more longitudinal in perspective. If the new technologies are a paradigm shift, then teaching will be a part of this shift, and research needs to investigate how certain teachers are able to consistently adapt their practice over time.

Digi-teachers seems a useful term and a broad category at present, especially as it is characterised by expertise that incorporates and adapts technology. It is very striking that these teachers have evolved their practice autonomously. Most importantly, they have not developed innovations because of any policy agenda or any training programme; essentially they are motivated by the life worlds of their students. This kind of engagement is both an indicator of expert teaching and a validation of teacher autonomy. At a practical level, schools would do better to invest as much in digi-teachers as in machines because innovative practice is created in individual classrooms.

Earlier in the book, much consideration was given to the formal status of expert teachers and what they might be called. This research showed that formal 'expert teacher' categories should not exclude other forms of developing expertise, or that such formal mechanisms are helpful if they are exclusive or reductive, by suggesting that any research on expertise should start with those formally identified as, for example, advanced skills teachers.

New technology, new media?

In the discussion in Chapter 3 about English as a subject, it was noted that the first National Curriculum for English included a chapter on media education and information technology. These two fields were somewhat lumped together as important future areas, but were not consciously conceptualised as part of a paradigm shift; their inclusion in a single chapter is, in its own way, part of that shift, an example of it as it was happening. In terms of the subject, the inclusion of media education was far more radical and challenging. Equally, the inclusion of teaching about the moving image in the revisions in the year 2000 was very demanding pedagogically for a workforce not actually trained in the study of the moving image (Goodwyn 2004c). Media studies has become firmly established as a major feature in many schools at Key Stages 4 and 5 since the 1980s, and the great majority of its teachers are English teachers. Here there is a very strong link to the research on digi-teachers who are largely, at least in their own view, 'self-taught'. English teachers who have 'become' media studies teachers have certainly accessed some training but, at the deeper level, they are both self-taught and have taken this direction because of their wish to engage with the life worlds of their students. I base these generalisations on experience of schools and English teaching, not on any major research study as I am not aware of one.

Clearly, teaching about the media is part of English teaching in England, and I have tried to contribute to that development since the requirement to teach media education came in, in 1988 (see Goodwyn 1992b, 2004a). An ongoing professional issue has pertained in two ways: first, who is qualified to teach about the media whether within English or media studies and, second, what kind of career exists for those who elect to develop expertise in this field of teaching?

If 1988 was the formal moment of recognition for media in English, then this comes after a long period of internal conflict about media in English, which has powerful resonances for developing expertise in the twenty-first century. Before any consideration of the expertise involved in teaching about the media, the question arises about what might be the point of such teaching and why it should be part of English. I have considered these questions in considerable detail elsewhere (Goodwyn 1992b, 2004a).

A brief consideration of the background to this issue is vital in understanding English as a subject and also in considering what expert English teaching is like in practice. It can be argued that the 'new technologies' have always been with us. The mass production of the book since Caxton has made English teaching possible in the way we conceptualise it today. However, the teaching of reading was originally concerned with ensuring that people could read the Bible and other sacred texts; the idea of literacy essentially stems from this intention. Equally, the mass production of newspapers since the eighteenth century has further developed the impetus for a literate population, but also raised the issue of understanding the nature of a media text; newspapers set out to persuade as well as inform. These two issues, the idea of sacred or canonical texts and the power of the mass media to influence citizens, have been a dominant concern in English teaching for a hundred years and they are ever more salient in the twenty-first century.

One text stands out as epitomising these two issues and in highlighting conceptualisations of teacher expertise. Leavis and Thompson's 1933 book *Culture and Environment* was written expressly to improve teacher expertise in English teaching. Leavis had recognised that the new technologies (not his term) were the beginning of a paradigm shift for citizens. His reaction was one of fear and disgust at the prospect of a mass media society, a society that would lose all its serious culture, washed away by a tide of popular films and trashy magazines filled with seductive advertisements, created to exploit and traduce the people. His ideas are still shared by many intellectuals and citizens alike; now their fear is of the internet rather than newspapers, although they still attract plenty of criticism of that kind.

In summary, Leavis proposed a very specific pedagogical set of practices formulated around a stance towards media texts of 'discriminate and resist'. For supporters of the critical literacy movement (see Lankshear and Knobel 2006), this sounds like an early version of empowering students. However, Leavis' stance was thoroughly elitist. All media texts, he proposed, were essentially trivial and to be rejected, and the more popular the more they must be discriminated against. He wanted English teachers to train the taste of their students to become elite readers for whom the English literature of the Great Tradition (as he decided to call it) would be the stuff of life. Therefore, that is what good English teaching meant for Leavis, to be evangelists for great literature and to instil critical resistance to all things merely popular.

Leavis was a huge influence and the key figure in the Cambridge school (see Chapter 3) and still is today. Through his absolute rejection of popular culture, he ironically made it worthy of study; indeed, he insisted, in that sense, that teachers took it seriously. By claiming that literature was the most important part of culture and that English was the most valuable subject to study, Leavis inspired generations of teachers. Looked at historically, he invented a form of media studies predicated on a kind of critical resistance to texts that remains a paradigm within contemporary media studies today, and within English.

There has not been much systematic research around the practice of media teaching in schools. Hart and Hicks (2002) undertook some small-scale work in England and also produced a valuable collection in which other researchers had applied Hart's approach in their own countries (see Hart 1998). I have also undertaken some small-scale work (Goodwyn and Findlay 2001) including case studies of English departments who were developing media studies.

In broad terms, English teachers consistently pay attention to newspapers and magazines as relatively straightforward, print-based texts; students are encouraged both to 'study' and analyse these texts and also to produce 'creative' work of their own. Obviously, technology allows for a much higher standard of production of such student-generated texts. The other consistent topic is advertising, many examples of which are contained within magazines and newspapers, but practice tends to include both moving image and other sources such as websites and products. There is evidence of other media-related activities such as leaflet analysis and production, web page design and so on. There is also a good deal of attention to the moving image, especially film, but it is essentially in support of textual study, typically of a novel or Shakespeare play; television adaptations are another much used resource. However, as I have argued elsewhere (Goodwyn 1998a, 1998b), the literary source is the dominant text, and opportunities for giving the film equal attention, for studying film per se or the phenomenon of adaptation are rarely taken up. Of course, some enthusiastic and knowledgeable teachers do go well beyond this rather limited practice. They are also the teachers who give students opportunities for much more challenging 'practical work'.

However, practical work in media education or media studies remains problematic in three main ways. First, there is an underlying view, strongly articulated by Masterman in the 1980s (Masterman 1980), that students only produce imitative and derivative work, and because of this, devoting precious curriculum time to such low-value products is undesirable. This view has been much countered in the 1990s and beyond (see Buckingham 2003). There is also an increasing body of evidence that the affordances of the new technologies are giving young people remarkable opportunities to be both creative and original, very often outside school, but also, with the right teacher, in curriculum time.

Second, practical work does not fit well in the National Curriculum for English, nor was it encouraged in any meaningful way during the periods dominated by the 'Strategies'. It is time consuming, it is more difficult to grade (I would argue not necessarily more difficult to assess; see Goodwyn 2004a) and it is, by its nature, very often group rather than individual work. In other words, all the things that make it so exciting and challenging for young people are not enabled by a rigid curriculum that is overly determined by individual outcomes. The latter, it is fairer to say, comes more from a high stakes testing regime than the actual curriculum content.

Third, practical work can involve a degree of technical expertise with equipment and/or software/hardware; an obvious example would be editing the moving image or creating web pages. These activities both require good, well-maintained equipment and knowledge of what they can do and how they can do it. This perceived level of technical expertise is offputting to many teachers. Inevitably, it is one distinction between teachers who have become media studies teachers and the traditional English teachers, the former become technically competent at least.

This last point highlights expertise in a rather different way and links back to the earlier discussion of digi-teachers. Does a teacher need technical expertise or conceptual expertise to engage young people in learning through the use of the new technologies? For many teachers, the answer is that they can conceptualise how to structure good learning experiences that are heavily reliant on the quick learning capacity and existing technical expertise of the students themselves. This pedagogy is one of enablement, trusting in students to take much responsibility for their own learning, respecting their capabilities. Put simply, the teacher remains the pedagogical expert; the students' own expertise in using the new technologies is in the foreground much more.

I would argue strongly from experience that this is a strong feature of very good English teachers and comes very much from the wellsprings of personal growth thinking and cultural analysis concerns. They enable their students to explore meaning in personally significant ways while encouraging them to adopt a critical and investigative approach to media texts and the contexts of their production in the real world.

Conclusions

The much heralded digital age is changing everything, include teaching. However, schools themselves change slowly and so does practice. The subject of English is being changed by this emergent digitally oriented environment that is pervading all aspects of life. What it means to be a very good teacher is thus powerfully and valuably challenged by such forces. Broadly expressed, teachers are developing additional expertise that generally extends and complements their more 'traditional' expertise; they are also critical of platitudes about the transformative potential of ICT, certainly as experienced in the limiting environment of the school, still based on a factory model of education. For a minority of English teachers, new, and distinct, expertise is probably emerging in a field such as media studies. However, we have no real empirical evidence based on actual observation that teaching approaches are radically different. New knowledge gained through acquiring technical expertise is not necessarily transformative of practice. A key aspect of media education or media study is 'practical'; we have little research into the way English teachers undertake this work and what its benefits are to students; it might well be very revealing as an aspect of expert teaching. I have argued elsewhere for the inclusion of media education within English, especially from ages 5 to 14, and twenty years after it was first included in the National Curriculum for English, that view has not changed (for a detailed argument, see Goodwyn 1992a, 2004a). On this basis, expert English teachers are very good at selecting the right media-related topics and texts and in applying a pedagogy that maximises the learning potential of their students. Equally, they see the new technologies (more generally) as part of the life worlds of their students, and adapt ICT fit to learning purpose in their classrooms.

Chapter 7

Working with others

Polly, Interview 5: *I enjoy being on my own in the classroom and it is nice to 'shut the door' as it were and be free just to get on with the job of teaching as good a lesson as you can on the day, and most English lessons I think are very enjoyable ... but you need some critical edge too, feedback from colleagues, collaborating over planning and just working with other teachers, whether student teachers or very experienced people, it keeps you on your toes.*

This chapter and Chapter 8 will explore the wider world of the expert teacher, the world beyond the individual's classroom. There are some creative tensions between being an expert teacher and what might be called an expert colleague; these are discussed below. There is also an issue of definition at times in determining what is the difference between working with others to develop and support them and what is developmental for the teacher 'doing the developing'. Working with others and enabling them is unquestionably developmental for the enabler. For the purposes of these two chapters, we will distinguish between how expert teachers can work with others (and be developed by such work) and how important it is that expert teachers seek out and benefit from professional development, usually offered by others. However, even then, some activities such as action research (see Chapter 8) seem very much an individual project of development. The best teachers are aware, however, that they can be drawn into supporting others to such an extent that their own development may be slowed down or even arrested; they know that a balance is important to achieve and is not, in itself, somehow a selfish act.

A paradox remains in education that the experience of teaching (see Chapter 1) often feels like an isolated experience despite a crowded classroom full of lively students. Teachers often 'give up' their break and lunch times to offer students additional activities or individual support. They also devote great amounts of time to either planning and reviewing curriculum materials or assessing students' work; in English, the latter activity is hugely time consuming, and both forms of work are typically done individually. 'Marking' is often undertaken in another crowded space, the staff room or 'work room', and there may well be occasional exchanges between teachers. There is no need to labour the point: teaching can be a very individual experience and it can be isolating partly because teachers give up much of their social time to students. One solution is professional development, the subject of the last chapter.

Another solution is for the teacher to recognise the 'danger' of isolation and to consciously overcome it. Before exploring some of the purpose and benefits of such an approach, it is essential to review one key issue about expert teaching. To start with a simple idea, the expert teaching that is the subject of this book is, unquestionably, expertise in teaching young people. To some extent, the book is predicated on a conceptualisation of young people as at certain developmental stages during their time in school. This positioning of young people is certainly open to some question in itself, and there is much debate about whether these 'phases of development' are more societal constructs than true biological or psychological stages. Expert teachers recognise and interact with individual students and so are much less rule bound by these factors. However, they cannot but be affected by the highly structured nature of schooling, which certainly treats young people as a kind of 'mass' and still operates the factory model.

Equally, teachers themselves are a 'mass', partly produced by schooling. Inevitably, many of them are successful products of the education system and, however idealistic about empowering young people, are caught up in the transmission of received notions of power and authority. Part of this process is socialisation into teaching, becoming part of the community of practice with its rituals and 'ways of doing things' (see Chapter 3). Considered descriptively, this is simply the process of becoming 'professional', i.e. developing an identity that conforms to the norms, conventions and expectations of both fellow professionals and 'clients'. As a positive process, this is highly developmental. Individuals engage in an intense period of learning while they come to terms with the formal elements of the process such as meeting the literal 'Standards' required in teaching and also acquiring much of the 'craft' knowledge that may be unwritten, especially in the situated context of a very particular school. Discussing teachers literally 'en masse' is not to dismiss their humanity or individuality; it is in fact to address the point that maintaining such individuality is a real challenge. Indeed, in the isolation of the classroom is where much of that identity is formed, so there is relative space for individuality. There is a certain folk lore understanding in teaching that 'once the classroom door is closed', the teacher can really be that individual, and there is much to be said for a good degree of autonomy for the genuine, self-monitoring professional.

Another point here, building on Chapter 2, is that experts are not all alike and certainly disagree. Reviewing how teachers develop, there is plenty of evidence that, using Dreyfus, novice teachers and competent teachers are in very generic stages. They are very similar to their peers. The acquisition of real expertise is relatively uncommon, and we simply do not know how many teachers deserve to be called expert teachers. We do know (Day et al. 2007) that teachers do not simply make linear progress towards excellence and may well have periods of regression. It seems probable that expert teachers become more 'individual' as they become more expert. By individual is meant more distinctive, more particular in behaviours and more fluent in performance so allowing more mental space for subtle action.

In Michael Eraut's discussion of professional performance, he considers a model developed for architects (Eraut 1994: 219): the stages are awareness, understanding about, ability to do, competence and excellence, not that different from Dreyfus and others. However, there is one more stage, 'finesse'. This stage is reached once an architect has achieved all-round capability, then become a specialist in some way and then become outstanding in that specialism; hence, what they add is that subtle but distinctive quality that is 'finesse'. Whether this is the best way to describe expert teaching has not been tested; in fact, there is very little empirical evidence of the distinctiveness of very expert teaching.

And we may enter some challenging epistemological territory if we pursue the logic of 'finesse'. To what extent is very expert teaching 'original', in the sense of going beyond what has been done before? In the way that Picasso is described, for example. Can there be even, say, genius in teaching? Currently, we do not know and, also, how would we 'know'? That which is original is often radical and threatening to the accepted norms. Would an Ofsted inspector recognise an extraordinary teacher; indeed, who is qualified to do so? This last discussion is highly and intentionally speculative. Some teachers are more often described as 'eccentric', 'charismatic', 'a real character' and so on, and these terms are vague and not necessarily even indicators of teacher quality. In the folk lore of teaching, individuality may well be recognised far more in this populist way than in any deep or epistemological manner. There has been a body of research concerned with teacher 'style' that has gone some way to characterising teachers more formally and more precisely, but its main concern was to categorise all teachers and not to distinguish expertise. The same is true of head teachers and styles of leadership, both middle and senior management. What we have less evidence of is the relationship between expert teaching and collegial working and benefit.

There is certainly no proven link between being a very good teacher of young people and a very good colleague. The much mentioned isolation of teaching is one factor here; most teachers have little time to enact being a good colleague. Some teachers conceptualise teaching as the only activity of value; other activities such as meetings are seen as wasting time and energy. Other, highly competent teachers are certainly very poor at supporting other teachers, especially novices. At one level, this may be ascribed to their unconscious competence (see Chapter 2); they have not only forgotten what it was like to be a novice, they are now overly critical of quite normative novice behaviours. Their own competence therefore makes them very incompetent mentors (see Goodwyn 1997).

At a simple level then, it can be argued that being a very good and, in a sense, self-sufficient teacher is an end in itself. However, much of this book is concerned not only with the expert teaching of English, but also with the status of such teaching and the importance of its influence. One obvious difference between an architect's ability to demonstrate 'finesse' and an English teacher's is that the architect produces plans and even a finished building, visible in the real world; lessons are fleeting things and not many teaching plans end up on the wall of the Royal Academy. This latter is not a facetious point; teaching can be individual to the point of secrecy, so much of what is important can remain hidden. In order for expert teaching to have more influence and more accessibility, it has to come out more into the educational 'open'. Both the advanced skills teacher (AST) and the excellent teacher have elements of this, as will be discussed below.

However, a more important starting point comes from a well-developed tradition in teaching in which the best teacher is characterised not as an isolated artist but as a member of a community of practice with shared values and goals; such a community is a network of collegiate understanding. One issue is both the importance and also the paradox of the reflective practitioner model. Schon's model, discussed in detail in Chapter 2, remains, rightly, hugely influential. Certain aspects of his theories have been more prominently discussed than others. The key emphasis in reflective practice is considered to be the individual teacher in 'dialogue with the situation'. This individual both reflects while in the action and retrospectively on the action. Initial teacher training (ITT) also sends out this message through its insistence on trainees generating mounds of evidence of their planning teaching and evaluation. All the above are important aspects of teacher development. However, because Schon tended to discuss individual practitioners through his case study approach, there is an impression that 'the situation' was an inanimate one, i.e. the architect wrestling with a design problem. In fact, Schon's situation was the work environment with all of its social features and dynamics. In a paper that he gave in 1987, he offers a telling commentary on this point. He states first, 'The experience in reflective teaching is that you must plunge into the doing, and try to educate yourself before you know what it is you're trying to learn', reminding us that this is really how professionals learn 'in action'. He continues with what at first seems to position such learners as very much isolated, even alone:

> But that plunge is full of loss because, if you've taken that plunge yourself, you know the experience. You feel *vulnerable*; you feel you *don't know what you're doing*; you feel *out of control*; you feel *incompetent*; you feel that you've *lost confidence*. And that is the environment in which you swim around, trying to design or trying to teach or trying to do whatever the hell it is you're trying to learn to do until you get to the

place where you can understand what people are saying to you (emphasis in the original).

And this is the key point, he is not just talking about the physical situation but also the social situation, as he explains further:

And you become angry and you become defensive. Or defensiveness, at any rate, becomes a very present danger... 'a clear and present danger'. And what's extraordinary is that, for the same students in this design studio, for example, after six months or a year, they were understanding perfectly well what was being said.

In other words, part of the challenge for the novice is to understand 'what was being said'. In ITT, this issue has been successfully addressed by ensuring that trainees have not just a mentor but a well-trained and empathetic mentor who has learned to be trainee centred as well as student centred. These factors are a vital element in prompting and sustaining reflection in the novice teacher. They are thus part of the trainee's situation; in England, newly qualified teachers (NQTs) should have a similar mentor. But for the competent teacher, say five years into teaching, what is the 'dialogue' with the situation? As she becomes more burdened with responsibilities, especially of a management kind, what is aiding her reflection on teaching? In England, there are some formal episodes that may help such as performance management and preparing for the threshold assessment, but these are infrequent occasions. In the right kind of school, there may be excellent opportunities for professional development (see Chapter 8).

Overall, it still 'comes down' to the individual teacher, and it is best to accept that and start from that premise. A useful concept that has emerged over the last thirty years is that of the extended professional, i.e. that teacher who is self-consciously extending what they do and becoming more important to their institutions and their colleagues. It might be argued that some of this thinking is implicit in the creation of ASTs and excellent teachers.

McKernan (1996: Ch. 2), drawing on Stenhouse's pioneering ideas (Stenhouse 1975), offers a useful summary of this idea beginning with the competent but 'restricted' professional.

The restricted professional has the following characteristics:

1. A high level of classroom competence.
2. Child-centredness (sometimes subject-centredness).
3. A high level of skill in handling children and in understanding them.
4. Derives a lot of satisfaction from personal relationships with pupils.
5. Evaluates performance in terms of own perceptions of changes in pupil behaviour and achievement.
6. Attends short courses of a practical nature.

On the other hand, the extended professional has all the qualities of the restricted professional, plus:

1. Views work in the wider context of school, community and society.
2. Participates in a wide range of professional activities (subject panels, teachers' centres, conferences).
3. Has a concern to link theory and practice.
4. Has a commitment to some form of curriculum theory and mode of evaluation.

Ibid.

Therefore, the extended professional has an enquiring attitude to the profession and to personal performance and a broad understanding of curriculum. Stenhouse argued, from the 1970s onwards, that the outstanding characteristic of the professional teacher (or administrator) is the capacity for autonomous professional self-development through systematic self-study, through the study of the work of other teachers and through the testing of ideas by classroom research procedure. This latter point concerning research, principally of the 'action research' kind, will be considered in Chapter 8 as part of professional development.

The essence of extended professionals is that they are working at greater depth through more reflection and in a broader context through working with others and through engaging with the much 'bigger picture' that exists, not just beyond their classroom, but beyond their school. This vision is very much that of the chartered teacher model developing in Scotland (see Chapter 2). It is very hard to prove that this broader vision has a direct improving effect on the individual's teaching, but teachers themselves insist that it does. Sometimes, this is more at the level of understanding their practice rather than changing it; teachers move from 'feeling' that this particular aspect of practice is effective to having much greater clarity about why it does and that they can now articulate their reasoning.

Advanced skills teachers and excellent teachers as extended professionals

It is important at this point to review whether the characterisation of the above roles is as an extended professional, and if so, to what extent? The well-established AST role has been strongly marked since its inception by 'outreach', i.e. spending a day a week in a different setting, typically another school, and working with others in a variety of formats. In this way, and without question, the AST role was designed for extended professionals. It must be said, however, that the selection of ASTs is still not based on much evidence that would allow for such a judgement. Assessors still visit a school to observe the candidate teaching and to examine their portfolio of evidence, which is essentially of a performance management kind. The assessor does interview some parents, possibly students and a senior colleague, usually the head teacher, and through these discussions may be able to learn about the wider professional skills of the applicant. There is something of a Catch 22 scenario in all this, in that an AST, once appointed, has plenty of opportunity to demonstrate such capabilities but much less so in the usual school setting. Performance management in schools has been chiefly driven by classroom performance, and this model may not do justice to really extended professionals.

The standards for ASTs and excellent teachers do promote the extended model. Taking one cluster of standards for the AST as a starting point (Guidance for ASTs 2009; see DCSF website at www.dcsf.gov.uk for all references below):

Team working and collaboration

P9 Promote collaboration and work effectively as a team member.

E13 Work closely with leadership teams, taking a leading role in developing, implementing and evaluating policies and practice that contribute to school improvement.

A2 Be part of or work closely with leadership teams, taking a leadership role in developing, implementing and evaluating policies and practice in their own and other workplaces that contribute to school improvement.

P10 Contribute to the professional development of colleagues through coaching and mentoring, demonstrating effective practice, and providing advice and feedback.

E14 Contribute to the professional development of colleagues using a broad range of techniques and skills appropriate to their needs so that they demonstrate enhanced and effective practice.

E15 Make well-founded appraisals of situations upon which they are asked to advise, applying high-level skills in classroom observation to evaluate and advise colleagues on their work and devising and implementing effective strategies to meet the learning needs of children and young people leading to improvements in pupil outcomes.

A3 Possess the analytical, interpersonal and organisational skills necessary to work effectively with staff and leadership teams beyond their own school.

This clearly characterises a professional who can contribute very significantly beyond their classroom. Some of the more elaborated examples reinforce this more clearly, making the important point, for example, that outreach work is not just teaching somewhere else:

The commitment to outreach is the distinctive feature of the Advanced Skills Teacher grade. Outreach gives ASTs the opportunity to have an impact in the wider educational community. Outreach work does not include the use of ASTs as teachers in the outreach school apart from specific instances such as giving a demonstration lesson which fall within professional duties.

The reference to 'demonstration' lessons is important, especially in relation to the development of teacher expertise in colleagues and will be developed below. Equally, the notion of working on 'model lessons' is explicated:

Working with other teachers on classroom organisation and teaching methods/providing model lessons

- leading continuing professional development activities;
- holding workshops on classroom management, differentiation, pace and challenge;
- matching teaching approaches to pupil learning styles;
- making a video of model lessons;
- acting as a consultant to teams developing strategies for pupils experiencing difficulties;
- supporting the operation of the literacy and numeracy hours.

One definite change in the AST role since its inception has been an increased emphasis on not only disseminating best practice but being knowledgeable about research and evidence-based change; this comes out even more strongly in the excellent teacher role (see below):

Disseminating best practice based on educational research

- identifying educational research to enhance existing practices;
- acting as a link with the local authority in implementing strategies for dealing with challenging behaviour and promoting inclusion;
- co-ordinating the assessment and analysis of results and developing action planning;
- co-ordinating the assessment and analysis for targeting underachievement and reducing disaffection.

Some aspects of the extended role fit more closely with established practices, but they nevertheless illuminate just how extended such professionals may become:

Producing high-quality teaching materials

- updating existing schemes of work and supporting their introduction;

- leading the introduction of new technologies, such as video conferencing, whiteboard technology, the use of the National Grid for Learning and the Internet;
- developing resource packs to support existing teaching.

Advising on professional development

- designing and delivering professional development activities;
- participating in the planning and delivery of focused in-service training days;
- identifying CPD activities needed to support local processes for improving teaching and learning.

Participating in the performance management of other teachers

- contributing to the development and introduction of the school's performance management policy;
- developing a code of good practice in the observation of teaching;
- undertaking observations and feedback in schools (not the AST's school).

This is an impressive and demanding list and again begs the question of where the training came from to enable an AST to be not only 'extended' but also so widely knowledgeable and practised. One absolutely key area (see below) for the expert teacher is whether they can bring their expertise into the open in a way that is meaningful to other teachers. For example, ASTs are expected to help less effective teachers:

Helping teachers experiencing difficulties

- observing and feeding back on the teaching of colleagues experiencing difficulties;
- providing a structured programme of advice and support;
- develop and sustain advanced beginners.

Mentoring newly qualified teachers

- providing a weekly discussion and overseeing personal action planning;
- formulating a handbook to provide support across the school;
- work closely with novices in training.

Initial teacher training

- providing exemplar lessons for trainee teachers;
- contributing to the assessment of students' teaching practice;

- participating in the training of teachers within teacher training institutions;
- acting as mentor to trainee teachers;
- leading the development of a school-centred initial teacher training scheme.

Although these elements might appear to be on some kind of continuum in relation to the gradual development of others, they elide just how very different they are contextually and in terms of the skills involved and the level of experience needed to undertake them successfully.

What, if anything, has the introduction of the excellent teacher role added to the AST? The main focus of the excellent teacher, within their school, is clearly to be the kind of extended professional that is in all respects a role model for colleagues. The following is a selection from the excellent teacher (ET) standards where the emphasis is on working with and/or influencing others:

- Be willing to take a leading role in developing workplace policies and practice and in promoting collective responsibility for their implementation.
- Research and evaluate innovative curricular practices and draw on research outcomes and other sources of external evidence to inform their own practice and that of colleagues.

Again, we see the emphasis on research and the necessity f the ET to have a wide understanding, far beyond the school, of how change is decided and implemented. The emphasis is also on bringing a critical, informed perspective to local practice:

- Have a critical understanding of the most effective teaching, learning and behaviour management strategies, including how to select and use approaches that personalise learning to provide opportunities for all learners to achieve their potential.
- Know how to improve the effectiveness of assessment practice in the workplace, including how to analyse statistical information to evaluate the effectiveness of teaching and learning across the school.
- Have an extensive and deep knowledge and understanding of their subjects/curriculum areas and related pedagogy gained for example through involvement in wider professional networks associated with their subjects/curriculum areas.

    1   Take a lead in planning collaboratively with colleagues in order to promote effective practice.
    2   Identify and explore links within and between subjects/curriculum areas in their planning.

This extended professional is both a subject (in some sense) expert and a teacher development expert in a broad sense. There is also an emphasis on 'wider professional networks', which will be considered in Chapter 8. Although it is not clarified with examples, there is a strong expectation that an ET can 'demonstrate' their expertise', for example:

- Demonstrate excellent and innovative pedagogical practice.
- Demonstrate excellent ability to assess and evaluate.

Finally, there is an emphasis on making strategic contributions to the development of the whole school and all its teachers:

- Work closely with leadership teams, taking a leading role in developing, implementing and evaluating policies and practice that contribute to school improvement.
- Contribute to the professional development of colleagues using a broad range of techniques and skills appropriate to their needs so that they demonstrate enhanced and effective practice.
- Make well-founded appraisals of situations upon which they are asked to advise, applying high-level skills in classroom observation to evaluate and advise colleagues on their work and devising and implementing effective strategies to meet the learning needs of children and young people leading to improvements in pupil outcomes.

The AST and the ET are unquestionably designed as roles that encompass the ideal of the extended professional. We will now examine some of these elements in more depth and detail, and will review the problematic nature of some of the assumptions underlying the rather formulaic descriptions of what ASTs and ETs should be able to 'perform'.

Mentoring and coaching

The expert teacher has great potential to develop others, and the profession has moved a long way in the last twenty years in its recognition of the crucial role of mentoring. It must first be restated that the expert teacher may have difficulty in appreciating the needs of the struggling novice.

In an earlier book of mine (Goodwyn 1992a), I attempt to articulate this issue through describing a recognisable scenario in which a student teacher observes the lesson of a very good teacher. The teacher is very modest, tells the student she does not really do planning any more and that this will be a very ordinary lesson. In fact, it is a very enjoyable poetry lesson in which the students become very animated and enthusiastic about writing and all produce poems. The student teacher finds herself reverting to 'pupil' mode and being inspired by the teaching and wanting to write a poem. As a future teacher, she learns nothing from the lesson, and the teacher herself has actually unintentionally 'hidden' her expertise and made the lesson look 'easy'.

What all teachers need to do when they first take on mentoring or coaching is to recognise that they need themselves to adopt a novice stance as a mentor, using the Dreyfus concept that one is continually a novice in some parts of a knowledge domain. Learning to be a mentor then has some of the features of Schon's plunge into new learning, which has a sense of initial loss. Mentoring is also a multifaceted role with any teacher, but especially so with novices and advanced beginners. Aspects of mentorship include:

- TEACHER who offers IDEAS/CONTENT;
- OBSERVER who provides ongoing FEEDBACK;
- COACH who focuses on SKILLS/METHODS and deliberate practice;
- ADVISER who provides both SYMPATHY and SUPPORT;
- COUNSELLOR who may be dealing with quite personal and psychological issues;
- linked to this is EMPATHY and SELF-KNOWLEDGE, where the teacher recounts formative experiences of their own;
- CRITIC who uses EVIDENCE to CHALLENGE and set targets and achievable goals;
- ASSESSOR, both DIAGNOSTIC and SUMMATIVE with a GATEKEEPER role at times.

Goodwyn (1992: Ch. 2)

This latter aspect, especially with trainee student teachers, requires close knowledge of professional standards and of working with partners, usually from a higher education institute (HEI). These standards, however definite looking on paper, have to be interpreted in the field and made meaningful to trainees, and also discussed with partners from HEIs. Good mentors are not necessarily very experienced teachers because recent, active memories of both the experience of learning to teach and of standards can be an advantage.

What is a limit, however, is likely to be that their own practice is less secure and their classroom performance less exemplary; again, this can be used as a learning tool for trainee and mentor. But the expert teacher really should be able to go beyond this level and, to paraphrase Bruner's excellent observation on skilful demonstration:

Experts are able to demonstrate things with great skill, but they often disguise difficulty unintentionally by making things look easy. A good demonstration is not one that makes the activity look easy but one that reveals its difficulty in a meaningful way.

Bruner (1986)

So, the expert teacher does not just act as a role model by demonstrating their excellent teaching, they reveal their expertise; this is what was missing from the example above. They are also able to recognise that the novice, in particular, cannot find mental space for too much new knowledge. The classroom is a confusing place for them, full of signs that they cannot read or may not even notice. The expert teacher will therefore want to focus their attention on the specific during an episode of observation, and this is where the English inflections will come out, for example in the particular way a class is helped to work on a poem through a series of readings of the poem, i.e. this is not JUST reading aloud, or roles are assigned in a group for a discussion of a short story, i.e. this is not JUST group work.

This valuable attention to specifics and to manageable elements of teaching does not reduce the mentor role to a 'tips for teachers'-style approach. The expert teacher is using expert demonstration of detail but in the context of a much more holistic and developmental relationship; the expert is more able to envisage what the novice needs to know at what stage and at what pace to include challenge as well as support. It is very important to distinguish this from 'coaching', however useful coaching may be in learning to teach.

In a relatively short time, the term 'coaching' has become common in schools in England. The emergent definition is of a very 'hands on', skills-based model of teacher development. The coach is expected to be sufficiently knowledgeable to 'diagnose' where their subject needs to improve and then to work closely on one or two discrete areas to make rapid improvements. At one level, this may be rather mechanistic and simplistic because the coaching is not taking place within a more holistic view of the teachers' development. However, if it is additional to what the mentor is providing, then that issue is resolved. It might also be more powerful if the teacher has identified their own issue and has invited the coach to support them. As a model, this is much closer to 'deliberate' practice, something that is regularly discussed in the literature of expertise (see Ericsson et al 2007). An expert teacher might therefore become an expert coach within their subject area or, more likely, more generically. This would be a very good way to become an extended professional, being an expert mentor in English and a coach of something specific such as questioning, speaking and listening activities and so on.

There is a possibility that 'coaching' may become exaggerated in both status and anticipated benefit. For example, in this quotation about the potential Master's degree for all new teachers in England, the Master's in Teaching and Learning (MTL), coaching features as follows:

> The MTL is a new professional qualification for teachers, designed to fulfil the Government's ambition to make teaching a masters-level profession. It aims to further improve teacher quality in order to raise standards in education, narrow gaps in attainment and give children better life chances. It is fully funded by Government. It will provide effective

structured professional development in the first years of a teacher's career, a time when we know many teachers feel under pressure and would value additional support. There will be significant benefits for schools – trained in-school coaches who support participants will be able to make a wider contribution to induction, training and development across the school; the programme should support an increasingly collaborative culture in professional development; and retention should be improved, especially in the early years. Above all it should improve teacher quality and support better teaching and learning across the school.

DCSF website

It is noticeable how the rhetoric moves from 'trained in-school coaches' to 'better teaching and learning across the whole school'. That would be a very desirable outcome, but the rhetoric elides a great deal, not least in defining what this training would be like and also which teachers might be able to take on the role that could lead to such dramatic school-wide improvements.

Observation and demonstration

The role of coach and/or mentor relies fundamentally on the two separate but complementary skilled activities of observation and feedback. Observation is now a well established practice in schools, but its purpose and intended outcomes are often very confused. A simple model would be novice observes expert then tries, with support, to use the expert as a model and to imitate the expertise. The expert then provides feedback on performance and the novice watches the expert again, before retrying. I would argue that this simply never happens in teaching. One very obvious reason is that the purpose of teaching is almost never 'demonstration'. The expert and the novice are more concerned with the outcomes for the children than the outcomes for themselves. This may well be a tribute to the deep professionalism of both teachers, but it underlies how difficult it is for expert knowledge to be disseminated in teaching as a profession; some ways forward are explored below and in Chapter 8. Another factor that the expert must pay great attention to is that, because of their fluent, seamless classroom performance, the novice not only notices little of what is happening but adopts the student mode and enjoys the lesson in a 'child-like' way. The other side of this coin is that the expert sees so many issues with the novice's teaching that their feedback can be hugely overwhelming and bewildering in its detail. This latter point makes skilled, selective feedback vital to the novice's development.

Observation remains a very powerful aspect of teacher development for both observer and observed, and there is still far too little time devoted to training teachers to become skilled and versatile observers. In one respect, observation is now potentially more effective simply because it is much more normative. The students themselves are more familiar with it, whether it be a well-known teacher from their school or a comparative stranger (inspector, visiting AST, HEI tutor, etc.). However, the students themselves are, and always will be, a dynamic in this situation. One way in which observation remains a crude activity in schools is simply that the students are aware that observation is taking place, but they do not know why and sometimes are not even introduced to the observer. It is not without irony that many teachers would feel uncomfortable introducing not only the observer but also that they are present to help them improve their teaching. This paradox, I would suggest, persists because of the folk lore expectation that once a teacher is trained they should be able to 'hold their own', etc. and that explicitly suggesting to students that they want to 'improve' may undermine their fragile authority. Such 'authority' is a sensitive issue, and NQTs in particular feel under intense internal pressure to prove themselves. In the long term, schools may be able to change this culture by aligning their policy on improving learning in their school by encouraging students to see observation of teachers as explicitly linked to improving their learning.

The students are also a powerful dynamic during observation, however used to it generically, because they have existing experiences and sets of relationships which unconsciously play on the situation. For example, if an expert is observing a novice and that expert is known to the students, then that existing relationship will be present in the classroom although the novice 'cannot see it'. The expert must recognise what their influence may be on the learning environment of the classroom. One interesting development has been the use of students as trained observers providing feedback on teaching and learning. This initiative is at a very early stage and its efficacy unproven, but it immediately offers one way to break down the 'fragile authority' issue. If students are themselves empowered to become part of the school's teaching and learning culture, then the learning environment is fundamentally inclusive of all participants.

At this stage, it is important to make a crucial distinction between two necessarily distinct if complementary modes of observation, the developmental and the judgemental. Put simply, far too much observation is either undertaken judgementally or is perceived by the observed to be so. Performance management is certainly a problematic here, as the observed teacher knows they have to provide a 'top performance' and that they will have very few opportunities to impress in this way. Behind this lies a culture of external inspection, which gave every lesson a simplistic overall outcome by either a single number or a grade. However satisfying to statisticians, this mode is both reductive and misleading. On current resourcing, the reality of schools is that snapshot judgements will continue to be made in this mode, but that does not mean they help with the promotion or dissemination of expertise. Most observation by teachers should be developmental and authentic, i.e. not dominated by a teacher self-consciously 'performing. I will argue below that 'demonstration' is a different kind of performance.

There are some simple factors that certainly enhance the power and benefits of observation. It needs to feel:

Invitational – the observer wants the observer to be present and trusts their motives and that the observer also feels a wish to be present and feels welcome;

Timely – the observed feels 'ready' and the literal timing is good and agreed in advance; there is time for feedback and further reflection;

Well planned as a lesson for observation – the observer really knows what will be going on and has agreed what to look for and knows how he/she will be introduced (this has been agreed in advance); this may necessitate having a lesson plan and the scheme of work, perhaps some details, about students whether in the form of data or prose; the observer has a good vantage point and knows whether to walk around and talk to students or not as suits the purpose;

Valuable as a tool for reflection – as well as the spoken feedback, will notes be appropriate, should the lesson be recorded in any other way, is any kind of list/set of standards going to help or hinder real reflection?

This latter point brings in a great new opportunity but a very vexed one at a practical level, that is the recording of lessons, especially on camera. There are currently ethical issues involved in the recording of any event involving minors, and this sensitive environment is most unlikely to change. Many schools have found ways to engage with parents so that policies are in place that are transparent and principled, which allow the taking of images and the use of moving image cameras for restricted and agreed purposes. Based on such ethically sound principles then, it becomes possible for schools and their expert teachers to develop approaches which maximise the benefits of technology. It is worth noting that the US National Board for Professional Teaching Standards (NBPTS) model of the highly accomplished teacher is absolutely dependent on the creation of a video by the teacher which they feel illustrates their best teaching; the video is therefore elaborated by the teacher to explicate exactly what the video has recorded. As a model, this has much to recommend it for all teachers at different stages in their development.

A camera in the classroom can be as disruptive as a human observer, especially if it is being operated by someone – therefore doubling the disruption. With the NBPTS model above, filming goes on over a year, and the US teachers find that their students become oblivious to what is happening. Some teachers ask students to act as the camera person and, at a practical level, this works well; ethically, it is awkward because these students should be learning rather than filming. In England, this might be an interesting aspect of a teaching assistant's work perhaps?

There are some ways around the disruption issue. The simplest is 'familiarity', with students becoming accustomed to the presence of the camera, and cameras themselves can now be so small as to be almost invisible. There is also much to be said for students themselves watching footage of their workings in the classroom. In English, this may be linked directly to the curriculum, for example filming speaking and listening activities, drama presentations and poetry readings, providing students with a chance to reflect on their 'performance' and evaluate what they achieved and how they might improve. More broadly and generically, students can observe themselves as learners, that is how they participated in group work or a classroom discussion. This latter point returns us to the consideration of school culture. If students and teachers alike are observing themselves to improve teaching and learning, then the camera is a valuable and familiar part of everyday life.

An important element in the use of recording is 'stimulated recall'. As was set out in Chapters 1 and 2, teaching has a high cognitive demand during performance; it is literally difficult to remember what happened during a lesson. A novice may only remember a couple of problematic incidents that loom large in their recall. An expert may equally only remember an unusual occurrence because otherwise everything went well as usual. In both cases, there is much more memory available, but it needs retrieving, and this may need to be a very deliberate and conscious action, perhaps best achieved by another viewer asking salient questions that prompt the recall. In other words, just recording a lesson does not reveal its complexity, but stimulated recall can do so. One new approach is to make the classroom rather more like a teaching laboratory. This approach is not absolutely new as an idea; what is new is that it is within the capabilities of individual schools to experiment with it.

A more radical solution, and one with even more ethical complexities, is a hidden camera. Some schools have designed a classroom with such a facility so that teachers can bring their class to this room for an 'ordinary' lesson, recording the whole thing without camera disruption or student self-consciousness. Students' parents may have given permission for such recording, but there are going to be some critics of an approach that may feel rather as though the students are being treated as laboratory rats. This decision rests on school culture, ethical leadership and treating teachers as proper professionals. If there are no issues with the students, that is that they are aware of the purpose of such filming, i.e. to improve teaching and learning, and there is parental permission, then the teacher should have their rights established. Each teacher should be filmed voluntarily and should be able to decide whether all or part of any filmed lesson becomes available to anyone else. Such footage might only be shared with a trusted mentor or be part of peer review so both teachers watch a lesson taught by the other and discuss them together. An expert teacher might record a lesson to replay with a novice, explaining as the lesson unfolds how decisions were being made 'in action' or asking the novice to predict what will happen next, etc. In each case, only two teachers ever see a filmed lesson, but it provides excellent developmental opportunities.

However, authentically filmed lessons have enormous potential for capturing and analysing expertise. Authenticity is very important. In England, many videos of lessons were made to support the pedagogic imperatives of the National Literacy Strategy; primary school shelves and English department stock cupboards are groaning under the weight of manuals, CDs, DVDs and other paraphernalia. There is much of value in these materials, not least many interviews with teachers talking about their work. However, the footage of classrooms, filmed at a very high professional standard with excellent sound, do not come over as authentic; classes of student teachers have burst into spontaneous laughter at the sight of the perfect children and their immaculate teacher. These lessons are better characterised as 'demonstrations' (more of this below). For practical purposes, these professionally produced films tend to irritate both novice and experienced teachers, partly because they are lacking in realism, but at least as much because they were made with an agenda that teachers did not necessarily share, being part of a huge top-down policy imperative (Goodwyn 2004a). School- and teacher-made videos can be technically very competent, especially if the teacher wears a decent radio microphone, and they have not only an authentic feel, but their purpose is local and shared; the teachers 'own' the material and use it as their professional judgement determines. In England, the relatively new phenomenon of *Teachers TV* (see website) has managed to produce some excellent material that sits relatively comfortably between the rock (of inauthenticity) and the hard place (low tech and local). This new resource will be considered in the last chapter, especially because some of its best material is very focused on capturing real expertise and analysing it in action.

Essentially, in the right school setting, locally captured footage has tremendous possibilities as a way of working with others. One immediate use is in providing training opportunities in observation. For example, a group of student teachers can watch and re-watch an expert lesson with the expert present and guiding them to really see what is happening. They can then take a copy away with them to study at leisure. In many lessons, it is only a few minutes that need to be discussed, and much more can be gained from intensive observation than a more 'blanket' approach. An English department's teachers could all film an individual lesson and then select five minutes from it to show at a department meeting, offering a commentary on why it reveals either good teaching, examples of good student learning or an issue they want help with, providing a real focal point for department discussion. These last two examples make the material much more public and undoubtedly require both professional confidence and mutual trust. This might be extended to a whole school staff meeting watching such material, or an expert teacher taking some examples along to their local teachers' centre or university for trainees to watch and discuss. In each instance, there is both the content to discuss and analyse but also the opportunity to improve teachers' capacity to observe teaching, especially the minute details that occur in experts' fluent performance.

The Japanese model of lesson study is worth mentioning here; it will be discussed in more depth in Chapter 8. In this model, teachers all plan a lesson together, teach it and then discuss how it went; this approach might be adopted by English teachers, and no technology would be needed. However, this mutual focus might be more on how we all teach the same challenging poem with each teacher recording the lesson in which they introduce it. This might apply to a Shakespeare play or a novel, or to a language lesson or using a film text. In this approach, English teachers are sharing common content and can focus on that, or on teaching styles and professional differences.

Another valuable and less obtrusive technique (from the students' point of view) is to use a still digital camera and capture snapshots from a lesson. This can be done through the observer's professional judgement, that is they consciously select key moments or aspects of the teacher's performance. Equally, they can focus on key moments in the learning of the class, taking shots of each group at work on a task over a period of time. Another approach is to use the camera in the way one might use an observation schedule, that is systematically and to a time frame, perhaps one image every minute, therefore capturing 'objectively' what was happening. Either approach, judgement led or systematic, provides rich material for discussion and reflection. Because the 'freezing' of a moment may capture what is typical, atypical or unusual, it provides an intense point packed with potential meaning. In a sense, there is no distraction of sound, and the camera lens may have been used to zoom in on facial and/or bodily expression. For the teacher who was observed, the image is a powerful mode of stimulated recall (see above), and this is valuable in itself; for the observer, it equally acts as an aide memoire to prompt questions, especially about detail or aspects of fluent performance.

However, the focus on such detailed images is not any easier than what appears to be the more demanding medium of video, because still images 'feel' more personal. One can freeze frame digital video and treat the image as still and, with decent technology, the image will be sharp and clear; however, this is a choice and the teacher observed could be in control of such decisions. For most people, 'photos' are either personal or very often linked to occasions of significance. Most people (not just teachers) are more struck by how they sound on video than by how they look; teachers particularly can be self-conscious about their voice. This 'shock' can be valuable in that it enables positive self-consciousness about the pitch of voice, pace of expression, conveying of emotion and so on; this is rich material in the hands of a sensitive coach. The still, silent image can 'feel' more personally revealing and invites scrutiny that may feel surprisingly uncomfortable, especially at first. Nevertheless, such images do provide excellent recall opportunities and a stimulus to professional discussion about many aspects of teaching. Images of students at work (with full permission) also provide excellent stimulus, allowing for more minute focus on body language and motivation or disengagement.

Learning environments

Still images of learning environments are also rich resources for reflection. As a visitor to many English departments during the years of the 'Framework for English', I was constantly struck by the visual landscape of English teachers. I could not take photos because of the permission issues, least of all as an occasional visitor. If there was an opportunity, I would sketch out the furniture arrangements of the room as from a bird's eye view, identifying how many vertical surfaces were available for 'display'. Although to state the very obvious, most classrooms have four walls and many windows, not only are teachers very inventive about what they use for display, but very many classrooms are not a simple rectangular shape; equally, they can have many pieces of furniture of all shapes, sizes and functions (some items were clearly dysfunctional). Having identified the display spaces, I would then make a sketch and annotate this with information. As most English teachers occupy one classroom for most of their teaching time, this room contains much individual choice in its representations. Such rooms are also, very often, 'home' for a class, and so some space may be devoted to them and linked to the pastoral system. In my observations, this would always be a relatively small space. I have never had a chance to discuss these visual details with colleagues from school, but I have made use of the idea of capturing the learning environment very often and with interesting results.

It would be easy to trivialise this form of observation by suggesting that the relatively casual and arbitrary decoration of a room is a set of random activities and extremely temporary as it is constantly subject to change and deterioration. Classrooms can be hopelessly scruffy, depressingly worn down places with no appearance of care about them; this, in itself, raises a powerful issue about the factory model of schooling. At even the simplest level, just capturing a good-looking classroom or an excellent display of students' work is linked to teacher expertise. These classrooms demonstrate both an emotional style of care for learning and also a recognition of what enables learners to learn. There is an immediate tension here as there is no suggestion that English teachers are all interior designers or that they can exercise immaculate control over their classroom which may well be used by many others. To the visitor, classrooms are strikingly full of what can only be called detritus and junk: old text books in piles, half empty shelves, pot plants in the last throes of a lingering death. The implication is not that mere neatness and orderliness are essential to good learning; expert teachers can enable such learning in almost any space and against all kind of odds. However, expert teachers do understand that, although the learning environment they create is principally pedagogic, that is it is in the heads of their students, it is much affected by the embodied nature of learning and circumstantial issues such as classroom furniture, layout and visual appearance. Hattie (2003) stresses the notion of the optimal learning environment, and Hay McBer (2000) similarly stressed the concept of a climate of learning.

The latter point raises the first valuable opportunity linked to still images of learning environments: does the visual learning environment match the pedagogic one? If it does, how does it? If it does not, why not and is that beyond the teacher's control or can conscious effort bring them into closer and more satisfying harmony? Again, many teachers love to display students' work but are not especially skilled in such exhibitions, and classrooms are often not designed with this purpose, any more than corridors which are also used for this purpose. One reason for devoting space to this issue is because schools and individual teachers have made huge strides in improving the look and 'feel' of the learning environment and are far more aware of the impact of such improvements on pupil engagement. When the comment is made (see above) that schools still suffer a factory model for learning, it is useful to contrast a picture of a Victorian school room with a contemporary one; one of the most salient differences is the bleakness and starkness of the nineteenth-century room with its large number of students in very neat rows.

Given this improvement in schools, it is revealing therefore to capture and analyse the learning environment. In Ted Wragg's book on classroom observation (Wragg 1994: 38), there is a page with photos of two contrasting classrooms. The images are obviously different at one level but, once teachers start to discuss the detail, they move rapidly into discussing the pedagogic messages implicit in the arrangements of furniture and the atmosphere and affordances of each room. Classrooms are places to work, and there is very often a strong message about what kind of work is done there and what is at hand to help such work. This is especially revealing in English because English is not a visually characterised subject such as science with the laboratory or art with its studios. In English, it is the community of teacher and learners that creates the visual landscape. This latter point is another element that teachers notice once they have images to analyse, that is whether their classroom does represent that community or only their own potentially eclectic selections.

The visual learning environment can be conceptualised as a rich semiotic and symbolic display revealing many meanings. Some are consciously constructed; some seem accidental (a film poster stuck on a cupboard door); many others reveal the dynamics of control bearing down on the space and its occupants. Items invite individual scrutiny, but combined make rich mosaics of meaning. My collection of 'sketches' cannot be dignified into a research project, but it allows me to make some comments. The great majority of English teachers' rooms are very highly decorated with barely a space to be seen. Therefore, from novice to expert, there is a shared activity that might imply a potential for expertise to be partly revealed through display. I do not have enough concrete evidence to support this hypothesis, but it is one that would be worth investigating at some time. In general, visual display in English can be defined as falling into three broad categories (this leaves out form notices, general school information, etc.).

One of the most consistent and most visually appealing categories is displays of student work. These displays take many shapes and forms but can be usefully subdivided into two types, displays about something studied, very often a Shakespeare play, a novel (frequently *Of Mice and Men* or *Holes*), a poet or collection of poetry, a genre such as 'Gothic and horror' and displays of some kind of creative activities including student poetry, stories and newspapers, the latter with much decoration and embellishment. The creative displays really can be like exhibitions and not only demonstrate highly skilled curation but also thoughtful preservation; they are put up to last. In a few classrooms, the display had become neglected and had begun to diminish the look of the learning environment. There is no question that judgement is needed about how long a display should last, and one link to expertise has to do with the relationship between such displays, their purpose and curriculum planning. Student displays mostly signify student and teacher success at the end of a sustained period of work along the lines of 'look what we have achieved'; it is likely that expert teachers are planning to give each class an opportunity to display success, and so co-ordination and forward thinking are needed. In these English classrooms, it was by no means dominated by the junior classes; there was interesting work from Key Stages 4 and 5. Some rooms had more than one space devoted to student work, but none had only student work.

The second category was very English specific in content, but is visible in many subject areas, that is 'subject-oriented guidance'. In English, this is mostly textual although graphics and font design add colour and shape. Almost anywhere in a room, you might see 'spelling rules', 'spelling strategies', 'writing paragraphs', 'twenty key literary terms', 'level descriptors' or 'attainment targets'; many of these are so dense as to be unreadable from even a few feet away. At no point in any lesson did any teacher refer to them; in no lesson at any point (as far as I could tell) did any student make use of them. What was striking was their collective 'presence' and their somewhat oppressive tone. Many of them were related to the objective-led pedagogy of the 'Framework for English' and its 'imperative to secure progression' (Goodwyn 2008). To the observer, they seemed to be there more to suggest that the teacher knew they had to show their knowledge of this imperative rather than that they believed in it or were going to use its visible resources in their actual teaching; in other words, they were highly symbolic and not at all, despite appearances, practical. To this observer, they were also a sign of the world order of the time and of the top-down pressure on English teachers to conform to certain narrow notions of what English should look like.

The third and most distinctive and identity-revealing category was what I have deemed 'personal decoration'. This can also be usefully subdivided. Every room had plenty of posters, usually with a link to the subject English; the majority were film posters (sometimes literary adaptations), some about youth culture, publishers' material promoting a particular book or series and so on. These posters were clearly personal choices of the teacher and added a distinctive look to their room, but they always had some professional relevance. But some rooms had a more intensely personal section usually close to the teacher's desk, which consisted of literary postcards, jokes and cartoons cut from newspapers, images of a film star; these displays seemed designed to project a personal distinctiveness and to make some of the personal identity of the teacher accessible to students. I would speculate that this is the teacher modelling both personal growth (this is how I came to be who I am) and some cultural heritage (here is some of my subject knowledge, possibly expertise).

Overall, the activity of decorating English classrooms is clearly important to the profession. Very clearly, for example, the celebration of student work does send out a strong message about English being student centred. Capturing and analysing the literal learning environment is an important aspect of working together because many teachers rarely spend time in colleagues' classrooms. When a lesson is being observed, it is an excellent opportunity to look at the three-dimensional nature of the space, layout, wall displays, etc., and images allow for focus and analysis in depth.

Display?

This last section has covered a relatively neglected area in relation to developing expertise. In essence, it has been about a concept of 'display', the exhibiting of learning for the benefit of learners. What part can the idea of demonstration play in developing expertise? It is worth noting that, in China, there is a well-established tradition, not much known in the rest of the world, of teaching 'competitions'; most of my knowledge comes from contact with Chinese teachers attending Master's programmes in England. According to them, these 'competitions' are highly prestigious and the winning of a kind of 'best teacher' prize is a great accolade. The competition involves teaching a kind of 'model lesson' in front of both a panel of judges and a considerable audience; there is a real class of students to teach, there on stage.

To many readers, this is likely to come across as a very undesirable demonstration of expertise; indeed, they might question whether any authentic expertise is on 'show'. However, it is a useful example in provoking some critical reflection. At one level, this form of teaching demonstration might be better thought of as a kind of entertainment. It is clearly popular and potentially reaches out to the public. Perhaps the students involved have a thoroughly enjoyable time.

There are of course depictions of English teachers in popular media: a very well-known Robin Williams charismatic depiction in *Dead Poets Society* or Paul Giamatti's rather melancholy failed writer in *Sideways*. In Robert Protherough's *The Making of English Teachers*, he includes a brief but intriguing section on fictional representations in imaginative writing (Protherough and Atkinson 1991: 5).

The fundamental point here is to challenge our assumptions about the way expertise in teaching can be made accessible to others. Much of the discussion above has centred on capturing it on video or still image; this is still an emergent use of technology. Two examples from other professions can also stimulate thinking.

Eraut points out that 'Most performing occupations offer considerable opportunity to observe master-performers at work both before and after initial training' (Eraut 1994: 38). He provides the example of surgeons:

> Practitioners have stated that learning to handle difficult cases is best accomplished in two stages: (1) watching several experts with differing approaches and having them explain their strategies and ongoing thoughts; and (2) practising while sharing one's thoughts with and receiving comments from an appropriately experienced mentor. Gaining access to experts' accompanying thought processes provides an essential new dimension to what would otherwise be pure observation.
>
> Ibid.: 38

The first comment fits very well with teachers, i.e. watching several different teachers approach the same 'difficult case'; this might be exactly what our example above, of English teachers all recording the way they introduce the same challenging poem, could offer. The second point exemplifies how a recorded expert lesson becomes much more powerful if the expert then adds a commentary. Such a commentary might be quite selective, especially if the intended viewers are novices; it might be much more detailed for an audience of peers.

Eraut also discusses how a 'promising musician' not only 'strives to see and hear famous players' but 'deliberately arranges to study with more than one teacher for substantial periods' (ibid.: 38). In music, there is also the concept of the master class, where the accomplished performer demonstrates how to play a piece and the other musicians try it themselves, not necessarily to copy the performance but to develop their own interpretation. For many English teachers, frequently overwhelmed with the day-to-day demands of the classroom, these ideas may seem practically impossible. However, if we pause for a moment and consider what a teacher 'costs' in crude terms, i.e. what it pays to train them, including the cost of their degree and then the possibility that they spend forty-three years in the profession on an annual salary, it is very probable that they 'cost' the state somewhere between £2 and 3 million depending what 'level' they reach in the profession. This crude financial analysis is simply meant to illustrate what an expensive asset a good teacher necessarily is to the system. Why should some professions devote so much more resources to their experts than teaching?

What can be taken from the musical master class analogy is not a simple replication but the recognition that expert teachers have that special quality desired by other teachers and that we should strive to make it available. Consider an English teacher leading the reading of a poem (including, possibly, their own performance of the text) and then orchestrating the class to explore and enjoy it, to engage with their emotions and reactions and develop their own meanings and critical judgements. This lesson would literally demonstrate some of the best qualities of the English teacher and the affordances of the subject. To create a demonstration lesson will require self-awareness in the teacher that that is an authentic purpose for the lesson. It might be possible for such a teacher to undertake such lessons to more than one observer, perhaps a group of novices. I was once asked by the deputy head if some visiting Norwegian teachers could observe one of my classes (he was rather vague about any details). Later that morning, fourteen Norwegian visitors quietly filed into my room and stood at the back for about twenty minutes and then quietly left. It so happened that my small bottom set of Year 10 students were sitting in an intimate circle discussing whether they knew any local legends or stories about ghosts and whether any might be true. They were so utterly absorbed that they took no notice of the visitors (they had been told that there might be a couple of guests). In the whole section of my lesson, I probably spoke for no more than four or five minutes, the rest was all the students. I offer this anecdote because it does show how students can be so absorbed with an interesting lesson that observers are of no interest; however, this example is also useful because it is atypical. A confident teacher can invite several observers to a lesson and plan for it to demonstrate something special for them. Generally, however, expert teaching is characterised by both fluidity and spontaneity, and these characteristics are most likely to be captured through recording a lesson and then creating a commentary where, in Bruner's phrase, difficulty is revealed in a meaningful way.

A final point about both the whole chapter but also especially about this last section is that expert teachers can work with others in many ways but also with each other. Capturing their 'best work' so that their peers can review and discuss it may be our 'master class'. Expert teachers have huge amounts to offer novices and others but, in a continually developing profession, they can be at least as helpful to each other. Teachers, however expert, do need help to continually develop – which is the subject of Chapter 8.

Chapter 8

Continuing to develop

Charlie, Interview 4: *The temptation is to just 'do enough' in the classroom and to put lots of energy into running the department and supporting new colleagues and so on, but that is not why I came into teaching and there is still nothing like the satisfaction of a really good lesson. I do think many teachers get a bit stuck and then tend to coast, that is an issue for the whole profession in my view, we have to find ways to stay fresh and continually challenged, in the classroom, not out of it.*

The ongoing learning of teachers themselves

In Hattie's typology of expert teaching, we have the descriptor 'Expert teachers are passionate about teaching and learning'. But how far does this passion extend to their own learning? One of the themes of this book has been its counterintuitive message that we need to make teaching more teacher centred, at least for some of the time. This is absolutely not in contradiction to teachers being student centred. All Hattie's characteristics describe expert teachers in relation to their students. However, it is appropriate to recognise a creative tension for teachers around the notion of being more teacher centred at times. Nothing illustrates this more clearly than the Cinderella that is professional development. Chapters 1 and 2 devoted much space to the notion of teaching as a profession and to new models of teacher recognition such as the advanced skills teacher and excellent teacher in England, the chartered teacher in Scotland and Wales and the highly accomplished teacher in the US. What is surprising is how rare these models are and how few teachers have a chance to gain these recognitions. Hattie makes the point:

> Expert teachers do differ from experienced teachers – particularly in the way they represent their classrooms, the degree of challenges that they present to students, and most critically, in the depth of processing that their students attain. Students who are taught by expert teachers exhibit an understanding of the concepts targeted in instruction that is more

integrated, more coherent, and at a higher level of abstraction than the understanding achieved by other students.

Hattie (2003: 15)

If this is a true measure of expertise, then how was it learned and how can it be developed in others? Hattie's continues in summing up his meta-analysis:

These studies have demonstrated the need for a focus on dependably identifying, esteeming and encouraging excellent teachers, wherever they may be. We do have excellent teachers in our schools in New Zealand, but we have a reticence to identify such excellence in the fear that the others could be deemed not-excellent. We work on the absurd assumption that all teachers are equal, which is patently not true to any child, any parent, any principal, and known by all teachers. Such an assumption of equality brings all teachers down to the latest press scandal about a teacher, and our profession needs and deserves better than this. Every other profession recognizes and esteems excellence (Queen's Counsels, Colleges of Surgeons, Supreme Court Judges) but in teaching we reward primarily by experience irrespective of excellence, we promote the best out of the classroom, and we have few goalposts to aim for in professional development, instead allowing others to define what latest fad, what new gimmick, what new policy will underline the content of professional development.

Ibid.: 15–16

There is the magic phrase 'professional development', and Hattie scathingly and rightly condemns as 'the latest fad…gimmick' the endless absurd tinkerings with teacher development that stem from so-called 'policy'. He goes on to argue:

Like expertise in teaching, we need a deeper representation of excellence in teachers, a greater challenge and commitment to recognizing excellence, and a coherent, integrated, high level of deep understanding about teacher expertise.

Ibid.: 16

The 'deeper representation of excellence' is certainly one potential purpose of professional development. We do not need to revisit in any depth the point that experience and long service are simply not enough to produce excellence; very typically, they produce competence. Hattie's concentration on what teachers do expertly in the classroom does not provide us with much insight into how they learn from outside their classrooms.

Back in 1991, Protherough and Atkinson made a determined start, in *The Making of English Teachers*, to outline what we know about how English teachers come, as it were, into being. Their book was written in the context of the late 1980s when teaching was being ridiculed by the right-wing press, and there was a strong policy move to make teacher training purely school based. One clear aim of the political right was to get rid of all that 'theory' allegedly so beloved of teacher educators. As a result, much of their book is taken up with an analysis of initial teacher education (ITE), and the last four chapters are devoted to case study examples of approaches to ITE, including a chapter on the Oxford Intern scheme that has proved itself over the last nearly twenty years (see Chapter 2). As discussed in Chapter 2, initial teacher training (ITT) has improved very substantially since that time and not by becoming entirely school based.

However, as a basis for some of their book, the authors identified and surveyed 110 'effective teachers of English' to gather their views about how they became English teachers. These teachers were identified essentially through contacting English advisers across England and also some well-established teacher educators with considerable experience of running postgraduate certificate in education (PGCE) programmes (ibid.: 3). The authors are very clear that it is not a 'scientifically based sample' and that their purpose was to be 'selective'. This model of peer nomination remains both valuable and problematic: how does one identify expert teachers of English in a 'scientific way'? The authors felt that their nominees were a very varied group, at different ages and stages; many had become heads of department, deputy heads or advisers and so had moved 'away' from the classroom. There were, of course, no advanced skills teachers (ASTs) in 1990 when the data were collected. All these nominees completed detailed questionnaires and some were interviewed.

The overall impression of this group is of energetic, passionate and committed professionals who retain that love and enthusiasm for the subject that has been much discussed throughout this book. Two more factual findings are especially relevant to the theme of this chapter. First, 17 per cent held advanced diplomas or certificates, 13 per cent had higher degrees in English, 26 per cent had higher degrees in education and a 'good number' were working towards such advanced qualifications; effectively, about 40 per cent had a Master's level qualification and a further proportion were working towards it. We have no accurate figures about this for either current English teachers (or teachers more generally), but there is absolutely no doubt that this proportion is far higher than is typical of teachers generally, and is unquestionably significant. One difference between that generation of teachers and the current one that has just left training (i.e. not strictly comparable to these generally very experienced teachers) is that very many have a number of 'M' level credits, in some cases up to a third needed for a Master's degree; this gives them a strong start towards completing a full Master's degree at some point. The pros and cons of this 'M' level work in initial training are considered more fully below.

The second statistic relates to their membership of professional bodies, of which a number were named in relation to English, and many belonged to two, but 84 per cent belonged to the National Association for the Teaching of English (NATE), and most considered this association to have been a formative influence on their development. The importance of professional associations and professional networking has received some recognition at policy level, and is now touched on in the standards for ASTs and excellent teachers, but is not part of a fully formed model of continuing professional education (CPD) or firmly rooted in the culture of the profession.

So, this group of 'effective teachers of English' were characterised by having advanced qualifications and membership of an important subject-based association. These two factors strongly support the idea that they were passionate about their own teaching and learning and were committed to CPD. On that basis, one would make a strong link between being a teacher so effective as to be nominated by knowledgeable peers, and some of that effectiveness being derived from various forms of CPD. Again, this cannot be claimed scientifically, but it is hugely probable. My own personal experience certainly fits in with this view for a number of reasons that will be illustrated below. However, it must be said that there is no evidence that a teacher *cannot* become expert unless they engage in CPD.

In Eraut's initial discussion of CPD (Eraut 1994: 5–14), he highlights the problematic nature of 'professional knowledge'. Most professionals, and certainly most English teachers, acquire their knowledge in practice and develop this after their initial training, however powerful that may have been, that is to say that knowledge is 'practical'. This immediately emphasises that such teachers must become or maintain an orientation to be a 'learning professional'. To refer back to the driving metaphor of Chapter 2, drivers do not necessarily improve with experience; indeed, there is the likelihood that that complacency leads to deterioration and the development, in common sense parlance, of 'bad habits'. Although this is highly undesirable, it is partly tolerated because most drivers are, as it were, casual; they are not professionals. Society will not tolerate coach drivers who drive badly. This point is even more emphatic if one were to include airline pilots as a form of driver. Therefore, a professional is expected to continue to learn, and there is a consensus that cumulative experience is not enough; this does not imply that new experiences do not develop new learning. An AST undertaking outreach may well be transferring knowledge to a different context, but they are also gaining new knowledge through that dialogue with a different situation. Eraut (1994) points out that the 'learning professional', however individually motivated, is not as powerful an orientation as the 'professional learner', i.e. someone dedicated, quite self-consciously, to learning consistently from all available sources of which practice is only one element. Even, therefore, if there is no fully established relationship between undertaking CPD and becoming an expert teacher, there is a huge degree of probability that there is an inter-relationship between what might be deemed 'learning in practice' and 'learning about practice'.

Continuing professional development

CPD takes many forms and ranges from the informal to the formal. There is evidence (Croos 2010) that very informal learning can take place in the staff room over a cup of coffee. There is plenty of evidence that certain kinds of CPD, especially that selected by policy-makers, is highly ineffective. Experienced teachers are familiar with the current spectrum of CPD, which can be outlined as:

- School-based, teacher-led sessions, e.g. team meetings, short skill-based sessions, working parties;
- Staff inset days often with internal and also external sources (it is very striking that teachers' entitlement to even these days, currently five per year, is only twenty years in duration);
- Performance management and peer review – although these are not necessarily designed as CPD activities, they can be catalysts to learning;
- 'Going on a course' – this model takes the teacher out of school to another provider, which may be a local authority, a university or a commercial organisation; typically, these are single day, 'one off' events;
- Long courses – this term is loose enough to encompass the range of courses that include simply a series of sessions to a complete Master's programme that might take several years to achieve. These courses can also have no accreditation or, as with a Master's, be fully 'award bearing'. For a very few teachers, such courses might include a PhD or a taught doctorate.

For the experienced teacher looking over this familiar list, the question to ask may well be how many forms of CPD have been genuinely available to you over your career. One striking absence from this list is any opportunity for sustained full-time study, something that was available twenty years ago, although only for a tiny minority. Also missing from the list is the term 'secondment'. There have been times when teachers kept their permanent post but undertook another role for an agreed period of time; a classic such role was the 'advisory teacher', and this was a feature of the profession during the Protherough research. This model involved working as a specialist adviser for several years, typically three, and then 'returning to the classroom'. There was a time when many outstanding English teachers undertook these roles, and it was a very different orientation to being an 'inspector' or a 'consultant'.

A final 'missing link' is the concept of 'sabbatical', that is time out from teaching to become refreshed. Certain Australian states have operated a system whereby a teacher was entitled, with every seven years of continuous service, to a term 'off' with full pay or, possibly, a whole year off with half pay.

In that time, the teacher could undertake further study or spend time in other schools and so on, but they could also spend that time reading or travelling. This model has several interlinked dimensions. One is 'refreshment'; teachers suffer from burn out and the retention rate in teaching is relatively poor (Day et al. 2007). In English, initial recruitment is good, but retention is especially low. This will be discussed further below. The second dimension is 'reward'; a teacher is being offered material recognition of their long service and of the system's need to retain them. The third, linked to the first, is 'well being'; teachers' mental and physical health is a relatively neglected concept. The PIT (pool of inactive teachers) is estimated at hundreds of thousands, and the ratio of 'returners to teaching' (apart from maternity/paternity leave) from the PIT is tiny. The final, and at least as important, dimension is 'autonomy'; the teacher is being trusted to decide what best to do with that time for the benefit of themselves and the future students in their charge. If this model seems economically naïve, it is not. The cost of this model would be rapidly overcome if more teachers stayed in the profession for longer, but equally if their capacity to teach well (not just cope) was enhanced and if their capacity for new learning was also improved.

All these forms of CPD have their pros and cons, however well intentioned, and the 'cons' make sustained professional learning very difficult. School-based sessions are often merely functional, i.e. there is a new directive, this is what we have to do to meet it or, more usefully, here are some new criteria for 'x' ('A' level, GCSE), how shall we interpret them? Most such sessions, and this even includes Master's level work, are taken either out of potential leisure time or at the end of the working day or a hurried lunch time. Whatever else might change, this aspect of teacher development needs to, and hence the argument for being more teacher centred at times. How can we develop real expertise without high-quality and sustained opportunities to do so? Other professions have much better developed systems for CPD and much higher expectations of its benefits (see Chapter 2). The expert teacher, especially a designated excellent teacher, should be leading some of these school-based sessions. One element that they will have to grapple with is how to enable their participants to engage in (in Hattie's terms) deep, rather than surface, learning. In other words, to move beyond sessions built on functional reactions to external change and to design learning about the essentials of teaching and learning.

There is much evidence that short courses (Eraut 1994; Day et al. 2007), especially of the one-day kind, are useful refreshment but are not really developmental. They can provide excellent networking opportunities but that is not normally their purpose. Longer courses, especially Master's programmes, certainly according to teachers, do make a very significant contribution to their knowledge and they lead to improvements in their practice. The latter are undertaken voluntarily, sometimes with school support, but often this is an individual decision and motivation is high.

This point about individual ownership of CPD and about authentic motivation are especially important in England as the circumstances of the subject and its teachers are changing. I would argue that the introduction of the excellent teacher is an exciting opportunity generally, but especially for English teachers. In Protherough and Atkinson's sample from 1991, there were 110 'highly effective teachers', many of whom had 'left' the classroom to join a local authority and/or higher education institution (HEI). This move is not to be decried; these are very important positions in themselves. However, the combined opportunities of the AST and excellent teacher, with their enhanced status and material rewards, would make it very probable that more of such a sample would still be in the classroom now. It is not a trivial point to say that they would also have been easier to identify as literally being more 'visible'. In any secondary school in England, one would expect to see at least one designated excellent teacher; what a powerful network for development that could become, especially if linked in to a supportive subject association such as NATE and with General Teaching Council for England (GTCE) backing (see discussion of NATE below).

Two further developments offer new possibilities, 'lesson study' and 'Teachers' TV'. Lesson study originated in Japan (Lewis et al. 2006) and offers a very simple but effective model with real focus on developing expertise (see Chapter 7). Essentially, a group of teachers meet and plan a lesson; they then all teach the agreed lesson and meet to evaluate the lesson and plan a new version or move on to another, different lesson. The group of teachers could be two or many more; it could be a whole English department or a subgroup. It could be teachers from more than one department planning not the same, but a complementary, lesson, i.e. looking at William Blake in English and in art for the same age group, even the same class possibly.

Such lesson study is in the teachers' hands and respects that autonomy. The time has to be mutually agreeable and can focus exclusively on issues of pedagogy and learning. Given all the earlier points about how teachers disagree, and experts even more so, there might be a danger of 'lesson design by committee', i.e. a lesson that no-one really believes in. I am not aware of research in this country to back up what follows, but I am sure it can be a very valuable process. It would seem that, on occasion, all agreeing to teach 'the same lesson' would be productive, as with the example in Chapter 7 of introducing the same difficult poem – the same lesson will not actually 'happen' because students are so variable – this difference in itself is powerful and offers much food for reflection. With a group working over time, the 'sameness' of the lesson could vary in an interesting way, i.e. lessons might be similar rather than replicas. Each teacher could introduce the same short story or teach the dreaded apostrophe and compare outcomes. Teachers could compare the outcomes of similar lessons, e.g. the writing produced by students. Over time, it might be a sequence of lessons. Most departments already have agreed schemes of work that provide opportunities for teacher comparisons. However, the focus on single lessons does allow for intense concentration on pedagogy and on aspects of expertise. It can bring novices, competent and expert teachers together to learn from each other about best practice in English teaching.

Finally 'Teachers' TV' is a very promising development. A channel devoted to helping teachers improve their work, broadcast on television and available online is a fantastic resource. The DCSF website states:

> Teachers TV is the first digital TV channel for teachers and it's available free of charge every day of the year. The channel is editorially independent and aims to reflect the views of the teaching community.
>
> The channel offers programmes aimed at both new and experienced primary and secondary teachers, as well as programmes and resources for headteachers, managers, governors, teaching assistants and support staff. There is information on continuing professional development, as well as general education interest programmes, including a weekly news round-up and documentaries, plus debates about the current issues in education. Curriculum-based programmes for use in the classroom also form part of the programming schedule.
>
> Teachernet website, DCSF

It offers many different kinds of resource, but it does focus on expertise in certain programmes, looking at how, for example, good teachers can become outstanding. It is a television programme and therefore elements of lessons being 'staged' can be present, but the programmes are not preoccupied by an agenda in the way the National Literary Strategy (NLS) material was and their authenticity is relatively strong.

The concept of Teachers' TV is still relatively new and politically fragile. However independent the channel is of government, nevertheless, it will be politicians who decide whether to continue the funding. In a few years' time, it may well be possible to evaluate its impact on teacher development in the long term.

English teaching and CPD, 1989–2009

Teachers' TV has content that is either specifically for English teachers or that might be used by English teachers in a specialist capacity, but much of its content is generic. It is, inevitably, focused on being up to date; it does not put current teacher development into any historical perspective. At times, this means a lack of perspective on where certain key ideas, for example 'reflective practice', have come from. Equally, it does not review some of the policy mistakes of the recent past.

This section of the book puts into perspective what happened to English teaching and the CPD element devoted to it, between 1989 and 2009. There is no precise evidence to compare the Protherough 1991 sample with the present English teaching community, but I do have much evidence of how English teachers have felt disempowered and deskilled; the irony of this is that much of this feeling is a direct effect of governmental policy intended to raise student and teaching standards. I am about to argue that a degree of deskilling, and certainly a reduction in autonomy, has occurred over this period, but chiefly because the decade 2010–20 looks much more promising, and so the CPD landscape may be much improved for all teachers from novice to expert.

However, English teachers will need to reflect on what has happened during the period 1989–2009 because of the legacy of government policy. The period 1987–1992 was important and was a very powerful stimulus to the profession. The now forgotten Kingman Report was at the centre of powerful debate about English (see Jones and West 1988). The report was generated initially by a typical right-wing concern in the mid-1980s with 'reading standards'. This 'concern' was overtaken, possibly confused, by a great deal of anti-teacher sentiment and media hostility, which suggested, in a loosely consensual way, that English teachers no longer taught grammar and that, therefore, standards of language use were falling. The further confusion that falling linguistic standards equate to falling moral standards was famously expressed by Norman Tebbit in 1985 when he said on BBC radio: 'If you allow standards to slip to the point where good English is no better than bad English, where people turn up filthy at school ... all those things tend to cause people to have no standards at all ... and once you lose those standards, there's no imperative to stay out of crime'. It would take a whole book to deconstruct what Tebbit does in those few words; however, for our purposes, it sums up the atmosphere of the times and unquestionably links to the production of the Kingman Report in 1988.

That report is far more than a footnote in the history of the subject and repays careful attention for its genesis, its conclusions and the CPD model that was created to implement those conclusions. Its genesis owed much to the political milieu and attitude towards schooling as exemplified by Tebbit's comments, but also to Her Majesty's Inspectors (HMI). In 1984 and 1986, HMI published two reports, *English 5–16, Curriculum Matters 1* and then *English from 5–16, The Responses to Curriculum Matters 1*. The 1984 report argued strongly for a much more language-centred approach to English teaching, was critical of teachers' lack of relevant subject knowledge and argued (without evidence) that there had been some loss of attention to language compared with the past. Whether accurate or not, these claims were not research or evidence based. There was a very angry reaction to this report, so much so that HMI took the unprecedented step of publishing a kind of rejoinder as a 'Response' to the responses. One aspect of the reaction to the 1984 document was the strong belief that the HMI's much vaunted independence had been compromised (Jones and West 1988; see especially

Harold Rosen's Introduction, pp. 1–14), that this was document produced from a political imperative but not a publically acknowledged one, hence the 1986, clearly defensive, response. This debate led to the setting up of the enquiry chaired by Kingman, with the report appearing in 1988.

It is also the only report on English teaching to have led to the making of a *Panorama* documentary that went out on prime-time television.

The key focus of the project was to investigate the level of 'Knowledge about Language' (KAL) currently extant among English teachers and to review the curriculum to see where teaching about language actually featured. The report followed the classic civil service model appointing a non-specialist chair, Sir John Kingman, a mathematician, and then a committee made up of individuals chosen via a completely opaque process and certainly ignoring some of the best minds in English education at the time. However, as with the Cox Committee which followed hard on its heels, the committee did a thoughtful job and produced some really fresh thinking. It was also emphatic that there was absolutely no evidence that a return to 'grammar teaching' was what was needed. However, it argued for more KAL for teachers in ITT, for serving teachers and for a National Language Project.

The report was published in 1988 and was generally well received in the profession, not least because it had intelligently identified a dimension of subject knowledge that English teachers were, and still are, concerned about. That knowledge is not merely about grammar. What English teachers then, and now, are often concerned with is their lack of a deep understanding of a linguistic knowledge of English, chiefly because their studies have been literature based. As discussed earlier in the book, English teachers come from a wide range of degrees, and some do have elements of language study; a minority have an actual linguistics degree, but generally they know most about and are most focused on literature. Since 1988, as with media studies, there has been a growth in English language 'A' level, and more English teachers have developed this aspect of their subject knowledge.

Kingman made a number of recommendations and the agenda was very ambitious; perhaps had the National Curriculum not overtaken it, then its recommendations might have been more fully realised. One recommendation was for the parallel development of resources and materials suitable for teachers to use in the classroom, with a complementary CPD programme designed to reach every English teacher. This was a three year (1989–1992), 'cascade' model. Each LEA (local education authority) would appoint at least one KAL advisor who would first be trained and then contribute to the design of the resources. In year 2, they would train a representative from every English department in the country. In year 3, that trained teacher would train their home department. The cascade model has been much derided as essentially a form of ongoing dilution, with each level of training becoming less effective. HEIs were also advised, not required, to adapt their ITT programmes, and many were very happy and excited to do so.

However, three major factors derailed KAL. Before the report was published, the Conservative government had decided to introduce a National Curriculum (NC) and the first subject was English (see Chapter 3 for details). Kingman was published in 1988; the CPD programme began in 1989, at exactly the same time as the Cox Report was published, defining the whole English curriculum. Inevitably, the introduction of the NC for English dominated English teaching during the period 1989–1992. The cascade model proved not very effective and there never was a National Language Project, so the KAL initiative, even though it was clearly acknowledged as important in the original NC for English, never became properly embedded. The most spectacular problem for KAL, however, was the political reaction surrounding its work that led to the *Panorama* documentary.

One of the major aims of the LINC (Language in the National Curriculum) project was to generate resources for English teachers that they could use in the classroom. These were going to be free to every English department and ITT department and were not therefore going to be published commercially in text book form. Just before they were to be published in their final form, after three years of development work, the Department for Education withdrew them, deeming them unsuitable for use by teachers. Essentially, ministers banned the materials. There was a significant reaction by the media in all this, but the public perception was that the whole exercise had been a costly (perhaps £20 million?) waste of time. The popular press pilloried the project, and the idea that these materials had been outrageously banned and repressed by political diktat went largely ignored. Those professionals who had seen the materials had found them very valuable indeed, and photocopied versions did find their way into many departments. Although the cascade model was not powerful, it did have some effect on receptive teachers and departments.

The banning of these materials was not only outrageous but a sign of things to come for English teachers and their opportunities for CPD. If the perception by the profession had been that HMI had been 'got at' in the 1980s, then that was small beer compared with this brutal and contemptuous political act of 1992. What ministers clearly felt was that Kingman and his committee had produced the opposite to their intentions; instead of a rigorous return to grammar teaching, English teachers were now officially encouraged to adopt a sociolinguistic approach throughout the curriculum. If Kingman had proved a political traitor, then his failings were nothing compared with those of Brian Cox, once the darling of the far right for his production of the 'Black Papers' in the 1970s (see Cox 1991). His NC not only adopted Kingman but was positively received by English teachers with its bold emphasis on creativity, a very broad range of literature and its celebration of diversity in language and texts. The 1989 Cox Report did underpin the first NC for English. By 1995, the NC for English had been radically revised several times, and almost all the more progressive elements had been removed; KAL was effectively elided.

So 1989–1992 was a very stimulating time and the KAL CPD programme, whatever its limitations, was part of that creative period. The period 1992–1997 was taken up with revisions to the NC, and any CPD was dominated by instrumental notions of how those revisions should be implemented, a very dull period. The government clearly felt that English teachers and English teaching needed 'telling' what to do. Two features of this period 1992–1997 also spelt out very prescriptive times ahead: the creation of Ofsted in 1993 and the steady increase in testing children in English between the ages of five and fourteen, culminating in the Key Stage 3 standard assessment tests (SATs).

Ofsted was forged in the heat of right-wing fulminations over standards in schools. The early 1990s were dominated by a concerted campaign to denigrate teachers and to assign blame for much of the country's social ills to the failure of schools. Ofsted was designed as a form of inspectorial attack, to pressurise schools to 'improve' or be closed. From 1993 to 2003, this model dominated schools and ITT. Over that period, hundreds of thousands of reports were written about individual schools, and many summaries created about whether standards were rising; many such reports were specific to English teaching. This Ofsted model was conceptualised as part of the national pressure for school improvement and was deliberately separated from any notions of support. All Ofsted did was make judgements and recommendations, never offering advice or developmental feedback. Many hundreds of thousands of English lessons were observed and recorded in Ofsted notebooks. I would argue that this was a huge opportunity missed to improve expertise. Some inspectors were subject experts and certainly were in a position to both provide useful feedback and also create an archive of good teaching. Even if much of this teaching was atypical because of being highly influenced by needing to 'display' to an inspector, nevertheless very good teachers are better than this implies. Ofsted might have created a huge evidence base of expert teaching (outstanding in their terminology) but that will not be the legacy of that period. The era of self-evaluation may well be a much more developmental one.

I would argue that the impact of Ofsted over that period was negative towards expertise in the profession generally; it was a model of compliance and certainly no stimulus to risk-taking or innovation. This problem was exacerbated in English by the steady pressure to teach to the tests. It is remarkable that English teachers resisted the tests for as long as they did. The government brought in the Key Stage 3 tests completely against professional advice and, for the first two years, schools simply boycotted them. By 1995, infuriated politicians 'solved' the problem by making the test legally the head teacher's responsibility and by outsourcing the marking. Thirteen years later (2008), the test finally collapsed under its own weight after several years of disastrously inconsistent marking and huge bureaucratic problems.

Very good teachers can 'teach to the test', and there is some evidence that they achieve good results while teaching much more than the narrow focus that the tests demand. The best evidence I have is personal and not systematic because of lessons I have been fortunate to observe during that period by experienced teachers and because of the research I have carried out, but much of it based on self-report (more of this below). It might be argued that 'teaching to the test' is actually a form of expertise and one necessary to all teachers, especially in a high-status subject such as English. First, it is because of expertise that English teachers refused to co-operate with the testing programme; they could see just how limiting the tests were and how they would become a barrier to real learning not a driver of learning. Expert teachers are very good at linking teaching with forms of assessment (see Chapter 5) when they believe the assessment is authentic and developmental. The Key Stage 3 tests epitomise everything that was wrong with the prescriptive models of the 1990s and the general move towards narrow outcomes at GCSE and 'A' level.

But the final period of 1997–2008 was even more dominated by merely functionalist CPD. The story of the NLS and its secondary incarnation, the Framework for English, is an extraordinary one. It is considered the largest policy-driven CPD programme of its kind in the world (Stannard and Huxford 2007). The NLS was designed to change the practice of every single primary teacher, not just subject co-ordinators, in every primary school, and the Framework was designed to have the same impact on every English teacher in every secondary school.

Essentially then, the project was designed to remodel the expertise of every relevant teacher to fit a government-designed set of outcomes. This model treats teachers as technicians in the most patronising sense; it goes against all proper models of professional development. It is also designed, I would argue, to be more about deskilling than improving expertise; such a claim needs some justification.

In the mid-1990s, the usual government concern with falling reading standards was once more enjoying heated debate. The new Ofsted machine was pressurising schools and the HMI produced a specific report in 1996 damning the teaching of reading in forty-five primary schools in the LEAs in London (Ofsted 1996). The government of the day (then in its last year in power) created a National Literacy Project, inviting fifteen LEAs to undertake some funded pilot work aimed at improving literacy standards. In parallel, the new Labour government in waiting set up its National Literacy Task Force, chaired by Michael Barber, whose 1996 book *The Learning Game* was to influence New Labour's education policies at every level (Barber 1996). *The Literacy Game*, by John Stannard and Laura Huxford, tells the fevered story of the next ten years, including the frenetic period between 1996 and 1998 when the NLS had its first full year of operation (Stannard and Huxford 2007). I undertook a steady stream of research projects at this time to try to understand the nature of English teachers' work and professional identity throughout this period, acting as an independent researcher not funded by any government body or quango.

However, before commenting on English teachers and their experience of CPD during that time, a comment must be made about the NLS in its primary orientation, but first about the term 'literacy'. Much has been written about the changing nature of literacy in the digital age (see Chapter 6), and this was something almost entirely missing from the conceptualisation of the NLS (see below for further comment). The rise of the term itself is very striking in relation to the teaching of English. For most of the twentieth century, literacy was almost always discussed in terms of its opposite, illiteracy, and especially in relation to adults. Its rapid global ascendance into a term that dominates policy and practice has been remarkable (Goodwyn and Findlay 2002). One explanation is that the rapid technological changes of the final third of the twentieth century destabilised traditional conceptions of literacy while at the same time demonstrating its importance. For some, this meant a desperate need to get back to the basics; for others an exciting prospect of deep change towards a more participatory democracy. It is notable that, in other English-speaking countries where there have been equally passionate debates about schooling, the term literacy has often been added to teachers' titles. In Australia, for example, English teachers routinely describe themselves as teachers of English *and* literacy; this is also common in New Zealand and Canada

But if less contentious, the *and* is revealing. The expertise of English teachers lies with the subject of English (see Chapter 3). The use of *and* suggests an additional element; this is somewhat paradoxical at first glance. However, in England, although the term is occasionally seen in job titles aimed at English teachers, the profession has adamantly rejected the term as a professional 'badge'. In my last survey (Goodwyn 2008), 98 per cent of respondents were adamant that English is quite distinct from literacy and that they did not wish to have the word in their job title.

This, I would argue, is strongly predicated on their professional identity and sense of authentic expertise. They believe that they are English teachers and there is no need for an '*and*'. Much of this stems from the NLS itself and also from the CPD model that it generated, which impacted on secondary English between 2000 and 2007.

Primary colleagues did not suffer from this issue. For them, the very first stages of the NLS were promising. They felt that literacy as a term and as a focus was absolutely right; many had felt uncomfortable with the way the term 'English' had been imposed on primary schools in 1989 (Goodwyn and Findlay 2002). Prior to 1989, they would have talked about teaching 'language' not English. They had also had problems with a more subject-dominated curriculum since 1989, making them feel as if they had to adopt a secondary model where subjects are all divided up rather than brought together in a topic-based approach. However, the imposition of the 'literacy hour' reduced much of the initial positive reaction. The literacy hour 'clock' was used in the training programmes of the NLS for the first few years and was featured in various training manuals that went with it. Stannard and Huxley (2007) make huge claims for the impact of the hour, but also for its symbolic power in being simple to understand and useful in a sound bite. They also state without demur that the whole CPD infrastructure was based on forcing teachers to change their practice first before they understood the principles. This exactly mirrors the introduction of the NLS itself, which was not based on the pilot studies of the fifteen LEAS (because none of them had had even a year of research) nor on existing research – the research justification was published much later (Beard 2000a).

The literacy hour clock is, indeed, easy to understand and certainly had symbolic power. It carries great prescriptive power in determining not only what teachers must do but for exactly how long, and it implies that, like the clock, they must be timed and watched. It is therefore more important, apparently, that they do what they are told to do in that hour than that they understand what they are doing. All schools had to conform to the literacy hour model or provide their own evidence that they did not need it, with armies of consultants ensuring compliance and with Ofsted never far away; compliance was the name of the literacy game.

The introduction of the 'Framework for English' was much the same. My survey of the first two years (Goodwyn 2003a) could not have been more emphatic. Experienced teachers in particular loathed the patronising training, the endless manuals and the mind-numbing PowerPoints they were subjected to on a regular basis. They always acknowledged that the documents associated with the Framework contained good ideas, but these ideas were neither new nor unwelcome, whereas the prescriptive nature of the pedagogical models was new and very unwelcome. By year three, the consultants were instructed to 'loosen up' during their training sessions, and this change came through in later surveys (Goodwyn 2008). Given that there was a revised National Curriculum for English in 2000, which included, for example, teaching about the moving image for the first time, it might have been a time for innovation and development; it was not.

Not only was existing teacher expertise marginalised, possibly diminished, but for novices, this was an especially difficult time. One feature of both the NLS and the Framework was script, that is models of scripted lessons and also scripted planning, i.e. here is the plan you need to teach this objective, made explicit at the scheme of work level and the lesson level. Scripted lessons and plans are very seductive to the novice as they provide apparently authoritative things to say and guaranteed ways to do them. What started off as the three-part lesson and became the four-part lesson suggested an utterly schematic approach to every lesson, taken as a single episode of learning, the components being starter, guided work, independent work, plenary session. When experienced teachers were trained 'how to teach' this model, they were exasperated (Goodwyn 2003a) by its rigidity but also its naivety: do not all lessons have a beginning, a middle and an end? The curious answer is 'yes but also not always', and the reasons for this paradox relate to best practice in authentic English teaching.

There are four main failings to the pedagogy of the Framework. The first is the rigidity of the four-part structure and especially its obsession with starters, often disconnected from the lesson per se and treated as a series of mini-lessons. This failing partly stems from an obsession with pace and the 'imperative to secure progression':

> There is clearly a balance to be achieved between providing classroom time to support the reading of longer texts and the imperative to secure progression. Having clear objectives lends pace and focus to the study of longer texts: there is less need to teach all possible angles on the text and more reason to focus on those aspects that cluster around the objectives. The aim is to provide enjoyable encounters, which serve the objectives well but do not demand a disproportionate amount of time. Teachers already a use a repertoire of techniques (such as the use of priority passages, support tapes, abridgement, televised extracts and recapitulation) to move quickly through longer texts without denying attention to the details and quality of the text.
>
> Framework document, DCSF website

The last point is an appropriate recognition of how very good English teachers do use a variety of techniques, recognising that teaching longer texts is a real challenge. However, English teachers have been increasingly frustrated with the emphasis on 'pace' and its negative effective on depth of learning and especially engagement with longer texts. The most recent look at literature teaching (Goodwyn 2008) found that English teachers were reduced to using far too many extracts to achieve limited teaching objectives and found it very difficult to generate real encounters with literature. In other words, the coverage of the curriculum is 'pacey' but superficial.

The third limitation of this pedagogical model is that it is far too teacher centred and didactic. One reason why very good English lessons do not always appear to have a 'start' is because students start working as soon as they come into the class. Certain aspects of English lend themselves remarkably well to developing pupil independence. Students may be engaged in an activity, often working collaboratively in a group with others, producing a magazine or newspaper for example, that takes several lessons. What the effective teacher does is to interact with each group to monitor progress and add in new ideas, but the whole class is busy. At selected points, the teacher will 'bring the class together' to review overall progress and key learning points. The final lesson in this sequence might be a series of pupil-led presentations and a whole class evaluation of the 'project'. The question 'where is the starter?' would be completely irrelevant during this learning sequence.

The fourth limitation of the Framework model was more at the strategic level and relates to the relentless production of material. The point was made in Chapter 7 about the inauthentic nature of the many videos produced to support the goals of the strategy. More generally, there was simply a relentless production of new goals, for example 'guided reading'. This initiative, which in itself may be a valuable pedagogical strategy, was supported by compulsory training, a manual of instruction and various supporting materials including videos. Before this initiative was embedded, another one was introduced with a similar training model. Overall, these four limitations add up to a deskilling, not a CPD, programme. The period 1997–2008 has not been a developmental period for English teachers, and they are emphatic that this has been their experience (see Goodwyn 2004a, 2004b, 2008).

Professional networks and expertise: the National Association for the Teaching of English

An inevitable side-effect of the monolithic strategy model has been to reduce teachers' opportunities for other forms of CPD, however good the individual teacher has been. In the Protherough sample discussed at the opening of the chapter, of those teachers nominated as highly effective by their peers, 84 per cent belonged to NATE. Over the period of the NLS and Framework, NATE's membership has declined and its offer of CPD activities has reduced. NATE seeks to represent English teachers, including primary colleagues, independent of any passing government strategy and as a voluntary organisation. It is a professional organisation and offers a range of publications to its members from a research-intensive journal to a range of very practical magazines and classroom materials. It is one of many such organisations that represent all the key subjects and interests of teachers. NATE's sister organisation, focusing very much on the primary phase, is UKLA (the United Kingdom Literacy Association); naturally some teachers belong to both. All such organisations have some level of national organisation and a variable level of local, typically regional activity. At national level, an annual conference is a high point.

All these organisations are similar in that their members choose to belong and they are marked by a passionate devotion to subject (or equivalent) teaching. This makes them true professional networks because the united focus is the sharing and dissemination of best practice. An interesting development in 2008 was the establishment of a Council for Subject Associations (CfSA), a body intended to raise the profile of all the associations and to enable them to share best practice as organisations. Its impact is yet to be evaluated and it will need a stable period to develop. It is notable that the GTCE (see Chapter 2) does not feature as an influence in the setting up or the maintenance of the CfSA.

In the standards for both the excellent teacher and the AST, mention is made of professional networks; standard E5 states:

> Have an extensive and deep knowledge and understanding of their subjects/curriculum areas and related pedagogy gained for example through involvement in wider professional networks associated with their subjects/curriculum areas.

It would seem likely that, in the post-Strategy, post-Framework period, the professional associations will once more become much more active in the CPD landscape. However, this remains to be seen. The changes in teacher expertise discussed in Chapter 6, i.e. the way to teach in the digital age, must be recognised by professional networks. New teachers in particular find it harder to see the value of an association that you have actually to join, and pay a subscription for, when you can get so much from the internet both immediately and often for free. The development of *Teachit* is a good case study in this respect (see *Teachit* website). It began as a few English teachers sharing lesson ideas for professional benefit, and it is now a powerful and well-established commercial organisation. It provides a very valuable service to the English teaching profession. However, a problematic element is that the material offered can be of low quality or of high quality; NATE would certainly pride itself on only producing 'high-quality' material. *Teachit* is a logical development of the internet and it, and variants on it, are here to stay. What will be the impact of Facebook, or blogging or twittering or whatever, on the future of professional networks? Associations such as NATE will need to engage with these forms of communication and also determine how to maintain a structure that enables good teachers to get together in real space and time to share (and argue) about best practice. One difference between NATE and its comparable associations and *Teachit* and its similarly commercial organisations is that NATE speaks for the profession of English teaching and has a collective memory. It remains, while governments come and go and while superficial initiatives relentlessly fail to deliver their promised nirvanas. It therefore plays a valuable and consistent role representing the best of English teaching. It was noted in Chapter 2 that some subject associations are developing their own chartered teacher models, something that NATE may explore in the future.

NATE is also part of the International Federation for the Teaching of English (IFTE), a loose confederation of the English subject associations from the English-speaking world. It holds a conference every four years, for example 2007 Canada, 2003 Melbourne, Australia, 1999 England (University of Warwick) and 1995 New York – 2011 is Auckland, New Zealand. Naturally, many teachers, however effective, might assume that something like IFTE is remote from their work. First, it need not be in an age of global opportunities and, second, for the teacher aspiring to be an outstanding professional, such an organisation represents a chance to review best practice from across the world.

One theme of this book is the global rise in attention to the quality of every teacher and especially towards recognising and developing the very best teachers. These best teachers are not in a vacuum. The subject of English is influenced by a matrix of factors and one of these is the influence of 'the international'. This takes many forms, from the publication of a seminal academic work based on research (consider Schon's influence) to the visit of one teacher to another teacher's school in a different country. There is an international set of networks and, for the teacher who wishes to be informed by best practice across the world, there is a great opportunity to develop. Another element in this internationalised world is the way policy initiatives interact across systems. The term advanced skills teacher came from Australia. Most English-speaking systems have developed a National Curriculum for English; Australia is introducing its version in 2010. For the well-informed professional, these movements help to both explain why change happens but also to appreciate positive change and to oppose and resist attempts to negatively impact on best practice.

IFTE brings together the subject associations from Australia, Canada, New Zealand, the USA and the UK. It is therefore representing teachers of English from around the world. Each individual association has a valuable website, produces journals, resources and holds conferences and CPD events. Earlier, we reviewed the STELLA project, which comes from the Australian Association of English Teachers (AATE), as a very remarkable model of teacher-generated evidence of excellent teaching. It may not be available often, but for an outstanding or aspirational teacher, attendance at either an international conference (which could be held in their own country) or more regular attendance at their chosen association's national event is clearly an excellent opportunity. However amazing are the affordances of the internet and now its social networking dimension, there seems no immediate advantage in reducing conference-style CPD events.

One element at such events is the reporting of research. Such events are typically attended by colleagues from teacher education and by researchers; these colleagues can be the same people, but by no means always. Other organisations also conduct research, for example government agencies, but also examination boards and even publishers. The presenters at a subject conference such as NATE know that the audience will be a varied one and by no means 'pure' researchers, and presentations will be intended to be accessible and connected to teachers' practical interests. Some of the audience will often be learning about research themselves through their participation in a Master's programme.

Research and developing expertise

The final element in this chapter on CPD and continuous development, and the final section of the book, considers the role of research in the development of expertise. This book is not a research book, but it is entirely 'research informed'. The AST and excellent teacher standards make it clear that such leading teachers need to know about research and to become disseminators of research to their colleagues.

> Research and evaluate innovative curricular practices and draw on research outcomes and other sources of external evidence to inform their own practice and that of colleagues.
>
> DCSF website

However, in the English standards for teaching, that is the only place in which research is directly mentioned. The document from Scotland about chartered teaching is a much more detailed, visionary and comprehensive piece than its rather reductive English counterpart and contains these kinds of insights:

> Accomplished teaching of the kind reflected in the Standard for Chartered Teacher is teaching in which the four central values and commitments permeate the work of the teacher in the classroom, the school, and beyond. The Chartered Teacher will be effective in promoting learning and committed to the development of all forms of professional action. In every sphere of his or her work the Chartered Teacher should be reviewing practice, searching for improvements, turning to reading and research for fresh insights and relating these to the classroom and the school. These should be informed by those moral and social values which give point to education, bringing to the task of educating others the resourcefulness which characterises all professional work, and undertaking all these actions collaboratively with colleagues and others in a shared and collegial undertaking. Approached in this way, the capabilities of the accomplished teacher become sustained and embedded in an integrated professional life. And it is because these central values and commitments are so pervasive that a generic standard has been adopted: that is, a standard that will apply at all stages of education, across all subjects and specialisms, covering all aspects of teachers' work throughout the country.
>
> Chartered teacher, p. 5, GTCS website

This kind of reference to research places it at the heart of the extended professional's role. Equally, when it is more explicit about how the chartered teacher demonstrates this approach, it states:

- engaging in professional enquiry and action research, and applying findings
- reflecting critically on research evidence and modifying practice as appropriate

- testing whether a particular theoretical perspective actually applies in practice
- interpreting changes to education policy and practice and contributing and responding to such changes.

Ibid.: 12

The argument is much clearer in this document and it also extends the conceptualisation of the teacher to that of a contributor to research. The excellent teacher standard above makes the expert teacher a user of 'research outcomes' and an evaluator of local innovation. The chartered teacher does all this but also engages in 'professional enquiry and action research' and tests 'whether a particular theoretical perspective actually applies in practice'.

In broad terms, the expression 'teachers as researchers' has steadily acquired more currency and more status. This movement has been evolving for at least thirty years, first crystallising in the work of Lawrence Stenhouse in the 1970s (for example, see Stenhouse 1975). Some of this 'teacher as researcher' movement has manifested itself in Master's level programmes, and many of those have adopted a school-based approach where the 'M' level work happens in the school itself with many teachers evaluating their own practice or introducing curricular change and attempting to monitor its effects. As discussed above, the last twenty or so years have not been very conducive to this approach because teachers have had little autonomy and have been oppressed by top-down policy and accompanying CPD.

However, a review of the Department for Children, Schools and Families (DCSF), Training and Development Agency (TDA) or GTCE websites would produce scattered but substantial references to research. The GTCE site is especially impressive, devoting a large section to research and to advising teachers on how to undertake it; for example, it explains about:

The National Teacher Research Panel

The GTC is a co-sponsor of the National Teacher Research Panel (NTRP). This is an independent group of practising teachers who work to ensure that all research in education takes account of the teacher perspective and increase the number of teachers engaged in research. The GTC co-sponsors are the Department for Children, Schools and Families (DCSF) and the National Council for School Leadership (NCSL).

GTCE website

The site also has regular and very well-produced summaries and syntheses of recent research.

On the DCFS website, there is much reference to research, partly because the Department commissions very substantial ongoing research projects, but these are mainly of interest to professional researchers. There is some attention to teacher research, for example one study that the NTRP undertook called 'Engaging teacher expertise', which examined:

> how to establish practitioner research as an effective and sustainable form of continuing professional development both for participating researchers and, through their research work, for colleagues within the schools and network. It was hoped that this would contribute to the development of the schools and the network as effective professional learning communities.

The project set out to identify:

- what motivates teachers to both engage in practitioner research and to sustain their involvement over time;
- what forms of support teacher researchers need for their work to be successful;
- and how the learning generated by practitioner research can be effectively shared with colleagues within a school and across the network of schools.

DfES (2006)

The report concludes, optimistically:

> Our conclusion is that it can indeed play an important part in helping our network and schools become strong professional learning communities. We have learned that a wide range of teachers have been motivated by participation in research, that there is a specific combination of support that is vital to success; and that a diverse range of communication approaches are needed for the research to reach a wider audience. Our hope is that the lessons we have learnt might make it possible for many more teachers to engage in and be sustained during their own research.

Ibid. (2006)

There is currently no evidence that this has happened, but the arrival of the excellent teacher role in England provides a very timely opportunity for some of their hopes to be realised. The above definitions very rightly give the teacher a high status in relation to properly critical use of research and as an active creator of knowledge through local research activity.

Before concluding the book with some thoughts on the vital link between developing teacher expertise and research, it is important to comment briefly on the proposed Master's degree in Teaching and Learning (MTL), potentially available to all teachers in England in the future. At the time of writing, much has been said and proposed (see section on coaching in Chapter 7) about the MTL, but there is still enormous uncertainty about its structure, its content and the extent to which it will be welcomed by the profession. It appears to offer beginning teachers (or novices) an opportunity over several years to undertake coaching and HEI-supported reflections on their emergent practice and to conduct school-based investigations of teaching and learning. There are merits in this approach, although it is in stark contrast to the chartered teacher model from Scotland or the US National Board for Professional Teaching Standards (NBPTS) model, where teachers start the programme when they are ready and are expected to have a considerable amount of practical experience. The merits of this approach may be considered to be:

- The needs of novices are being taken seriously;
- The induction to the profession is rightly being seen as taking several years, not an ITT then newly qualified teacher (NQT) model;
- The support of a coach could be very developmental;
- The coach might be an 'excellent teacher' or AST;
- HEI involvement maintains continuity from PGCE (perhaps less so from other routes e.g. graduate teacher programme);
- HEI involvement provides academic credibility and access to libraries and published research;
- The status of the profession may be raised to compare more favourably with others;
- The MTL does not replace more HEI-based Master's programmes, which teachers could take later in their careers.

However, this is very much a best case scenario; there is, for example, nothing in the proposals about the role of excellent teachers or ASTs as coaches. Looked at holistically, the MTL appears not to be truly a Master's level programme or to be practically feasible; financial models in particular seem unworkable.

It is difficult to critique a policy that is not finalised or a model that is not transparently clear or tested in practice. A final comment then is that it may yet prove to be a step change in improving teacher expertise in England.

The expert teacher who is an extended professional will not need an MTL, but they will need to continue to improve, and participating in research is one of the most powerful ways to do so. There is not space to discuss research methodologies and projects in a book like this, but rather to make a brief case for its importance.

The extended professional is highly effective but also self-critical and reflective, an encourager and motivator of colleagues, but devoted to self-development. Research, especially action-type models of research, are an intense form of CPD. Action research is now a robustly established model, and there are many useful texts to support teachers (see Hopkins 2002;

Costello 2003; McNiff and Whitehead 2005a, 2005b). Action research is by no means the exclusive territory of the excellent teacher; all teachers can benefit as Stenhouse argued back in the 1970s. The action research model is especially suited to the expert teacher as it can be captured as simply as:

- plan;
- act;
- observe;
- reflect,

thus fitting very closely with Schon's notion of reflection on the action. The key difference between action research and reflective practice is that the focus is on producing evidence of some kind, whether highly qualitative or including some quantitative element. The action research model is typically described as like either a spiral or a cycle with the practitioner going 'round' the above four processes and then, very possibly, going around again, deepening understanding at each completed cycle. I would argue that action research is at its best when the participant or participants are working towards an outcome that can be articulated to colleagues. The act of articulation and dissemination is crucial if the outcomes are to become a form of knowledge that can benefit others. It would be a significant step forward if some of the best English teachers could undertake research about their own teaching.

It has been argued throughout the book that the expert teacher is a role model and should be knowledgeable about research and policy and act as a critical disseminator of both. These skills should have been developing as an undergraduate and should have been extended by initial training; they are not new skills per se. At one level, following Dreyfus, the expert teacher needs to embrace the novice phase as regards research; it is an entirely different form of expertise, even more radically removed from teaching than becoming a mentor. If the expert teacher's expertise is to extend into research, it will be a gradual and cumulative development. It requires entering a different community of practice and going through those Dreyfus stages. We do not have descriptions of expert teacher researchers even if they are active in the profession. Much more likely is that we have teachers, whether experts or not, who have acquired extensive experience and reached some level of competence. One of the real dangers with the 'teachers as researchers' movement is that it elides the difficulty of undertaking any form of research and the need for support, especially training with a practical component; this can be addressed through the right kind of MA work. It also elides a very fundamental issue about educational research and its own paradigm wars. There are many books about the challenge of undertaking research with real human beings in real settings where the number of variables operating is dauntingly impossible to measure.

Therefore, the nature of teacher research is rightly, at present at least, small scale, local and specific. It is also, almost always, not supported by additional funds, so the teacher is finding ways through their expertise in teaching to find time to do research and analyse findings; they are the resource. This individual effort can be much enhanced through collaborative working, which is highly recommended.

However, it is right to conclude the book by recognising again the inevitable paradox of teaching: the teacher is almost always working with others but they are students; the teacher is the key, often singular, professional. We therefore know that much teacher expertise exists in the action of practice and that we are a long way from capturing it fully. Therefore, we need more teachers, perhaps all teachers, to be thinking about the kinds of research that investigate expertise, at least partly 'for its own sake', that is for teacher-centred reasons, as well as for the students. Despite the paradox outlined above, teachers are working together more, technology is enabling better study of teaching, and we are, as Hattie's study shows, beginning to understand and describe expert teaching in meaningful detail. Put simply, we need more English teachers to study themselves and their peers, and we now have better ways to engage with this as a project; the STELLA initiative is a good example of a teacher-led focus on capturing and reflecting on what we mean by good English teaching.

This book has endeavoured to cover a great deal of ground and many issues about expertise in teaching and about expert English teaching specifically. It has tried to avoid, at all times, the patronising simplicities of recent imposed models of pedagogy. Teachers are not technicians, and their skills are not easily reducible to formulaic or scripted models of teaching; there is no one size that fits all. The best teachers are reflective, thoughtful, critical but also enthusiastic, passionate and committed, but perhaps a little too modest for their own good. I have argued consistently that more attention needs to be given to teachers themselves, and that a profession with more teacher centredness would ultimately be more beneficial to students over the long term. Whether we call such teachers, 'expert', 'excellent' or 'highly accomplished' does matter, but it matters far less than trying to understand and describe that expertise and finding multiple ways to represent it meaningfully to the profession. As Hattie reminds us:

> Like expertise in teaching, we need a deeper representation of excellence in teachers, a greater challenge and commitment to recognizing excellence, and a coherent, integrated, high level of deep understanding about teacher expertise.
>
> Hattie (2003: 16)

One challenge for the future is for English teachers to step forward into the spotlight of excellence and to accept that this bold act will benefit not only many students but also, through sustained effort and enthusiasm, their fellow English teachers.

Bibliography

Adams, A. and Brindley, S. (eds) (2007) *Teaching Secondary English with ICT.* Maidenhead: Open University Press.

Allen, N. (2002) 'Too much, too young? An analysis of the Key Stage 3 National Literacy Strategy in practice'. *English in Education*, vol. 36, 5–15.

Andrews, R. (ed.) (2004) *The Impact of ICT on Literacy Education.* London: Routledge Falmer.

Atkinson, T. and Claxton, G. (2000) *The Intuitive Practitioner: On the value of not always knowing what one is doing.* Maidenhead: Open University Press.

Barber, M. (1996) *The Learning Game.* London: Routledge.

Barber, M. and Moushed, M. (2007) *The McKinsey Report: How the world's best performing education systems come out on top.* New York: McKinsey.

Barnes, D., Barnes, D. and Clarke, S. (1984) *Versions of English.* London: Heinemann.

Beard, R. (2003) 'Not the whole story of the National Literacy Strategy: A response to Dominic Wyse'. *British Educational Research Journal*, vol. 29, 917–928.

Beard, R. (2000a) 'Research and the National Literacy Strategy'. *Oxford Review of Education*, vol. 26, nos 3 and 4, 421–436.

Beard, R. (2000b) 'Long overdue? Another look at the National Literacy Strategy'. *Journal of Research in Reading*, vol. 23, 245–255.

Benner, P. (1984) *From Novice to Expert: Excellence and power in clinical nursing practice.* Menlo Park, CA: Addison-Wesley.

Beverton, S. (2003) 'Can you see the difference? Early impacts of the primary National Literacy Strategy on four secondary English departments'. *Cambridge Journal of Education*, vol. 33, 217–245.

Beverton, S. (2000) 'Implementing the National Literacy Strategy: How are teachers managing?' *Topic*, Spring, issue 23, 1–7.

Black, P.J. and Wiliam, D. (1998) 'Inside the Black Box: Raising standards through classroom assessment'. *Phi Delta Kappan*, vol. 80, 139–148.

Blake, D., Hanley, V., Jennings, M. and Lloyd, M. (2000) 'Superteachers: The views of teachers and head teachers on the Advanced Skills Teacher grade'. *Research in Education*, 63, 48–59.

Brookes, W. (2005) 'The Graduate Teacher Programme in England: Mentor training, quality assurance and the findings of inspection'. *Journal of In-service Education*, vol. 31, no. 1, 43–62.

Brookes, W. and Goodwyn, A. (1999) 'What Literacy Means: An initial enquiry'. *The English and Media Magazine*, 39, 43–47.

Brown, S. and McIntyre, D. (1993) *Making Sense of Teaching*. Milton Keynes: Open University Press.

Bruner, J. (1986) *Actual Minds, Possible Worlds*. Cambridge, MA: Harvard University Press.

Buckingham, D. (2003) *Media Education: Literacy, learning and contemporary culture*, London: Polity Press.

Collins, H. and Evans, R. (2007) *Rethinking Expertise*. Chicago, IL: University of Chicago Press.

Connelly, G. and McMahon, M. (2007) 'Chartered Teacher: Accrediting professionalism for Scotland's teachers – a view from the inside'. *Journal of In-service Education*, vol. 33, no, 1, 91–105.

Cooper, P. and McIntyre, D. (1996) *Effective Teaching and Learning: Teachers' and students' perspectives*. Buckingham: Open University Press.

Costello, P. (2003) *Action Research*. London: Continuum.

Cox, B. (1992) *The Great Betrayal: Memoirs of a life in education*. London: Hodder and Stoughton.

Cox, B. (1991) *Cox on Cox: An English curriculum for the 1990s*. London: Hodder and Stoughton.

Croos, P.S. (2010) *Interactive approaches to teacher practice and professional development*. Unpublished doctoral thesis, University of Reading.

Cullingford, C. (1995) *The Effective Teacher*. London: Cassell.

Cullingford, C. (ed.) (1999) *An Inspector Calls: Ofsted and its effect on school standards*. London: Kogan Page.

Day, C., Sammons, P., Stobart, G., Kington, A. and Gu Qing (2007) *Teachers Matter: Connecting lives, work and effectiveness*. Maidenhead: Open University Press.

DCSF (2009) *Professional Standards for Teachers*. London: DCSF.

Departmental Committee of the Board of Education (1921) *The Teaching of English in England: Being the report of the departmental committee appointed by the President of the Board of Education to inquire into the position of English in the educational system of England (Newbolt Report)*. London: HMSO.

DES (2001) *The Framework for Teaching English, Years 7, 8 and 9*. London: HMSO.

DES (1986) *English from 5–16, The Responses to Curriculum Matters 1*. London: HMSO.

DES (1985) *Better Schools*. London: HMSO.

DES (1984) *English 5–16, Curriculum Matters 1*. London: HMSO.

DES (1975) *A Language for Life: Report of the committee of inquiry appointed by the secretary of science and education under the chairmanship of Sir Alan Bullock (Bullock Report)*. London: HMSO.

DfEE (1999) *Teachers Meeting the Challenge of Change: Technical consultation document on pay and performance management*. London: DfEE.

DfEE (1998) Green Paper. *Teachers: Meeting the challenge of change*. London: The Stationery Office.

DfES (2006) *Engaging Teacher Expertise*. London: DfES.

Dixon, J. (1967) *Growth through English*. Oxford: Oxford University Press.

Dreyfus, S.L. and Dreyfus, H.L. (1986) *Mind over Machine: The power of human intuition and expertise in the era of the computer*. New York: Simon and Schuster.

Eagleton, T. (1975) *Literary Theory: An introduction*. Oxford: Blackwell.

Eisner, E.W. (1985) *The Educational Imagination: On the design and evaluation of school programmes*. New York: Macmillan.

Ellis, V. (2007) *Subject Knowledge and Teacher Education: The development of beginning teachers' thinking*. London: Continuum.

English, E. (2003) 'All Change! The National Literacy Strategy and its influence on the teaching of reading'. *Studies in Training and Learning*, vol. 4, 18–23.

English, E., Hargreaves, L. and Hislam, J. (2002) 'Pedagogical Dilemmas in the National Literacy Strategy: Primary teachers' perceptions, reflections and classroom behaviour'. *Cambridge Journal of Education*, vol. 32, 9–26.

Eraut, M. (1994) *Developing Professional Knowledge and Competence*. London: Falmer Press.

Ericsson, K., Charness, N., Feltovitch, P. and Hoffman, R. (eds) (2007) *The Cambridge Handbook of Expertise and Expert Performance*. Cambridge: Cambridge University Press.

Frater, G. (2000) 'Observed in Practice. English in the National Literacy Strategy: some reflections'. *Reading*, vol. 34, no. 3.

Goldstone, R.L., Schyns, P.G. and Medin, D.L. (1997) *Perceptual Learning: The psychology of learning and motivation*. vol. 36. San Diego, CA: Academic Press.

Goodson, I. and Ball, S. (eds) (1984) *Defining the Curriculum: Histories and ethnographies*. London: Falmer Press.

Goodson, I. and Medway, P. (eds) (1990) *Bringing English to Order*. London: Falmer Press.

Goodwyn, A. (2009) *Expert Teachers and Innovative uses of Technology*. Paper given at the Annual Conference of the New Zealand Association for the Teaching of English.

Goodwyn, A. (2008) *Student Teachers and Literary Reading*. Paper presented at BERA, September 2008.

Goodwyn, A. (2004a) 'What's in a frame? The English Framework – Three years on'. *English, Drama, Media*, issue 2, 39–43.

Goodwyn, A. (2004b) 'Literacy versus English: A professional identity crisis', in Goodwyn, A. and Stables, A. (eds) *Learning to Read Critically in Language and Literacy Education*. London: Sage, pp. 192–205.

Goodwyn, A. (2004c) *English Teaching and the Moving Image*. London: Routledge.

Goodwyn, A. (2003a) 'Literacy or English: The struggle for the professional identity of English teachers in England', in *English Teachers at Work: Narratives, counter-narratives and arguments*, Australian Association for the Teaching of English/ Interface. Kent Town: Wakefield Press.

Goodwyn, A. (2003b) 'Breaking up is hard to do: English Teachers and that LOVE of Reading'. *English Teaching, Practice and Critique*, vol. 1, no. 1, 66–78.

Goodwyn, A. (2001) 'Second tier professionals: English teachers in England'. *L1 – Educational Studies in Language and Literature*, vol. 1, no. 2, 149–161.

Goodwyn, A. (2001) 'Who Wants To Be a Super Teacher? The perils and pleasures of recognising expertise in English teaching'. *English in Australia*, vol. 129–130, 39–50.

Goodwyn, A. (2000a) 'Texting; reading and writing in the intertext', in Goodwyn, A. (ed.) *English in the Digital Age*. London: Continuum, pp. 78–96.

Goodwyn, A. (2000b) '"A bringer of new things": An English teacher in the computer age?' in Goodwyn, A. (ed.) *English in the Digital Age*. London: Continuum, pp. 1–21.

Goodwyn, A. (1998) 'Broadening the Literacy Horizon', in Goodwyn, A. (ed.) *Literary and Media Texts in Secondary English*. London: Cassell, pp. 1–23.

Goodwyn, A. (1998a) 'Literature: The writing on the wall is now on the screen', in Kooy, M., Janssen, T. and Watson, K. (eds) *Fiction, Literature and Media: Studies in language and literature, international perspectives on mother tongue education*. Amsterdam: Amsterdam University Press, pp. 39–50.

Goodwyn, A. (1998b) 'Adapting to the Textual Landscape: Bringing print and visual texts together in the classroom', in Goodwyn, A. (ed.) *Literary and Media Texts in Secondary English*. London: Cassell, pp. 129–150.

Goodwyn, A. (1997) *Developing English Teachers: The role of mentorship in a reflective profession*. Milton Keynes: Open University Press.

Goodwyn, A. (ed.) (1995) *English and Ability*. London: David Fulton.

Goodwyn, A. (1992a) 'English Teachers and the Cox models'. *English in Education*, vol. 28, no. 3, 4–10.

Goodwyn, A. (1992b) *English Teaching and Media Education*. Buckingham: Open University Press.

Goodwyn, A. and Fidler, B. (2002) *Advanced Skills Teachers: The emergence of the role*. Paper given at the BERA Annual Conference, Exeter.

Goodwyn, A. and Findlay, K. (2004) *Subject Teaching and ICT Literacy*. Coventry: BECTA.

Goodwyn, A. and Findlay, K. (2003) 'Shaping literacy in the secondary school: Policy, practice and agency in the age of the National Literacy Strategy'. *British Journal of Educational Studies*, vol. 51, no. 1.

Goodwyn, A. and Findlay, K. (2003b) 'Literature, literacy and the discourses of English teaching: a case study'. *L1 – Educational Studies in Language and Literature*, vol. 3, no. 2.

Goodwyn, A. and Findlay, K. (2002) 'Secondary Schools and the National Literacy Strategy', in Goodwyn, A. (ed.) *Improving Literacy at KS2 and KS3*. London: Paul Chapman Publishing, pp. 45–64.

Goodwyn, A. and Findlay, K. (2001) 'Media Studies and the establishment'. *The International Journal of Media Education*, vol. 1, no. 1, pp. 23–40.

Goodwyn, A. and Findlay, K. (1999) 'The Cox Models Revisited: English teachers' views of their subject and the National Curriculum'. *English in Education*, vol. 33, no. 2, 19–31.

Goodwyn, A., Adams, A. and Clarke, S. (1997) 'The Great God of the Future: Views of current and future English teachers on the place of IT in English'. *English in Education*, vol. 31, no. 2, 54–62.

Goodwyn, A., Protopsaltis, A. and Fuller, C. (2009) *Harnessing Technology Strategy: Celebrating outstanding teachers*. Report to BECTA.

Green, B. (1993) 'Literacy Studies and Curriculum Theorizing: Or, the insistence of the letter', in Green, B. (ed.) *The Insistence of the Letter: Literacy studies and curriculum theorizing*. London: Falmer Press, pp. 195–225.

Grossman, P. (1990) *The Making of a Teacher: Teacher knowledge and teacher education*. New York: Teachers' College Press.

General Teaching Council for Scotland (2009) *The Chartered Teacher*. Edinburgh: GTCS.

Halsall, R. (ed.) (1998) *Teacher Research and School Improvement*. Buckingham: Open University Press.

Harrison, C. (2002) *Key Stage 3 National Strategy: Key Stage 3 English: Roots and research*. London: HMSO.

Harrison, C., Comber, C., Fisher, T., Haw, K., Lewin, C., Lunzer, E., McFarlane, A., Mavers, D., Scrimshaw, P., Somekh, B. and Watling, R. (2002) *ImpaCT2: The impact of information and communications technologies upon pupil learning and attainment, ICT in schools*. Research and Evaluation Series, No. 7. London: Becta/DfES.

Hart, A. (ed.) (1998) *Teaching the Media: International perspectives*. Mawaha, NJ: Lawrence Erlbaum.

Hart, A. and Hicks, A. (2002) *Teaching Media in the English Curriculum*. London: Trentham Books.

Hattie, J. (2003) *Teachers make a difference: What is the research evidence?* Paper presented at the Australian Council for Educational Research Conference.

Hickcox, E.S. and Musella, D.F. (1992) 'Teacher performance and appraisal and staff development', in Fullan, M. and Hargreaves, A. (eds) *Teacher Development and Educational Change*. London: Falmer Press.

Hoffman, R.R. (1998) 'How can expertise be defined? Implications of research from cognitive psychology', in Williams, R., Faulkner, W. and Fleck, J. (eds) *Exploring Expertise*. New York: Macmillan, pp. 81–100.

Hopkins, D. (2002, rev. ed.) *A Teacher's Guide to Classroom Research*. Maidenhead: Open University Press.

Hunt, G. (2001) 'Democracy or a Command Curriculum: Teaching literacy in England'. *Improving Schools*, vol. 4, 51–58.

Hutchings, M., Mansaray, A., Minty, M. and Smart, S. (2009) *Excellent Teacher Scheme Review*. London: DCSF.

Ingvarson, L. (2008) *Recognising Advanced Teaching: What's working? Why?* Teaching Australia and Business Council of Australia Symposium, 15 October 2008, available online at www.acer.ac.uk (accessed January 2009).

Ingvarson, L. and Chadbourne, R. (1997) Reforming teachers' pay systems: The Advanced Skills teacher in Australia'. *Journal of Personnel Evaluation in Education*, vol. 11, 7–30.

Jones, M. and West, A. (eds) (1988) *Learning Me your Language: Perspectives on the teaching of English*. London: Mary Glasgow Publications.

Kleinhenz, E. and Ingvarson, L. (2004) 'Teacher accountability in Australia: current policies and practices and their relation to the improvement of teaching and learning'. *Research Papers in Education*, vol. 19, no. 1, 31–49.

Kress, G., Jewitt, C., Bourne, J., Franks A., Hardcastle, J., Jones, K. and Reid, E. (2005) *English in Urban Classrooms: A multimodal perspective on teaching and learning*. London: RoutledgeFalmer.

Kyriacou, C. (2001) *Effective Teaching in Schools*. London: Nelson Thornes.

Kyriacou, C. (1997) *Effective Teaching in Schools: Theory and practice*. London: Nelson Thomas.

Lankshear, C. and Knobel, M. (2006) *New Literacies: Everyday practices and classroom learning*. Maidenhead: Open University Press.

Lave, J. (1988) *Cognition in Practice: Mind, mathematics and culture in everyday life*. Cambridge: Cambridge University Press.

Lave, J. and Wenger, E. (1991) *Situated Learning: Legitimate peripheral participation*. Cambridge: Cambridge University Press.

Leavis, F. and Thompson, D. (1933) *Culture and Environment*. London: Chatto and Windus.

Lewis, C., Perry, R. and Murata, A. (2006) 'How Should Research Contribute to Instructional Improvement? The Case of Lesson Study'. *Educational Researcher*, vol. 35, no. 3, 3–14.

Livingstone, S. (2009) *From Page to Screen? Critical reflections on the prospects for ICT in education*. Paper presented at ESRC funded seminar series, Oxford.

Marshall, B. (2000) *English Teachers – The Unofficial Guide: Researching the philosophies of English teachers*. London: Routledge.

Masterman, L. (1980) *Teaching about Television*. London: Macmillan.

Mathieson, M. (1975) *The Preachers of Culture*. London: Allen and Unwin.

McBer, Hay (2000) *A Model of Teacher Effectiveness*. London: DfEE.

McKernan, J. (1996) *Curriculum Action Research: A handbook of methods and resources for the reflective practitioner* (2nd edn). London: Routledge.

McNiff, J. and Whitehead, J. (2005a) *Action Research for Teachers*. London: David Fulton.

McNiff, J. and Whitehead, J. (2005b) *All You Need to Know about Action Research*. London: Sage.

Millard, E. (2004) 'Is love all you need? Thoughts on the pedagogical preferences of English teachers'. *English, Drama, Media*, issue 2, 5–10.

Millard, E. (1997) *Differently Literate: Boys, girls and the schooling of literacy*. London: Routledge.

Millman, J. and Darling Hammond, L. (1990) *The New Handbook of Teacher Evaluation: Assessing elementary and secondary school teachers*. London: Sage.

Misson, R. and Morgan, W. (2006) *Critical Literacy and the Aesthetic: Transforming the English classroom*. Urbana, IL: NCTE.

National Curriculum Board of Australia (2009) *The Shape of the National Curriculum: English*. Barton: NCB.

National Curriculum Board of Australia (2009b) *Framing Paper Consultation Report: English*. Barton: NCB.

National Research Council (2008) *Assessing Accomplished Teaching: Advanced level certification programme*. Washington, DC: The National Academies Press.

Ofsted (2003) *Advanced Skills Teachers: A survey*. London: HMSO.

Ofsted (2001) *Advanced Skills Teachers: Appointment, deployment and impact*. London: HMSO.

Ofsted (1996) *The Teaching of Reading in 45 Inner London Primary Schools*. London: HMSO.

Perrot, E. (1982) *Effective Teaching: A practical guide to improving your teaching*. London: Longman.

Preston, C. (2004) *Learning to use ICT in Classrooms: Teachers' and trainers' perspectives*. London: TTA.

Protherough, R. (1989) *Students of English*. London: Routledge.

Protherough, R. and Atkinson, J. (1994) 'Shaping the Image of an English Teacher', in Brindley, S. (ed.) *Teaching English*. Buckingham: Open University Press.

Protherough, R. and Atkinson, J. (eds) (1991) *The Making of English Teachers*. Buckingham: Open University Press.

Protherough, R., Atkinson, J. and Fawcett, J. (1989) *The Effective Teaching of English*. London: Longman.

QCA (2000) *The National Curriculum for English*. London: QCA.

Rodgers, C. and Scott, K. (2008) 'The Development of the Personal Self and Professional Identity in Learning to Teach', in Cochran-Smith, M., Feiman-Nemser, S. and Mcintyre, D. (eds) *The Handbook of Research on Teacher Education*. New York: Routledge.

Sampson, G. (1921) *English for the English*. Cambridge: Cambridge University Press.

Schon, D.A. (1987) *Educating the Reflective Practitioner*. San-Francisco: Jossey-Bass.

Schon, D.A. (1987) *Educating the Reflective Practitioner*. Presentation at AERA, San Francisco. Available at http://resources.educ.queensu.ca/ar/schon87.htm.

Schon, D.A. (1983) *The Reflective Practitioner: How professionals think in action*. New York: Basic Books.

Selinger, E. and Crease, R.P. (eds) (2006) *The Philosophy of Expertise*. New York: Columbia University Press.

Shulman, L. (2004) *The Wisdom of Practice: Essays on teaching, learning and learning to teach*. New York: Jossey Bass.

Shulman, L.S. (1987) 'Knowledge and Teaching: Foundations of the new reform'. *Harvard Educational Review*, vol. 57, no. 1, 1–22.

Shulman, L.S. (1986) 'Those who understand Knowledge Growth in Teaching'. *Educational Researcher*, vol. 15, no. 2, 4–14.

Slee, R. and Weiner, G. (eds) (1998) *School Effectiveness for Whom? Challenges to the school effectiveness and school improvement movements*. London: Falmer Press.

Squires, G. (1999) *Teaching as a Professional Discipline*. London: Falmer Press.

Stannard, J. and Huxford, L. (2007) *The Literacy Game: The story of the National Literacy Strategy*. London: Routledge.

Stenhouse, L. (1975) *An Introduction to Curriculum Research and Development*. London: Heinemann.

Stones, E. (1992) *Quality Teaching: A sample of cases*. London: Routledge.

Sutton, A., Wortley, A., Harrison, J. and Wise, C. (2000) 'Superteachers: From policy towards practice'. *British Journal of Educational Studies*, vol. 48, no. 4, 413–428.

Taylor, C. and Jennings, S. (2004) *The Work of Advanced Skills Teachers*. Reading: CfBT.

Turner-Bisset, R. (2001) *Expert Teaching: Knowledge and pedagogy to lead the profession*. London: David Fulton.

Watson, D.M. (1993) *The ImpaCT Report: An evaluation of the impact of information technology on children's achievement in primary and secondary schools*. London: Department of Education and King's College London.

Watson, N., Torrance, N. and Earl, L. (2002) 'Front row seats: What we've learned from the National Literacy and Numeracy Strategies in England'. *Journal of Educational Change*, vol. 3, 35–53.

Woods, P. and Jeffrey, B. (1996) *Teachable Moments: The art of teaching in primary school*. Buckingham: Open University Press.

Wragg, E.C. (1994) *An Introduction to Classroom Observation*. London: Routledge.

Wyse, D. (2003) 'The National Literacy Strategy: A critical review of empirical evidence'. *British Educational Research Journal*, vol. 29, 903–916.

Index

'A' level examinations 35, 65, 66, 67, 73, 106, 110, 159, 163, 166

about this book: aim of addressing teachers directly 3–4; author's experience 2–3; rationale for writing 1; structure 6–8; target audience 1–2, 5; teaching English, case studies of 3

action research 99, 129, 134, 173, 174, 176–7

Adams, A. and Brindley, S. 114

adult needs, cultural heritage and 69, 87

Advanced Certificate in English Teaching (ACE) 55, 56

Advanced Skills Teacher (AST) 4, 5, 8; affective terms, absence of 49–50; AST2 model 46–7; Australian origins 46, 172; collaboration with others 49; continuous professional development (CPD) 156, 157, 160, 171, 176; data-rich school environments 49; development of others 49; effective, extended professional 14, 15, 16, 27; Excellent Teacher Scheme (ETS) 50–52; excellent teacher standards 47–8; exemplary aspect 48–9; expertise and models of expert teaching 37, 38, 41, 42, 44, 45, 46–52, 55; extended professional, concept of 47, 134–5; high level skills, possession of 46; implementational aspect 49–50; longevity in England 47; managerialism, discourse of 49–50; outside classroom work 49; policy, characterised in terms of 45; reflection, absence of requirement for 49–50; reports and reviews on standards 47; research for, importance of 173; teaching and learning, emphasis on 48; teaching English 63, 64, 76, 77, 88, 101; working with others 132, 133, 136, 137, 138, 139, 143

AI (artificial intelligence) 33

Andrews, R. 121

approved training providers (ATPs) 115, 116

assessment: authenticity 103, 105, 106, 108; burden of assessment load 102; change in assessment framework 106; characteristics of 103; classroom monitoring and 101–2; curriculum design as assessment design 102–3, 106–7; design for 106; GCSEs in English, effects of introduction of 107–8; holistic teaching 102–3; integrity 103–4, 105, 106, 108, 110; interest 103, 104–5, 108; monitoring and 101–10; practices of, discussions on 108; Programme for International Student Assessment (PISA) 6; satisfaction with outcomes 103, 105, 108; standard assessment tests (SATs) 98, 165–6; technical vocabulary of 108

Association of Science Education (ASE) 40, 41

Atkinson, J. 58

Atkinson, T. and Claxton, G. 36

Australia 158, 167, 172; Australian Association of English Teachers (AATE) 55, 172; South Australia, Government website 46, 47; Standards for Teachers of English Language and Literature in Australia (STELLA) project 7, 55–6, 98, 172, 178

Barber, M. 166
Barber, M. et al. 5, 13
Barnes, D. et al. 69, 70
Beard, R. 95, 168
BECTA *see* British Educational
  Communications and Technology
  Agency
Benner, P., development model 34–7
Better Schools (DES, 1985) 26
Beverton, S. 20, 97
The Bible 125
Black, P.J. and Wiliam, D. 108
Blake, W. 160
British Educational Communications
  and Technology Agency (BECTA) 121
Brookes, W. 17
Brookes, W. and Goodwyn, A. 97
Brown, S. and McIntyre, D. 23
Bruner, J. 140, 153
Buckingham, D. 127
Bullock Report (1975) 71

Cambridge School of English 70, 126
Canada 167, 171, 172
cascade model of resource provision 163–4
Caxton, W. 125
Certificate of Secondary Education
  (CSE) 107, 109
CfBT Education Trust 47
CfSA *see* Council for Subject
  Associations
Chartered Scientist status 40, 41
Chartered Teacher status 7, 8, 23, 88,
  101, 134; attributes, professional
  and personal 44; benefits of
  42; collaboration, commitment
  to 43; continuous professional
  development (CPD) 154, 171, 173,
  174, 176; expertise and models of
  expert teaching 38, 41, 42–4, 45,
  46, 48; leadership, commitment
  to 43; personal commitments
  42–3; professional development,
  commitment to 43; professional
  knowledge and understanding 43–4;
  professional values 42–3; promotion
  of learning, commitment to 43;
  self-evaluation, commitment to
  43; social and educational values,
  commitment to 43; standard for,
  components of 42
Chartered Teachers (Scotland) 154,
  173, 176

Chaucer, G. 31
Children, Schools and Families, Dept.
  for (DCSF) 23, 38, 39, 135, 161,
  174; website 48, 50, 142, 173, 174
China 151
coaching 139–42
collaboration: importance of 88–90;
  team working and 135–6
Colleges of Surgeons 155
collegiality 131–2
Collins, H. and Evans, R. 2
communities of practice 63–7, 132
competence model of teaching 22–3, 26
Connelly, G. and McMahon, M. 41
continuous development 172; action
  research 176–7; 'advisory teacher',
  role of 158; Australian Association
  of English Teachers (AATE) 172;
  cascade model of resource provision
  163–4; challenge of longer texts 169;
  Council for Subject Associations
  (CfSA) 170; didactic nature of
  'Framework for English' 169; *English
  5–16, Curriculum Matters I* and
  Responses to Curriculum Matters I
  (HMI) 162–3; English *and* literacy,
  distinction between 167–8; English
  teaching and CPD (1989–2009)
  161–70; excellence, representation
  of 154–5; excellent teacher,
  opportunities in introduction of 160;
  expertise, development of 154–5;
  failings of 'Framework for English'
  169; forms of CPD, availability of
  158–9; 'Framework for English',
  introduction of 168–9; full-time
  study, opportunity for 158; higher
  qualifications, significance of 156,
  157; individual ownership of CPD
  160; initial teacher education (ITE)
  156; International Federation for
  the Teaching of English (IFTE) 171,
  172; Kingman Report (1988) 162–4;
  Knowledge About Language (KAL)
  163–5; Language in the National
  Curriculum (LINC) 164; learning
  and practice, inter-relationship
  between 157–8; 'lesson study',
  development of 160–61; *The Making
  of English Teachers* (Protherough, R.
  and Atkinson, J.) 155–6; Master's
  degree in Teaching and Learning
  (MTL) 175–6; materials for

'Framework for English', inadequacies of 170; membership of professional bodies 157; National Association for the Teaching of English (NATE) 157, 160, 170–72; National Council for School Leadership (NCSL) 174; National Language Project 163, 164; National Literacy Task Force 166; National Teacher Research Panel (NTRP) 174–8; Ofsted, formation of 165; ongoing learning 154–8; paradox of teaching 178; passion about teaching and learning 154; pool of inactive teachers (PIT) 159; Postgraduate Certificate in Education (PGCE) 156; professional development (CPD) 157, 158–61; professional development (CPD), Cinderella nature of 154–5; professional knowledge, problematic nature of 157; professional networks 171; professional networks, expertise and 170–72; pros and cons of CPD forms 159; quality of every teacher, global rise in attention to 172; reflectiveness 176–7; refreshment, dimension of 159; research and development of expertise 172–4; research and extended professional's role 173–4; reward, dimension of 159; 'sabbaticals', concept of 158–9; scripting 168–9; 'secondment', concept of 158; self-criticism 176–7; short courses, refreshment through 159; spectrum of CPD 158; teacher expertise, marginalisation of 168–9; teacher research, nature of 177–8; teachers as researchers 173–4; 'Teachers' TV, development of 160, 161; teaching to tests 165–6; US National Board for Professional Teaching Standards (NBPTS) 176; well-being, dimension of 159
Cooper, P. and McIntyre, D. 23
Costello, P. 176
Council for Subject Associations (CfSA) 170
Cox, Brian 75, 77, 94, 95, 103; 'Black Papers' 164; Cox Committee 163; Cox models, comments on 86–7
Cox Report (1991) 68–71, 164
CPD see continuous development
Croos, P.S. 158

cross-curricular model 68–9
CSciTeach 40–42; aims of 41; Association for Science Education (ASE), awarding body 40–41; benefits of 41–2; definition of 40–41
Cullingford, C. 16, 23
cultural analysis model 69, 70, 71, 87, 94, 96, 104, 128
cultural heritage model 69, 70, 71, 87, 94, 96, 104, 151
Culture and Environment (Leavis, F. and Thompson, D.) 126
curriculum: authenticity 100; balance in, importance of 96; curriculum design and 96–101; curriculum knowledge 67–8; design prescriptiveness 98; interference with English, articulation of 95–6; lesson planning and curriculum design, differences between 97; micro level innovation, possibilities for 98; ownership of planning 100–101; planning for novices and accomplished teachers 96–7; reflective cycle, good planning and 99–100; schemes of work (SOWs), designs based on 98–9; school year, distinctive features of 98

Day, C. et al. 24, 25, 27, 71, 131, 159
Dead Poets Society 151
demonstration 136, 140, 141, 142–7, 151, 173
Developing a Knowledge Base within a Client-centred Orientation (Eraut, M.) 11–12
Developing English Teachers (Goodwyn, A.) 55
Dewey, J. 20
digital technologies: adaptation into pedagogy 115–16; balanced use of ITC in English lesson, example of 120; British Educational Communications and Technology Agency (BECTA) 121; challenge of 111–12; change, challenge of 128; in context 111–12; Culture and Environment (Leavis, F. and Thompson, D.) 126; digi-teachers 120–24; expectations of 115–16; ICT and English lessons, examples 118–20; ineffective use of ITC in English lesson, example of 118–19; Information and Communication

Technology (ICT) 44, 111, 112, 115–18, 121–4, 128; information technology, National Curriculum (NC) and 125; intellectual interface with 113–14; lesson observation notes, ICT and English lessons 118–20; media education, National Curriculum (NC) and 125; media innovation 125–8; media teaching, practice of 126–7; New Opportunities Fund (NOF) 114–18, 120–21; physical interface with 113–14; policy and practice 114–18; policy and practice, future considerations 124–5; practical work with 127; predominance of ITC in English lesson, example of 119–20; qualitative experience 117–18; quantitative findings 116, 117; research in practice of media teaching 126–7; self-teaching in 123, 124; student centred digi-teaching 123–4; teacher expertise, support and development of pedagogies using ICT and 124; teaching and technologies 112–14; technical or conceptual expertise, question of 122–3, 128; technological innovation 125–8
display, concept of 151–3
Dixon, J. 69, 70
Dreyfus, S.L. 57, 111, 130, 140, 177
Dreyfus, S.L. and Dreyfus, H.L. 33, 34, 37; model of teaching expertise 33–4, 37, 57, 111, 130–31, 140, 177

Education and Skills, Dept. for (DES) 26, 71
Effective Teaching (Kyriacou, C.) 24
The Effective Teaching of English (Protherough, R., Atkinson, J. and Fawcett, J.) 1
Eisner, E.W. 19
Ellis, V. 67, 71
English, E. 20, 97
English, E. et al. 97
English 5–16, Curriculum Matters I and *Responses to Curriculum Matters I* (HMI) 162–3
English for the English (Sampson, G.) 61–2
English in the Urban Classrooms (Kress, G. et al.) 71
English Language Arts 53, 54

English Literature 62, 107
English Teachers – The Unofficial Guide: researching the philosophies of English Teachers (Marshall, B.) 71
English teaching: adult needs model 69; automaticity 72; Bullock Report (1975) 71; common sense view, teacher aptitude and 60–61; as community of practice 63–7; contested subject 62; Cox Report (1991) 68–71; cross-curricular model 68–9; cultural analysis model 69; cultural heritage model 69; curriculum knowledge 67–8; disagreements within communities 67; *English for the English* (Sampson, G.) 61–2; formulations of 62–3; gatekeeping 60–61; graduate teacher programme (GTP) 65, 66; *Growth Through English* (Dixon, J.) 69, 70; historical perspective 62; initial teacher education (ITE) 59–60; initial teacher training (ITT) 59, 60; initial training 58–61; inspirational experience, reflection on 73–4; late development of 65; legitimate peripheral participation 64–5; listening, importance of 73; models of English 67–74; National Curriculum (NC), introduction of 68; National Writing Project in US 73; Oxford 'internship' model 59; personal growth model 68, 69–70; personal subject construct 71, 72, 74; PGCE 60, 61, 66; professional identity 71–2; reading, importance of 72–3; reflection in action 60; self-awareness 72; skills approach to 69–70; speaking, importance of 73; specialist knowledge 63, 64; standards, reductive nature of 58; subject knowledge, depth of 58–9; subject knowledge audits 66–7; Subject Knowledge Enhancement (SKE) 65–6; subject of English, 'quicksilver' nature of 61–3; Teacher Training Agency (TTA) 60; *Versions of English* (Barnes, D. et al.) 69, 70; writing, importance of 73
Eraut, M. 9, 10, 11, 40, 60, 100, 131, 152, 157, 159
Ericsson, K. 18, 65
Ericsson, K. et al. 32, 99, 141

Examination Board Specifications 62
Excellent Teacher Scheme (ETS) 50–52, 138, 139
Excellent Teacher status 4, 7, 8, 17, 27, 31, 38, 41, 45; excellent teachers as extended professionals 134–5; Hattie's definition of 49–50; opportunities in introduction of 160; standards for 5, 47–8
expertise: acquisition of 32–3, 130–31; advanced beginner stage of development 34–5; Advanced Skills Teacher (AST) 5, 46–52; Benner's model of development of 34–7; Chartered Teacher status 7, 8, 23, 38, 41, 42–4, 45, 46, 48, 88, 101, 134, 154, 171, 173, 174, 176; competent stage of development 35; CSciTeach 40–42; definition of 31–3; *Developing English Teachers* (Goodwyn, A.) 55; Dreyfus Brothers model of teaching expertise 33–4, 37, 57, 111, 130–31, 140, 177; English model of 37–40; excellent teacher standards 5, 47–8; expert English teachers, models of 52–7; expert stage of development 36; Guidance on teacher excellence (DCSF) 38, 39; individuality in 2; *The Intuitive Practitioner* (Atkinson, T. and Claxton, G.) 36; models of 33–7; National Board for Professional Teaching Standards (NBPTS) 52–5, 56; novice stage of development 34; *From Novice to Expert* (Benner, P.) 34–7; practical knowledge and 2; professional action 44–5; professional standards, criteria in England 38; proficient stage of development 35–6; Programme for International Student Assessment (PISA) 6; qualified teacher status (QTS) 33, 38; review of, time for 4–5; Standards for Teachers of English Language and Literature in Australia (STELLA) project 7, 55–6, 98, 172, 178; student achievement, link to individual teacher 5; susceptibility to generalisation 2; teacher 'performance' 6; title for 'expert teachers', challenge of finding 45; top-down implementation of 5; Variations in Teachers' Work, Lives and their Effects on Pupils (VITAE) project 23–4, 55

Framework for English 5, 62–3, 94, 95, 120, 121, 148, 150, 166; didactic nature of 169; introduction of 168–9
From Novice to Expert (Benner, P.) 34–7

gatekeeping 60–61
General Certificate in Education (GCE) 109
General Certificate of Secondary Education (GCSE) 35, 98, 103, 107–8, 109, 110, 159, 166
General Medical Council 13
General Prologue to The Canterbury Tales (Chaucer, G.) 31
General Teaching Council for England (GTCE) 7, 14–15, 160, 170, 174; role of 13–14
General Teaching Council for Scotland (GTCS) 14, 23, 38–9; Chartered Teacher status, vision for 173
Geography Association (GA) 39–40
Giamatti, P. 151
Goldstone, R.L. Schyns, P.G. and Medin, D.L. 37
Goodson, I. and Ball, S. 67
Goodson, I. and Medway, P. 61
Goodwyn, A. and Fidler, B. 50
Goodwyn, A. and Findlay, K. 71, 111, 126, 167
Goodwyn, A. et al. 7, 114, 122
Goodwyn, Andrew 5, 7, 10, 12, 20; continuous development 167, 168, 169, 170; curriculum and assessment 94, 95, 96, 97, 98, 101, 106; digital technologies 111, 121, 122, 125, 127, 128; English teaching and subject communities 60, 62, 70, 71, 72, 73; expertise and expert teaching 45, 55; working with others 132, 139, 140, 146, 150
graduate teacher programme (GTP) 17, 65, 66, 97
Grossman, P. 58
Growth Through English (Dixon, J.) 69, 70
Guidance on teacher excellence (DCSF) 38, 39

Hamlet (Shakespeare, W.) 85
Harrison, C. 95
Harrison, C. et al 121
Hart, A. 126

Hart, A. and Hicks, A. 126
Hattie, J.: characteristics of expert
    teaching 7, 28–30, 43, 46, 48,
    49–50, 72, 75–6, 154–5; classroom,
    multidimensional nature of 90; on
    content knowledge 29; deep learning
    29, 30, 76, 105, 159; excellence
    in teachers, recognition and
    representation of 178; expert problem
    solving 81; facets of expert teaching
    29; optimal learning environment,
    notion of 148; on passion and
    enthusiasm 34; professionalism and
    passion in teaching 79; seminal review
    of research evidence 28; 'situated'
    nature of expert teaching 103; on
    subject knowledge 58–9, 72
Hay McBer Report (2000) 6, 23, 148
head of department (HOD) 27, 76, 78,
    79, 89, 100
Hickcox, E.S. and Musella, D.F. 26
higher education institutes (HEIs) 17,
    140, 143, 160, 163, 176
HM Inspector of Schools (HMI) 28,
    162, 164, 166
Hoffman, R.R. 37
Hopkins, D. 176
Hughes, E. 91
Hutchings, M. et al. 50

Information and Communication
    Technology (ICT) 44, 111, 112,
    115–18, 121–4, 128; English lessons
    and ICT, examples of 118–20; skills
    in 122
Ingvarson, L. 46
Ingvarson, L. and Chadbourne, R. 46
initial teacher education (ITE)
    59–60, 156
initial teacher training (ITT) 58–61, 64,
    97; continuous development 156,
    163, 164, 165, 176; ITT trainers 94;
    standards for 17; working with others
    132, 133, 137–9
International Federation for the
    Teaching of English (IFTE) 171, 172
The Intuitive Practitioner (Atkinson, T.
    and Claxton, G.) 36
isolation, feelings in teaching of
    129–30

Japan 147, 160
Jones, M. and West, A. 162

KAL see Knowledge About Language
Key Stages 14, 67, 90, 95, 97, 98, 106,
    125, 150, 165, 166
Kingman, J. 163, 164
Kingman Report (1988) 85, 162–4
Kleinhenz, E. and Ingvarson, L. 46
Knowledge About Language (KAL)
    163–5
Kress, G. et al. 71
Kyriacou, C. 23, 24, 26

Language across the Curriculum
    71, 94
A Language for Life (DES 1975) 71
Language in the National Curriculum
    (LINC) 164
Lankshear, C. and Knobel, M. 114,
    121, 126
Lave, J. 67
Lave, J. and Wenger, E. 63, 64
learning environments 83, 96, 113,
    115, 117, 143, 148–51
The Learning Game (Barber, M.) 166
Leavis, F. and Thompson, D. 126
legitimate peripheral participation
    64–5
Lewis, C. et al. 160
LINC see Language in the National
    Curriculum
The Literacy Game: the story of the
    National Literacy Strategy (Stannard,
    J. and Huxford, L.) 94–5, 166
The Literacy Hour 97
Livingstone, S. 121
Local Education Authorities (LEAs)
    163, 166, 168
London School of English 70

McBer, H. 148
Macbeth (Shakespeare, W.) 104
McKernan, J. 133
McKinsey Report (2007) 5, 13, 19, 24
McNiff, J. and Whitehead, J. 176
The Making of English Teachers
    (Protherough, R. and Atkinson, J.)
    58, 151, 155–6
Marshall, B. 71
Masterman, L. 127
Master's degree in Teaching and
    Learning (MTL) 141, 156, 158,
    159, 175–6
Mathieson, M. 11, 70
media innovation 125–8

Member of the City and Guilds of London Institute (MCGI) 42
mentoring 137, 139–42
Millman, J. and Darling-Hammond, L. 26

National Association for the Teaching of English (NATE) 3, 157, 160, 170–72
National Board for Professional Teaching Standards (NBPTS) 23, 52–5, 56, 144, 176
National Council for School Leadership (NCSL) 174
National Curriculum for English 61, 62, 68, 94–5, 106, 125, 127, 128, 168, 172
National Curriculum (NC) 62, 76, 89, 95, 109, 163; introduction of 27, 68, 164–5
National Grid for Learning (NGfL) 115, 137
National Language Project 163, 164
National Literacy Project 166
National Literacy Strategy (NLS) 5, 20, 62, 76, 97, 98, 120–21, 146, 161, 166–8, 170
National Literacy Task Force 166
National Research Council 53, 55
National Teacher Research Panel (NTRP) 174–8
National Union of Teachers (NUT) 14
National Writing Project in US 73
NBPTS (National Board for Professional Teaching Standards) 23, 52–5, 56, 144, 176
NCSL see National Council for School Leadership
New Opportunities Fund (NOF) 114–18, 120–21
New Zealand 155, 167, 171, 172
Newbolt Report (1921) 61, 95
newly qualified teachers (NQTs) 33, 35, 59, 77, 88, 89, 97, 133, 143, 176
NLS see National Literacy Strategy
NTRP see National Teacher Research Panel

'O' level examinations 107
observation, forms of 2, 15, 16, 17, 18, 20, 34, 49, 55, 70, 142–7, 148
Ofsted (Office for Standards in Education) 5, 15, 16, 23, 28, 47, 52, 62, 66, 95, 131, 166, 168; formation of 165
ongoing learning 154–8
originality 131
Othello (Shakespeare, W.) 31
Oxford 'internship' model 59, 156

Panorama (BBC TV) 163, 164
paradox of teaching 10, 129–30, 143, 178
Perrot, E. 23
personal growth model 68, 69–70, 87, 93, 109, 110
personal subject construct 71, 72, 74
Picasso, P. 131
Plato 18
pool of inactive teachers (PIT) 159
Post Threshold Teachers, standards for 38
Postgraduate Certificate in Education (PGCE) 2, 3, 59, 60, 61, 66, 72, 76, 97, 156, 176
Power Points 111, 113, 168
The Preachers of Culture (Mathieson, M.) 11, 70
Preston, C. 115
Privy Council 40
Professional Development Record 39
professional identity 55, 65, 71–2, 166, 167
professionalism: accountability and standards 26–8; applied science model of teaching 19; appraisal, purposes of 26–7; art model of teaching 19; autonomy, tension between use of 'standards' and 15–17; being a 'professional' 9–13; *Better Schools* (DES, 1985) 26; challenge of 'status' as a professional 9; client service element 12; competence model of teaching 22–3; content knowledge 29; context of effective teaching 24; craft model of teaching 19–20; *Developing a Knowledge Base within a Client-centred Orientation* (Eraut, M.) 11–12; development function of appraisal 27; effective teaching 18, 23–6; *Effective Teaching* (Kyriacou, C.) 24; entering a profession 12; expert teachers, Hattie's characteristics 28–30; extended professionalism 134; facets of expert teaching 28–9; General Teaching Council for England (GTCE), role of 13–14;

graduate teacher programme (GTP) 17; Hattie's model of expert teaching 28–30; initial teacher training (ITT), standards for 17; intrinsic concerns for students 10; language of professionals 12; managerial function of appraisal 26–7; measurement effective teaching 24–5; National Board for Professional Teaching Standards (NBPTS) 23; National Curriculum (NC), introduction of 27; National Union of Teachers (NUT) 14; origins of term 'professional' 10–11; paradigm shift in concept of teaching 18–19; paraprofessional roles 10; passenger perspective on teaching 10, 22; passion in teaching, professionalism and 79; process of effective teaching 24–5; product of effective teaching 25; public accountability function of appraisal 27; qualified teacher status (QTS) 17; reflective practice model of teaching 20–22; regulatory body, importance of 13–14; restricted professionalism 133; standards, accountability and 26–8; standards, illusion of objectivity of 22–3; 'standards', tension between accountability and use of 15–17, 26–8; system model of teaching 20; Teacher Training Agency (TTA) 27–8; teaching, conceptualization of 18–20; teaching as profession 13; teaching English 79–80; Training and Development Agency (TDA) 14; unions, role of 14–15

Programme for International Student Assessment (PISA) 6

Protherough, R. 58, 151, 158, 162, 170

Protherough, R. and Atkinson, J. 151, 155, 160

Protherough, R., Atkinson, J. and Fawcett, J. 1

qualified teacher status (QTS) 17, 33, 38

Queen's Counsel 155

reading, importance of 72–3

The Reflective Practitioner: how professionals think in action (Schon, D.A.) 20

reflectiveness: continuous development 176–7; reflection in action 60;

reflective practice model of teaching 20–22; reflective practice (RP) 20, 21; social situations, reflective teaching in 132–3

Roberts, G. 40

Rodgers, C. and Scott, K. 71

Romeo and Juliet (Shakespeare, W.) 45

Rosen, H. 163

Royal Academy 132

Royal Charters 40, 41

Royal Geographical Society 39

Royal Shakespeare Company 78

'sabbaticals', concept of 158–9

Sampson, G. 61

SATs (standard assessment tests) 98, 165–6

schemes of work (SOWs) 98, 99

Schon, D.A. 20, 21, 34, 36, 81, 88, 91, 132, 140, 177

Schulman, L. 86

Science Council 40, 41

'secondment', concept of 158

self-awareness 72

self-criticism 176–7

self-sufficiency 132

Selinger, E. and Crease, R.P. 2

Shakespeare, W. 31, 45, 65, 66, 91, 98

The Shorter Oxford English Dictionary 11

Shulman, L.S. 23, 63, 68, 96

Sideways 151

SKE see Subject Knowledge Enhancement

Slee, R. and Weiner, G. 17

social situations, reflective teaching in 132–3

Social Workers 92, 93

Socrates 18

Squires, G. 19

standard assessment tests (SATs) 98, 165–6

standards: illusion of objectivity of 22–3; tension between accountability and use of 15–17, 26–8

Standards for Teachers of English Language and Literature in Australia (STELLA) project 7, 55–6, 98, 172, 178

Stannard, J. and Huxford, L. 94, 166, 168

Stenhouse, L. 133, 134, 174, 177

Stones, E. 23

Students of English (Protherough, R.) 58

Subject Knowledge Enhancement (SKE)
    65–6
Sutton, A. et al 50
system model of teaching 20

Taylor, C. and Jennings, S. 47
TDA *see* Training and Development
    Agency
Teacher Training Agency (TTA) 27–8,
    60, 115
Teachernet website 161
*Teachers Matter: connecting Lives, Work
    and Effectiveness* (Day, C. et al.) 24
'Teachers TV' 146, 160, 161
teaching assistants (TAs) 10, 17,
    124, 161
teaching English: absolute attention to
    individual students 90; adult needs,
    cultural heritage and 87; affective
    dimension 83; atmosphere and mood,
    monitoring of 83; autonomy 88;
    challenging students, dealing with
    79–80; character differences 79;
    collaboration, importance of 88–90;
    commitment 80; contextual factors
    76–7; Cox models, comments on
    86–7; cultural analysis, key aspect
    87–8; cultural pressures, distortions
    of 87–8; decision-making during
    lessons 80–81; depth of knowledge
    of each student 90; developmental
    aspects of collaboration 89–90;
    differences between novice and
    expert teachers 77–8, 92; English
    and literacy, distinction between
    167–8; expertise, reflection and
    84–5; external pressures, reflections
    on 108–10; group dynamics 81–2;
    humour 80; importance of the work,
    attitudes towards 80; importance
    of their subject to expert teachers
    92–3; individuality of students
    82–3; innovation and reflection
    85–6; introduction to observations
    on experienced teachers at work
    76–9; knowledge and expertise
    81; multidimensional nature of the
    classroom 90; negative pressures,
    reflections on 108–10; optimal
    learning environment 83–4; personal
    as part of subject domain 90–91;
    personal growth as starting point
    86–7; perspective on lessons, length
    of 84; philosophical dimension 86;
    political pressures, distortions of
    87–8; practical experiences of 75–93;
    problem-solving 81; professionalism
    79–80; reflection in action 84–6;
    repetition, reductive nature of 88–9;
    respect, vital importance of 90–91;
    role models 80; situatedness 81–2;
    solutions 91–2; style differences
    79; support for novice colleagues,
    commitment to 88
Teachit westite 171
team working and collaboration 135–6
Tebbit, N. 162
technological innovation 125–8
Training and Development Agency
    (TDA) 14, 28, 60, 174
Turner-Bissett, R. 19

unconscious competence, paradox of
    22, 36, 131
United States 52, 172; National Board
    for Professional Teaching Standards
    (NBPTS) 23, 52–5, 56, 144, 176

Variations in Teachers' Work, Lives
    and their Effects on Pupils (VITAE)
    project 23–4, 55
Versions of English (Barnes, D. et al.) 69, 70

Watson, D.M. 121
Williams, R. 151
Woods, P. and Jeffrey, B. 23
working with others: ASTs as extended
    professionals 134–5; becoming
    a professional, process of 130;
    best practice based on research,
    dissemination of 136; on classroom
    organisation 136; coaching
    139–42; collaboration and team
    working 135–6; collegiality 131–2;
    communities of practice 132; creative
    tensions 129; demonstration 142–7;
    display, concept of 151–3; excellent
    teachers as extended professionals
    134–5; extended professionalism
    134; 'finesse' 131, 132; helping with
    teachers experiencing difficulties
    137; high-quality teaching materials,
    production of 136–7; initial teacher
    training (ITT) 132, 133, 137–9;
    isolation, feelings in teaching of
    129–30; learning environments

148–51; mentoring 137, 139–42; newly qualified teachers, mentoring of 137; observation 142–7; originality 131; performance management of other teachers, participation in 137; 'phases of development' 130; professional development, advising on 137; on provision of model lessons 136; real expertise, acquisition of 130–31; reflective teaching 132–3; restricted professionalism 133; self-sufficiency 132; social situations, reflective teaching in 132–3; socialisation into teaching 130; structured nature of schooling 130; on teaching methods 136; team working and collaboration 135–6

Wragg, E. 149
Wyse, D. 95

YouTube 123